ALSO BY GUSTAVO ARELLANO

¡Ask a Mexican!

ORANGE COUNTY

A Personal History

GUSTAVO ARELLANO

SCRIBNER

New York   London   Toronto   Sydney

Portions of this book have previously appeared in the OC *Weekly*—a chunk of
"Becoming the Mexican" and stray, genius lines too good to leave for a fish wrap, is all.

To Jacinto "Chinto" Saldivar, who came to this country with nothing, was whiter than most *gabachos,* raised four awesome boys despite never really learning English, was the hardest worker anyone will ever meet, and whom God called earlier this year for reasons no one will ever understand.

The land of the orange blossom,
With its mountains, vales and hills,
Its wealth of olive, fruit and oil
And sunny, singing rills;
The home of the palm and
poppy, the blue Pacific too,
Orange County, Nature's
Wonderland, is calling,
Calling you.

—*From a 1921 Orange County
Board of Supervisors pamphlet*

CONTENTS

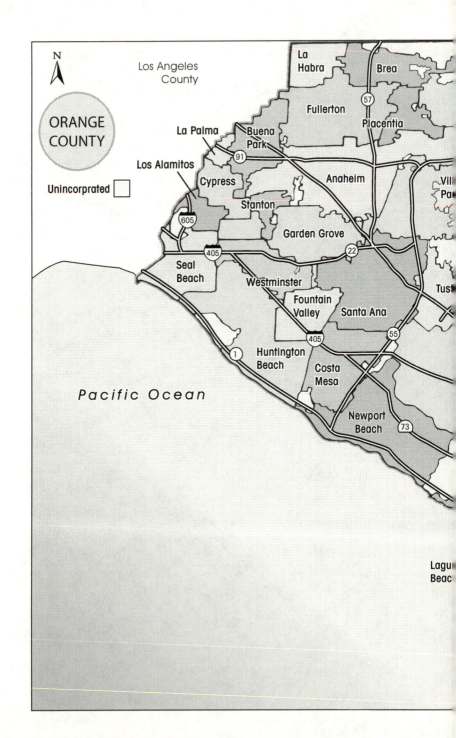

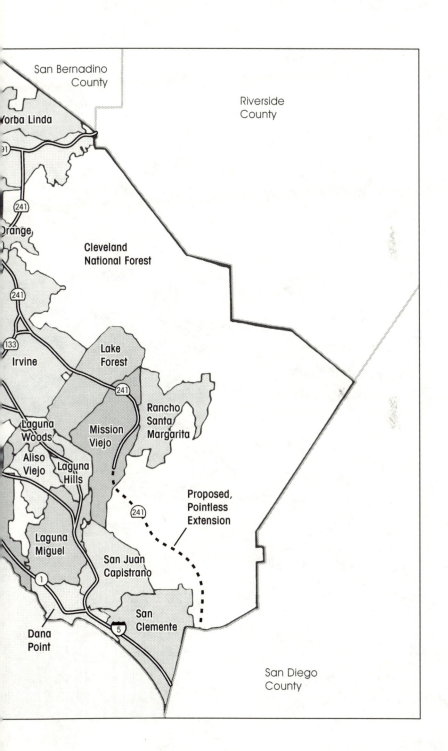

I'VE BEEN
TAKING NOTES

This Is How We Do It in the OC
(Don't Call It That)

I've seen the Mexican future of this country, the coming Reconquista—and it's absolutely banal.

Our looming takeover is spreading across America and will resemble the neighborhood where my parents live in Anaheim, California, Mexico. The houses here all feature the same basic design: three bedrooms, two baths, a long living room connected to the dining room, divided from the kitchen by a bar. Half of the houses keep pools, the others backyards. Garages jut out from the dining room. Depending on the garage's layout, the driveway either gently curves or rises upward at a dramatic angle, guaranteeing your car's undercarriage a daily scratch. About twenty years ago, this section of Anaheim was mostly white, baby boomers and their parents. Today? All Latino, save for the white man across the street who let his yard turn brown years ago.

Trembling yet? Really, the only way you would know it's a Latino neighborhood is due to a very American phenomenon called conspicuous consumption. Every house has at least four cars parked outside: all nice, mostly large SUVs with a smattering of Toyotas occasionally parked on front lawns. Those lawns feature palm trees or roses—no cactuses yet—and the richer house-holds erect ornate fountains and stonework to rival the Alhambra. No Mexican flags flutter above doorways, no roosters crow at dawn—at least not since Dad gave ours away because the cock kept assaulting dogs.

I moved out a couple of years ago at age twenty-seven, no longer content to share a bunk bed with my teenage brother. But a Mexican mother's breakfast beckons even the most prodigal of sons, so I return every Sunday morning to marvel at how Ozzie and Harriet our lives are—how absolutely banal. The Mexican conquest of the United States might not get televised, but it comes with a steaming bowl of menudo.

Don't believe me? Consider one Sunday, around November 2007.

I speed in around nine thirty in the morning, and damnit! No one is home.

Start dialing cell phones. Elsa, my school administrator of a sister, is organizing workshops for college-bound students—most of them Vietnamese, in a school that's majority Latino. Twenty-one-year-old Alejandrina settles in for a Starbucks study session—she wants to be a nurse, or maybe a teacher. Gabriel, the seventeen-year-old baby of our clan, who already towers over us all, is with Mom at a dentist's appointment. My father? No answer.

Where's the remote? The usual detritus of *Householdus ameri-canus* clutters the living room—water bottles, newspapers, back-packs. A *Guitar Hero* ax stands by the marbled fireplace. Jesus looms over me in the form of a huge oil painting bought at the swap meet—still don't know why Mami replaced our family por-trait in favor of the Savior, considering she shows up at Mass as often as a Jew. To my right in a bookcase are small framed portraits of Elsa in her cap-and-gown from the University of California, Los Angeles, Alejandrina's high school graduation picture, and a younger Gabriel wearing a New York Yankees baseball cap (he's a

Los Angeles Dodgers fan now—ah, front-runners). Ken Burns's *Baseball* series is on the top shelf, missing episode 7. And smack-dab in the middle is a photo of me grinning, holding a half-eaten tamale. Speaking of tamales, I toss three in the microwave—one dessert, one pork, one made with cheese, chicken, and jalapeños, all leftovers from our Thanksgiving dinner.

The doorbell rings. It's my father. He's dressed for work—jeans, cowboy boots, baseball cap—and his smile bends an increasingly salt-and-pepper mustache.

"Wassappenin', macho man?" Papi booms in heavily accented English. I turn away, embarrassed. "*Ven, ven, ven*—gimme a hand-chake!" We embrace. He beams.

"*¿Dónde estaba?*" I ask. "Where were you?"

"*En la cafeteria,*" he responds, his inexplicable nickname for a doughnut shop about five minutes away.

As long as I can remember, my father has spent *his* Sunday mornings at JAX Donuts House, a run-down coffee house across the street from Anaheim City Hall. Gentrification, redevelopment, and changing demographics have yet to kill this eyesore: when Starbucks usurped JAX's original location, the owners moved a couple doors down, and its mostly Mexican clientele followed. The Cambodians who own the small store don't fry the best doughnuts (if you ever stop in, order the cinnamon roll and ask for a hell of a lot more frosting), yet thirty to forty middle-aged Mexican men regularly hang out there every weekend—not to harass passing pickups for the chance to pound nails, but to live the good life. They're all men from Jerez, a city of about fifty-six thousand in the central-Mexican state of Zacatecas. More specifically, almost all of the men are from El Cargadero, the tiny village where my mother was born and whose migration to Anaheim captures the postmodern Mexican experience as well as anything.

But when these men meet, they don't chatter about politics or immigration reform. They gossip. "*¡Chismean como viejas!*" my mom has sighed numerous times. "They gossip like old ladies!" It's true: these burly machos, naturally light skin eternally sunburned due to years working outside, chatter almost exclusively about the goings-on in El Cargadero—who's marrying whom, which son or daughter got in trouble or went off to college, stories of their childhood. That their Mexican hometown is now three-quarters empty doesn't bother anyone.

On this particular Sunday morning, my father discussed an upcoming trip to his native Jomulquillo, a village just south of El Cargadero. He's in charge of the *comité Guadalupana*, a group of people who live in the United States but raise funds for a celebration in Jomulquillo for the feast day of the Virgin of Guadalupe on December 12. For the past four years, my father and others have raised thousands of dollars just so a brass band can play for twenty-four continuous hours, a childhood tradition they fondly remember but which died for a time as Jomulquillo hemorrhaged its residents to *el Norte*.

"*¿Quieres dar dinero?*" he asked. "Do you want to give money?" I forked over a $20 bill.

"*¿Se acuerda lo que le dije?*" I responded. "Do you remember what I told you?"

He agreed earlier in the week to answer questions for this book (*gracias* for reading it, by the way), but Papi's clothes suggested other plans. Of course he remembered, but there was grass to mow, palm trees to trim, roses to prune.

"*Ven durante la semana pa' comer lonche—entonces platicamos,*" he said while walking out the door toward the toolshed in our backyard. "Come by during the week to eat lunch—then, we'll talk."

About a half hour later, my mom and brother arrived from the dentist. Gabriel—showing off his immaculate 2006 Air Jordans—is upset. "Where's my music?" he bellowed. I promised him hip-hop and oldies songs from my iTunes months ago, but the memory stick that allows me to bootleg went kaput, and I haven't been able to steal a new one from my friend.

"And where's my game?!" I borrowed *Grand Theft Auto: San Andreas* about a year ago, but killing cops to Hank Williams's "Hey, Good Lookin'" is too much fun so I always conveniently forget to return it. Gabriel pushes me away and plops onto the couch, immersing himself in the *Los Angeles Times* sports section as the Oakland Raiders are losing another close one. "Oh, did you see that one-handed catch by Jerry Porter?" he yells at one point. My brother, the man-child, never removes his sunglasses.

My mom sits next to us and begins darning socks. "You work too hard," she teases, her English better than my father's but still lacking considering she has spent the past forty-five years in *los Estados Unidos*.

"*¿Dale una limpiesita a tu computadora, no?*" she says, pointing at my ink-smeared MacBook. "Don't you want to clean your computer?" Even for a Sunday morning, Mami dresses like a businesswoman on Casual Friday—sweater, dress pants, an earth-toned outfit nicely contrasting with her porcelain skin and coiffed hair.

My father barges in from outside. "*Luz, hasme de comer,*" he commands. "Make me food to eat."

"*Sí, Lorenzo,*" she says, in a tone that any casual observer could immediately deduce she has repeated thousands of times over a thirty-year marriage.

Mami grabs my copy of the *New York Times Magazine* and skims through it.

"*Te 'sta dolienda tu mano,*" she says. "Your hand's hurting." Unconsciously, I was massaging a finger.

"*Nomás* the tip *de mi dedo.*"

"*Aver.*" She motions, grabbing my right index finger and examining its frayed cuticle. She tells me I'm cutting my nails too short, which means that the skin underneath the nail chafes against the keyboard.

"Baby," Gabriel snorts.

"¿*Se acuerda lo que le dije?*" I ask Mami.

Mom tries to beg off the interview, claiming she needs to travel to Costco and load up on groceries. Actually, she does: a Mexican family is a hungry family.

"*Pues,* okay," I reply. I check my e-mail. "FUCK YOU ILLEGAL ALIEN WETBACK SCUM BITCH," it rants. The Raiders score a touchdown. Alejandrina returns with a double soy latte, no foam, for my dad. Canaries chirp in the background.

Just another day for the Arellanos in America. Our heaven. Your hell?

Do me a favor, folks fretting about whether Mexicans will ever become Americanized—fume about something else. Worthy choices: Al Qaeda. John McCain as president. The choking ways of the Chicago Cubs.

There's no real reason why what you just read and anything that follows relating to my personal life should ever have been published (reviewers: there's a pull quote for *ustedes* if ever there was one!). The immigrant saga, the coming-of-age rebel yell, the portrait of the artist as a young *hombre*—the memoir portion of this book uses those clichés of American letters to tell its tale. But the sad beauty of this country is that we forget. We forget that dumb ethnics assimilate, that they share the goals and dreams of any *Mayflower* descendant. It takes a snot-nosed, presumptuous minority to kick the United States in its amnesiac britches every couple of years—consider this your ass boot.

Self-important rant continues on page 13—but first, a word from our sponsor:

Take a flight into Orange County, from anywhere in the East, and witness our rise and fall. Select a window seat, preferably on the left side—don't fly United, do fly Continental—and sleep for a couple of hours until the deserts of the American Southwest transform into Southern California's drought-stricken Cleveland National Forest. The slight bump of the Santa Ana Mountains blesses its trees with the illusion of waves and peace. Serenity. But squint hard enough, and you might just see charred hillsides, remnants of the apocalyptic fires that cover Orange County in smog-fueled smoke every couple of years. Whoops—watch out for turbulence!

The tranquillity of Orange County's last undeveloped woodlands quickly dissolves into reality. Soon, kidney-shaped housing developments dominate the landscape: blobs and blobs sidling up to the forest, spreading across hills and valleys. Though these communities lie as docile as sleeping puppies, the curves are too neat, too surgical. Unnatural. You notice the houses—manorlike, most two stories, with Mission Style tiled roofs, the hard-earned equity of the county's upper-middle class. These preplanned palaces all look alike—neat, danger-free. Yes: banal.

A roadway pops up—that's State Route 241, the Foothill Toll Road, built just over a decade ago. It feeds into much larger arteries, streams of cars clogged in places, just slow in others. Farther away, you glimpse at the 55 Freeway, which connects commuters from those Stepford foothills to the Pacific Ocean. Although the airplane slowly descends, the houses actually become smaller. They're less ostentatious. The streets, however, continue to crawl over the land like varicose veins.

Soon, the enormity of Orange County greets you: It's a grid. Up and down, east and west, as far as you can see, the fifth most populous county in the Republic looks like a giant plaid shirt in industrial-park white and global-warming green. Unlike the terrain you just passed, this section bustles with architectural diversity—strip malls, neighborhoods, the occasional five-story skyscraper. Before you stretch thousands of acres of the most fertile soil in America—fifty years ago. Now? Mostly asphalt, the bounty of agriculture sacrificed for families seeking their slice of stuccoed tranquillity.

Non-native trees line boulevards, parks dot the vanilla vista. See that big slab of green in the middle of everything? That's Mile Square Regional Park, where Ronald Reagan kicked off his 1984 reelection before an audience of at least sixty-five thousand happy souls. Now? It's a good place to pick up a cheap blow job.

The airplane's wheels screech into landing position. You see more: cars, parking lots, office complexes. Few people on the sidewalks. You cross Interstate 5, the mighty 5, which connects America's Pacific states but is mostly known in Orange County for gridlock, always gridlock—shite, why can't they build more freeways? Wait, we did. Well, what about the public transportation system? Don't the buses continue to display a massive medal decal claiming a government agency deemed it America's best public transportation system? Yep? So why does a fifteen-minute car trip last an hour and a half on a bus? What a crock—where were we? Right—Orange County is perfect!

Make sure the stewardess isn't looking and scoot over to the right side of the airplane—lean over that fat, sleeping passenger if necessary. Look for Disneyland's Matterhorn—it's easy to spot; it's the only white-capped anything round these parts that isn't a KKK hood. Nearby is the famous Big A of Angel Stadium, which houses the Los Angeles Angels of Anaheim (don't ask why they're called that, just yell at the owner). You'll cross the remnants of the Santa Ana River, the waterway once deemed the most dangerous river west of the Mississippi by the Army Corps of Engineers, now tamed to little more than a concrete gulch.

Slink back to your seat and look south again. More hills—beyond them is South County, where moneyed people now flock to escape the urbanizing, minority-heavy north and central portions of Orange County. The far-off meadows look gorgeous, but more civilization creeps toward them every year. You might spot two historic blimp hangars that developers plan to tear down for retail. And the giant expanse of nothing? A former marine base that trained generations of Americans and welcomed Vietnamese refugees but now houses a hot-air balloon shaped like—wait for it—an orange!

More hills graded by bulldozers unfold, getting prepped for more developments. More houses leading toward Newport Beach, where parents buy children luxury cars for their fifteenth birthdays and plastic surgery for their eighteenth. Just below you is the 405 Freeway—the fifth freeway passed in less than ten minutes.

Finally! The Pacific! On the horizon! But just as visions of a siliconed beauty swapping sand with you on our trash-strewn beaches enter your mind, a hard bump—you've landed at John Wayne Airport, known in airport code as Santa Ana Airport (SNA), but called John Wayne by the natives because no one in Orange County dares identify anything reputable with a city that's 80 percent Mexican.

Welcome to the end of the West: Orange County, California, 789 of the most influential square miles in America. Fittingly, here to welcome you, just in front of where departing passengers pick up their luggage, is the Duke himself: John Wayne—rather, a nine-foot statue of him. Stetson, boots, kerchief, vest, holster. He's looking down toward you, wearing a crack of a smile—more Ringo Kid than Ethan Edwards. But the man born Marion Morrison isn't all pleasantries: Wayne's arm rests near a gun. Bullets are missing from his gun belt. A massive American flag hangs above.

Wayne was born in Iowa and raised in Glendale, California, but OC lore maintains that the county created the movie star. The story goes that the man born Marion Morrison forsook USC football for an acting career after sustaining a shoulder injury while body surfing at Newport Beach's notorious Wedge. Wayne spent his final years as the county's kind, crazy uncle, usually haunting bars in Newport Beach with his slurring, gentlemanly manners. But Orange County's custodians didn't care about Wayne the Orange County Resident—they renamed the airport after his screen persona. A blurb on the airport's Web site lionizes Wayne the Statue as a "man of humility, of honesty, and a hero of the American West [who] was a symbol to the world of the traditional American values." The statue itself bears a brave message: JOHN WAYNE LEGENDARY AMERICAN. When the legend becomes sad fact, bronze the legend.

But few people stop to appreciate Wayne—not the chubby tourists, they're all busy trying to wave down family members in the madness just outside. And not the dour Homeland Security personnel, the brown-skinned janitors and Asian shopkeepers. And so the man stands alone, a relic, a monument of Ozymandian excess.

This is how we do it in the OC, bitches. Or so the television show says—I certainly never saw it. And don't call us that, *por favor.*

You really are in Paradise. Sunny most of the year, with only the occasional catastrophic earthquake. Right on the Pacific Ocean and free of a major port, which means the only pollution to worry about is the millions of gallons of partly treated sewage the local sanitation districts flush onto our beaches daily, and the recycled poo water they filter into our taps. The county's developers consistently leave thousands of acres of open space free from their cookie-cutter visions—beautiful canyons and sagebrush-swept hills that house animals and various flora, perfect for hikes—as long as we accept the thousands of houses they build everywhere else.

Orange County is just hours from desert, mountains, forests, Los Angeles, and Mexico, but you can find almost anything within the county's boundaries. Like multiculturalism? America's largest city with an all-Latino city council is here—Santa Ana, the county seat, a place where whites stubbornly cling to their last neighborhoods and some hold Halloween on a separate day so that brown kids won't swarm their streets. The largest community of Vietnamese outside Vietnam lives in Little Saigon, where refugees continue to fight Ho Chi Minh. Muslims can enjoy Anaheim and Garden Grove, home to many mosques and much FBI monitoring. Chinese live in Irvine, which hosts a university that's part of the prestigious University of California system and that conservative bloggers call the most anti-Semitic campus in America. But don't bother stopping by OC (it's okay to call it *that*) if you're African-American—we only have a couple of thousand, which make up about 2 percent of the county's population. They know better.

Rest assured, religiously inclined folks can find their type of holy rollin'. The kitschy go to the Trinity Broadcasting Network in Costa Mesa, the world's largest televangelism network, located within a Barry Bonds homer from South Coast Plaza, America's most prosperous mall (but don't call it a mall). Theological troglodytes worship at Calvary Chapel Costa Mesa, where the original Jesus Freaks, transformed by their baptisms in picturesque Corona Del Mar State Beach, began preaching the End Days. If you're compassionate and your bigotry is soft, drive down to Lake Forest and Saddleback Church, home for the mega-phenomenon called the Purpose-Driven Life®. Want to roll with Jesus in a Mercedes? Try the Crystal Cathedral, America's original purveyor of the prosperity gospel, where life-size statues of religious icons provide endless photo ops to awestruck tourists and simple Passion and Nativity plays turn into multimillion-dollar extravaganzas. Supporter of pedophiles? Our Roman Catholic diocese can accommodate your needs. Hate Mexicans? *Hola*—that's the *real* county faith.

Beach bums of the world, unite! Huntington Beach, Seal Beach, San Clemente, Laguna Beach, Newport Beach—all rightfully promote their endless waves, but don't bother looking for the playgrounds immortalized by the Beach Boys and other surf-rock gods: developers overpriced our coasts years ago, erecting seaside resorts where once existed trailer parks and nine-hole golf courses. They've yet to touch the real jewel, Trestles, just south of San Clemente at Orange County's southernmost tip, but hang ten there while you can—county politicians want to extend that 241 toll road you flew over to trample through the purty place.

Queer? Hang out in Laguna Beach, which elected the country's first openly homosexual mayor way back when but is now rapidly gentrifying the gays, artists, and day laborers out of town. Tim Leary—who started an international hippie mafia in Laguna's canyons—must be rolling in his cosmic joint.

Your grandparents probably know about San Juan Capistrano, where the swallows returned every year as the old Ink Spots song once weeped, but must now look elsewhere to build their mud nests as that once rustic town continues to modernize. If you're young and can throw a football eighty yards while on your knees, the cities of Mission Viejo and Rancho Santa Margarita feature powerhouse prep squads whose kids annually earn Division I scholarships. If you can throw a football far and then dunk a basketball during the winter, you'll live in those cities but commute to Santa Ana to attend Mater Dei High School, a Catholic prep academy, which is the largest Catholic high school west of the Mississippi and employs statutory rapists the way Notre Dame once notched football championships.

Don't bother coming here if you're liberal—Republicans rule everything, from the courts to the sheriff's office to the Board of Supervisors and the district attorney's office. We're so conservative, the only way a Republican beat Minuteman Project founder Jim Gilchrist in a 2006 congressional race was by calling him a communist—seriously! A communist! There's a reason Reagan once said we're the place where "all the good Republicans go to die," and it ain't because of our hometown boy Adam Gadahn, Al Qaeda's token American terrorist.

If you're just a dull person, we have many cities with little history, little anything other than peace of mind and overpriced homes—La Palma, Foothill Ranch, Aliso Viejo, and the Little Lagunas: Niguel, Woods, and Hills. Anaheim has historically lapped up much of the national recognition earned by Orange County—the Ducks, Angels, and Disneyland are here—but the true economic powerhouse is Irvine, home to multinationals such as Blizzard Entertainment (makers of *World of Warcraft*) and Taco Bell. Country-lovin' folks will enjoy the canyon communities— Modjeska, Santiago, and Williams canyons are particularly pretty all year. Just be on the lookout for mudslides, m'kay? Stay away from Stanton, our eternal joke: it first incorporated in 1911 so—I kid you not—other cities didn't turn it into a sewage dump.

A geezer? Live in either of our Leisure Worlds—we created those before Dennis Hopper ever discovered Ameriprise. And if you're that old standby, the middle class? Tough luck—it doesn't exist anymore. The subprime mortgage scandal of 2007? Mostly started here.

Orange County is postsuburbia: thirty-four distinct cities of various sizes but none dominating over the rest. Yet each interconnects to create a petri dish for America's continuing democratic experiment.

Back from commercial, continued from page 6:

In the past couple of years, my homeland has emerged as an exaggerated, much talked-about microcosm of the United States. The hype is right: Orange County is the Ellis Island of the twenty-first century. What we've experienced in our century-and-change of official existence is coming to your town, if it's not there already. And the primary lesson Orange County can teach you is my family's four-generation journey—the Mexican invasion.

But first a history lesson, and history in the United States always begins with the Europeans. Orange County is no different. Yes, we had our Injuns—the Tongvas in the northern section, Acjachemen down south (Americans call them Gabrieleños and Juaneños, respectively, after the Spanish mission that tamed the tribes)—but the U.S. government doesn't list our Indians as officially recognized tribes, so I'm ignoring them, too.

Orange County, as we understand it, originated just a bit south of Orange County, in a serene stretch of wilderness near what is now Marine Corps Base Camp Pendleton. There stands a small, weed-choked plaque stating, "Near this spring the first Christian baptism in Alta California was performed by Padre Francisco Gomez."

On July 22, 1769, about 150 Spaniards and their mules trudged north through what was then called Alta California at the request of Father Junípero Serra. Serra had just established the first of California's twenty-one famed missions in San Diego. But the padre wanted more—he ordered Don Gaspar de Portolà to trek north ahead of him and explore the virgin country.

Just like his superior, Portolà sent a scout ahead of *him:* José Francisco Ortega. The two reunited in a village of about fifty Indians near the site of the above-mentioned spring. The natives presented Portolà and his party with two girls. They were sick, and the Indians asked the Spaniards to heal them.

Instead, Portolà told the priests to baptize the girls—christened Maria Magdalena and Margarita—in the name of Jesus and the Spanish crown. "We did not doubt that both would die and go to heaven," wrote Father Juan Crespi, who also accompanied Portolà, in his diaries. "With this, the only success that we have obtained, we fathers consider it well worth while the long journey and the hardships that are being suffered in it and that are still awaiting us. May it all be for the greater glory of God and the salvation of souls."

For decades, wealthy Orange County men reenacted Portolà's

trek through the county in a ritual that was half–Boy Scout, half–historical appreciation, and all cheese. Cristianitos ("Little Christians") Road, the closest road to this landmark, is named after the girls. Ortega earned a road, too: Ortega Highway, one of the more treacherous lengths of Southern California, a place where murderers frequently dump bodies. Fitting. Most of South County is named in Spanish—the cities, streets, and schools—in honor of these men and their Age of Discovery. Too bad the residents' cities don't honor the conquistadors' descendants the same way . . . but we digress.

Shortly after Portolà's expedition, Serra established Mission San Juan Capistrano just north of Cristianitos Creek. Until Mexico won its independence from Spain in 1821, Orange County was the mission, a couple of renegade Indian villages, and little else. After the Mexican government took control, officials divided the county into ranchos to reward military officers. The Californios—as these scions of Spain called themselves—went on to raise thousands-head herds of cattle, among the largest in the world at that time.

But not until 1840 did Orange County enter American letters, courtesy of Richard Henry Dana Jr., author of the maritime memoir *Two Years before the Mast*. The New Englander's time in the county was minimal—just caught a couple of tanned cowhides thrown down the cliffs of what's now Dana Point by mission peons. Nevertheless, Dana was so impressed with Orange County that he deemed San Juan Capistrano "the only romantic spot on the [Pacific] coast," a fact repeated in nearly every history of Orange County and reiterated here for obligatory purposes. When the Gold Rush hit California in 1849, thousands of miners came, many clutching a copy of Dana's tome as a guide. To this day, schoolchildren get bused from across Southern California to glimpse the *Pilgrim*, a replica of the boat Dana sailed on. (The docents never mention his Mexican-bashing, but again—we digress.)

The Gold Rush ended Orange County's Californio days—that, and devastating droughts and floods that cursed the region during the 1850s. Unscrupulous Americans—immigrants!—claimed the ranchos as their own and litigated many Californios into bankruptcy. These Americans tried playing ranch boss for a couple of years, but Orange County didn't see the rise of white communities until 1859, when a group of Germans from San Francisco purchased one hundred acres to create a socialist grape-growing commune named Anaheim in the county's first bilingual conflation (*heim* is German for "home," and the *Ana* refers to the Santa Ana River).

More towns followed. Santa Ana, Orange, and Fullerton are among the oldest, while others such as Newhope, Olive, and Paularino now only exist as street names. As more towns popped up, residents voted to secede from Los Angeles and create Orange County in 1889. Outsiders and even most residents assume the name describes the bounty of orange groves that first earned the county its wealth, but that tale is more of an urban legend based on a lie. As the county's historian emeritus Jim Sleeper put it, "The organizers of Orange County chose that name for the sordid purpose of real estate. They argued that Eastern people would be attracted by the name and would rush to that county to buy orange ranches, forgetful, or perhaps ignorant, of the fact that there were more than a hundred other places in the United States named Orange." Indeed, orchards were just sprouting around central Orange County when the county incorporated, but the promise of orange blossoms was enough for speculators to sell settlers from across the United States on communities that hadn't yet seen sawdust.

For about seventy-five years, this was Orange County—a cornucopia where sugar beets, lima beans, avocados, but mostly citrus groves made a few farmers rich and kept towns small and rural. Interviews with old-timers have them remembering the days when they heard the crash of ocean waves in Fullerton, about twenty miles inland, at night. There was little in the sense of a county identity other than as a seller of its produce to a hungry nation.

World War II introduced the twentieth century to this pastoral. The U.S. military annexed tens of thousands of acres of farmland, creating an air force base in Los Alamitos, the aforementioned blimp hangars in Tustin, and an army air base in Costa Mesa; the marines constructed an air base in El Toro near the heart of the county; and the navy opened a weapons station in Seal Beach. Hundreds of thousands of Americans passed through Orange County on their way to the Pacific theater. The mild temperatures and untapped potential enticed GIs to stay after they smashed the Japs, and farmers paved over their fruit trees and fields for the cash crop of tract houses.

This post-WWII population boom transformed Orange County from vast nothingness into hyper-suburbia. In 1940, 130,760 people lived in Orange County; by 1950, 216,224 were here. The population increased to 703,925 ten years later; 1,420,386 was the census count for 1970. Cities incorporated quickly, creating makeshift municipalities in a region a bit over a century old.

Disneyland opened its gates in 1958, introducing the country to a radically transformed Orange County, one governed not by farmland tranquillity but Progress. Aerospace giants—Rockwell, Lockheed Martin (partially named after Orange County native Glenn Martin), and Boeing opened factories that employed thousands. The county gained two state universities—California State University, Fullerton (originally known as Orange County State College), and the University of California, Irvine. The latter was the focal point of a new plan to introduce master-planned communities in the county's southern regions, where ranchers still herded cattle and the living had changed little after two centuries.

The county needed a vision, a philosophy to foster a sense of shared identity between the old-timers and newbies. Enter conservatism. Quickly, Orange County became nationally notorious for its right-wingers, ardent housewives and blue-collar husbands who wanted the United States out of the United Nations and God-fearing men in office. When local boy Richard Nixon—born at the upper northeast extreme of the county in Yorba Linda to Quaker parents—spoke of a Southern strategy, it was code for attracting the county's voters and their fellow suburbanites.

But as Nixon rose and fell, his homeland further evolved. The Vietnam War brought hundreds of thousands of refugees to El Toro and Camp Pendleton. Despite efforts by the government to disperse the Vietnamese, many of them settled in central Orange County and re-created Indochina as best they could, much to the chagrin of the other residents. But it wasn't just Vietnamese who were overrunning OC: Muslims, Koreans, Chinese, and refugees from the Soviet bloc also swooped in. And the most dramatic demographic rise involved Latinos, who had stayed in segregated barrios well into the 1960s.

Even as Orange County expanded and exhibited more signs of losing its backwater reputation through the 1980s—a performing arts center, luxury resorts in South County, a football team with the Los Angeles Rams—residents bemoaned the loss of their dreamland. Many of the county's aerospace factories started shutting down in the early 1990s, and the marines announced plans in 1993 to leave El Toro for civilian use by the end of the decade. And shock gripped God's People when Orange County—the Promised Land!—declared bankruptcy in 1994, the largest local government default in American history.

Even more stinging, however, was the 1996 election of Loretta Sanchez—a Mexican woman Democrat, the three most egregious OC sins, in that order—to a congressional seat. Sanchez's victory over incumbent Bob Dornan sent shock waves up to Congress, where Dornan demanded the Republican-dominated House investigate his claims that illegal Mexicans had handed him defeat.

White people began moving away, and ethnics transformed the petit bourgeois strongholds of Orange County—Central and North—into postmodern ethnic enclaves. Privatized freeways— a first in the United States—sprung up to serve the new communities that burrowed their way into South County's last open spaces.

It took two bands—Anaheim's peppy No Doubt and the political hard-rock Rage Against the Machine, fronted by Irvine resident Zack de la Rocha—to rehabilitate Orange County in the mind of mainstream America. Though No Doubt's and RATM's focus was on rebelling against their staid homeland, the rest of the country interpreted their melodic warnings to mean coolness was bubbling in the land of milk and Mickey. Soon came more bands, television shows, movies, clothing lines. Celebrities and the nouveau riche started buying second homes along the coast or in South County. By the start of the new millennium, Orange County was becoming what *USA Today* memorably, lamely called "America's Capital of Cool," the place where rich, young people partied and made beaucoup bucks. The Angels won the 2002 World Series, allowing sports fans to see this new Orange County. Finally! there was a civic identity that didn't involve people distinguishing us from Los Angeles. To say one was from *la naranja* now carried a certain hip cachet. Then, the Minuteman Project came along to remind the world about our rotting core.

And today? The houses keep rising, although there's little room left except skyward. The sleepy towns are now a mess of 3 million souls—if Orange County incorporated as a city, its population would trail only that of New York and Los Angeles. The Republicans still rule, but consistently shoot themselves in the foot and might permanently lose power within a generation. Whites still live here, but now number less than half of the county's residents, with Latinos making up a third and Asians almost 20 percent. It's projected that Latinos will be the majority of county residents in thirty years, an inconceivable thought even a decade ago. In Orange County!

The Indians? They're still around, although split into feuding factions and having to fend off attacks from the Catholic Church and politicians who want to deny them the chance to open a casino. Orange groves? Less than one hundred acres. Just this past summer, San Juan Capistrano officials booted an eighty-four-year-old Mexican man who had tended forty acres of orange trees for the past thirty-eight years so that the city could construct a maintenance yard. Time doesn't care for the past in Orange County—booms and busts go fast, and today's trends become tomorrow's latest built-over shopping plaza.

Thus concludes my history of Orange County, at least the short version. I doubt you want to read about the minutiae of our mega-burb—how Katella Avenue, one of the county's main roads, is named for Kate and Ella, the daughters of a prominent Anaheim farmer. That the Yorba family was one of Orange County's most important early settlers. And what about the ancient legend that the reason the Angels didn't win for decades was because their stadium was built on an Indian burial ground? Too bad that story is baloney; Anaheim Stadium was actually built on an old orange grove, a grove where my uncle gathered *naranjas* as a twelve-year-old—but I digress yet again. All good trivia—but hardly reason enough to read my book, *¿qué no?*

Municipal histories are fascinating mostly to those who live there; the public at large demands a connection, a reason to read about a place far away. With that in mind, I present to you the Orange County that witnesses, initiates, and fosters movements that transcend our borders and influence the arc of American life—even the world. Hell, there's even an Orange County in China modeled after us. The fact that commies look upon Orange County as an ideal for good living indicates that something about my homeland is weird and vital.

Our conservatives, our churches, our "real" housewives, anti-immigrant fools, and captains of avarice—all are mini-manias for major swaths of the country. So we've notched the television shows, *muchos* articles, increased tourism, even a Jack Black flick—but never a serious book outside academia's necessary-but-boring realm. Nothing has exposed Orange County in its unadulterated, bizarre, fascinating whole—until now (sorry, *Meet* The OC *Superstars: The Official Biography!* doesn't count).

Oh, local historians have regaled readers with tales of pioneers and the halcyon days when the John Birch Society reigned and the county smelled like a giant can of Tropicana. But the victors write history, goes the aphorism, and nowhere is that more true than in Orange County. Local histories follow a tight OC Story, positivist in predestined steps and outcome. Good for retirees, terrible for the macro view. We don't care for the fact—we print the legend. Meanwhile, American historians have long dismissed the county as America's fundamentalist wild, reviled as the place that spawned Nixon, ridiculed for the perfection that drew so many to find lives of leisure. We're historical ether—invisible but dangerous.

My family has witnessed the transformation of Orange County from a place where segregation forced my great-grandfather and grandfather to flee for their lives from flying potatoes, to a society in which my mother had to drop out of school in ninth grade to pick strawberries, to a phenomenon that has fostered my strange existence. I'm getting paid *mucho dinero* by a New York publishing company to present a life experience and county history which is crucial to understanding America to readers who might not want to believe it. Believe it. Families like mine are integral to this equation in that we qualify as old-timers and as the county's perpetual outsiders at the same time. And we are this country's newfound menace. We are natives; we are the ruin. We are the Zeligs, participating in or weathering many of the county's crucial moments, partners in the forging of this Brave New America, one that extends all the way to two tiny mountain villages in central Mexico.

The structure of this book is simple—chapters alternate between my family's binational trek and my memoir with the county's history, and one complements the other. Sprinkled throughout are blurbs that explain Orange County's cities and major points of interest—consider them the jalapeños on the nachos. Read this book as a guide to the past and a manual for the future. As Orange County goes, so goes my family, and as my family has traversed through a century of assimilation and resistance, so will the United States—not the easiest of transitions, but always moving forward. Toward the fruit of knowledge—not an apple, but an orange. Picked by a Mexican, of course.

Flying Potatoes, Anchor Babies, and Kidnapped Teen Brides: The Mirandas Go North

Hunger was all Plácido Miranda thought about when he and his two sons finally hopped off the train in the afternoon. For about two months and almost two thousand miles in the fall of 1918, the men had walked, ridden burros, and stowed themselves away in freight cars from their home village of El Cargadero in central Mexico to their awaiting utopia: San Bernardino, California. They begged for food, slept in coal piles, and fended off bandits, customs officers, and other shady characters along the way. In El Paso, the Mirandas put a penny in a slot machine and received a passport that allowed them to enter the United States legally.

It wasn't the first time Plácido and his sons had left El Cargadero—nestled high in the mountains in the Sierra Madre Occidental, which crosses the state of Zacatecas—for the riches of *el Norte*. Eighteen-year-old Antonio and his father had labored a couple of months every year for the past decade in the copper mines of Arizona alongside dozens of other men from their village; twelve-year-old José helped them by fetching water. While wielding a shovel and pick was strenuous and paid pennies, it still offered more than Mexico. But Plácido didn't want his sons to become miners, so the three trekked west.

As the train dropped off the *cargaderenses* and chugged away toward Los Angeles, the Mirandas wandered around town. They hadn't bathed or eaten properly in weeks. None had traveled west of Phoenix before. Exhausted and disoriented, the men decided to rest in a small park. Plácido had heard from other *cargaderense* men that Southern California was nothing but oranges and opportunity, and those rumors were panning out. Orchards dominated the town, and the air was almost suffocating with the sickly-sweet scent of just-harvested citrus. Trucks filled with migrant men passed by the Mirandas, returning from the groves. Plácido didn't know anyone in San Bernardino—just had the address of a farmer his friend swore treated Mexicans well.

A greeting party arrived: a mob of white teenage boys, hurling rocks as sharp as their unintelligible insults. The Mexicans fled, which angered the teens. More kids rushed in, all carrying rocks. The Mirandas didn't have time to feel the pelts and ran fast.

The chase spilled over from park to street, street to business areas, business areas to orange groves, to residential neighborhoods and back to the groves, where the two sides darted between the trees. Plácido and his sons didn't dare fight back—to challenge a *gabacho* in *los Estados Unidos* meant certain deportation, if not worse. This hide-and-seek continued for nearly an hour, until the teenagers ran out of rocks and walked away. The Mirandas rested again, now *really* lost.

About fifteen minutes passed before the teens returned, now armed with potatoes. Another chase. The potatoes hurt more than the rocks, so big and tough and lumpy were they. The same routine: run, hide, then run again. For another hour. Thankfully, evening was falling, and the teenagers tired of their game, but not before mouthing words the men didn't understand but knew weren't welcoming.

Night fell. The Mirandas retraced their chase. Potatoes littered the trail. They gathered the spuds and kindled a fire. Plácido and his two boys ate comfortably that night and hugged each other for warmth while sleeping underneath an orange tree. The following morning, they caught the train for the safer environs of Orange County. The men never dared stop in San Bernardino again.

Anaheim: Truly the heart of Orange County, and not just because this is my hometown. Most major national and international events in Orange County happen at Angel Stadium, the Honda Center, or the Anaheim Convention Center. It's home to the county's largest immigrant populations—significant numbers of Somalians, Arabs, Romanians, Filipinos, Samoans, Germans, and Mexicans keep enclaves here. And of course, there's Disneyland, which makes its might known to residents every election cycle or whenever anyone argues for affordable housing near its park. To the far east is Anaheim Hills, people who don't like to associate with us ethnics in the lowlands. Losers. **Best restaurant: Kareem's,** makers of the best falafel outside of Detroit in the United States. *1208 S. Brookhurst Street, Anaheim, (714) 778-6829.*

A couple months before finishing this book, I experienced the most vivid dream: I won a contest in which the main prize was the ability to fly. After traveling to Cambodia and Croatia, I decided to stop by El Cargadero.

I finally arrived in the late afternoon, around the time cinematographers describe as the "golden hour" because the sun bathes everything in a soft, radiant glow that transforms even the ugliest mug into a GQ man. El Cargadero sits on the slope of a mountain, so rays either enveloped houses or cast them in shadows.

The first few minutes of my dream played out like a colonial fantasy. All the houses were mini-estates, protected by wrought-iron fences, looking out toward cobblestone streets. Fountains, marble, tile: the people of El Cargadero entertained splendidly. Many bobbed in warmed swimming pools, sipping from bottles of rum and tequila. Kids frolicked in bathing suits, while the older folks lounged on couches. Inexplicably, a freeway overpass identical to the section of California Interstate 980 between Oakland and Berkeley ringed the town. The weather was warm, humid. I tried to eavesdrop on conversations as I hovered above, but all I heard were the laughs of contentment.

I landed and began walking the streets. Streetlights flickered on, lending a beautiful shine to the village. People greeted me warmly but were surprised—I hadn't strolled around El Cargadero in years. I knew everyone for a good reason—my mom was born here in 1951, and the people who dwelled in El Cargadero were the friends, family, and enemies I grew up with in Anaheim. There was my girlfriend from high school. Up the street gobbling tacos was my junior high bully. The college professor whose books I owned but whom I never quite got around to interview for this book walked past me and waved hi. The aunt I never knew, the girl I never married—it was *This Is Your Life* as imagined by Univisión.

I asked for and received directions to the spacious, centuries-old, two-story, blue house of José Miranda, the poor twelve-year-old who ran from those flying potatoes so many years ago. My maternal grandfather—*mi* Papa Je. If you ask me right now, I can give you detailed directions on how to get there from anywhere in the United States via car, burro, or plane. In my dream, I couldn't find it.

The dream had been happy-go-lucky to this point, but melancholy seeped in as I continued around El Cargadero. The paved roads turned to dirt, and cars transformed into horses that neighed nervously. Houses grew cracks before my eyes. People vanished one by one; those who were left continued with their activities as if nothing had happened. I walked for what felt like hours, but the sunset never turned to night. I trekked through valleys, next to rivers, up mountains, even to the large reservoir on the outskirts of El Cargadero, looking for my *abuelito*'s house, but no luck.

I ran into my father. He had just entered town after a day of driving a big-rig truck. He was tired.

"*Oiga, pa',*" I asked. "*¿Donde esta la casa de mi abuelito?*" "Hey, Dad—where's my grandfather's house?"

"*Ya no esta,*" he replied, shaking his head. "*Ya no esta nada.*"

I woke up. Usually, I can easily fall back to sleep if disturbed, but too much bothered my mind—the sadness of existence, the reality of knowing that the sights, feelings, and happiness I'd just experienced were never going to return and never truly existed. A feeling of unpardonable guilt seeped in, and I cursed God even as I thanked him.

Pardon my hyperbole. El Cargadero *does* exist, is still where God plunked it about 250 years ago. It's one of forty-six villages (from here on called *ranchos* because that's how *cargaderenses* refer to their village) that make up Jerez de García Salinas, a *municipio* (the Mexican equivalent to a county) in southwest Zacatecas of about fifty-six thousand people. During its heyday in the 1950s, El Cargadero's population was about a thousand; nowadays, El Cargadero is a cipher, a memorial to the tragedy that is modern Mexico and the indomitable wanderlust of the human soul.

By rural Mexico's standards, El Cargadero is well-off. A river runs through it and keeps plants green all year. The town's church, San Rafael, features gold gilding and an elegiac design on the outside, with massive saint statues inside. The main plaza, topped with a corrugated-iron roof, serves as a great place to chat the day away—it's named El Migrante. The Migrant. Streets are narrow, many houses two stories, and always well-maintained. Small businesses on every block. Around El Cargadero is undeveloped wilderness, and if you take the main road—excuse me, *only* road— in at night, halogen lights give El Cargadero the appearance of a high school football field from afar. The closest rancho is a couple of miles away.

Cargaderenses are proud of their town, bragging to everyone within earshot they're better than the other ranchos of Jerez—and whiter, too. The big sports are baseball and—bizarrely—volleyball. Soil is still fertile, a nice rebound from the environmental devastation unleashed about 125 years ago, when the trees that gave the town its name (*el cargadero* translates as "the carrier" and refers to the men who carried lumber down the mountains to the town in the 1800s) were deforested for good. Residents maintain a library, and there's even a computer lab boasting PCs that were brand-new around 1997. El Cargadero is modern enough to have also spun off a suburb—Cieneguitas de Fernandez, a rancho up the mountains colonized by *cargaderenses* in the 1930s.

It's the type of village *Lonely Planet* raves about if the surrounding country is Bhutan. The kind of place that American politicians praise for its small-town virtues when it's in Iowa. Problem is, about three-quarters of the homes and businesses are shuttered. Almost everyone is gone—the only people left are the old, the young, and the delusional. Everyone else is in the States—California, mostly, and brave souls in Chicago, North Carolina, Denver, and even abroad. But the vast majority of *cargaderenses* live in Anaheim, California—easily over a thousand of us, probably closer to two thousand. All chasing our grandparents' childhood Mexican dreams.

＊   ＊   ＊

BUSINESS

Many billionaires, and too many millionaires, but few of the companies based in Orange County matter much—and those that do are frightening. Allergan makes various pharmaceutical products but is most famous for Botox, which has blessed a generation of MILFs with tight faces. Although Taco Bell's parent company is in Louisville, Taco Bell itself is in Irvine, while its lesser cousin Del Taco is down the 405 Freeway in Lake Forest. Broadcom is one of the country's more important semiconductor manufacturers, but its founders are being investigated by the SEC for backdating stock options. And we were a major part of the subprime-mortgage scandal that nearly threw the country into a recession. So many ills to blame our captains of industry for, so please do.

No one knows who first migrated from El Cargadero to Anaheim, but I know it wasn't my maternal great-grandfather, Plácido Miranda. By the time Papa Plácido and my Papa Je reached Anaheim in 1918, at least two *cargaderense* families—and they weren't alone—resided in Anaheim. Honestly, no one in our rancho has ever bothered to pay attention. Long ago, El Cargadero merged with Anaheim to create a hybrid—beyond mere binationalism and closer to cultural osmosis, a permanent, natural (at least to us) evolution of a people struggling to survive in between two squabbling societies. It's the story of modern Mexican migration—hundreds if not thousands of Mexicans from the same village, city, state, or region bringing their hometowns and mores en masse to the United States. El Cargadero isn't unique—it's the rule by which to understand America's new immigration.

But many *cargaderenses* still wonder about those roots. Why Anaheim? Why so many? Angelina Veyna, a Chicano-studies professor at Santa Ana College, says her grandparents arrived in 1918 because they were fleeing the Mexican Revolution and a family friend told them Orange County's citrus industry needed pickers.

That's the reason why my Papa Plácido originally set sight on Anaheim—that, and that there were already *cargaderenses* living in the city. See how circular this investigation gets? Here's the one fact everyone from El Cargadero can agree on: by the time Plácido's son José Miranda reached Anaheim in 1918, my Papa Je was more American than Mexican.

He was born in 1906 to Plácido Miranda and Maria Bermudez, but Bermudez disowned my Papa Je when he was just two. No one has ever clearly explained the abandonment. My maternal grandmother claims times were tough in El Cargadero, and Plácido was heading north to Arizona, where other men from the rancho were already breaking rocks in the Morenci Mine, one of the largest copper mines in the world. She always ends this version of the story with a cryptic line: Maria screaming to Plácido, just as he was leaving for Arizona, *"¿Pues llevátelo, no?"* "Well, take [José], no?"

That's not the story one aunt told me, whom I'm not identifying because she swore me to secrecy. Apparently, my Papa Plácido fathered a child with another woman right after José's birth. Typical Mexican man. Humiliated, Maria Bermudez wanted nothing to do with Plácido or my Papa Je. Whatever the real story, my great-grandfather placed José in Arizona when he was about four and put him in the care of the boy's aunts, Romana and Agustina Miranda. They raised my Papa Je as a son while Plácido slogged away in the copper mines. Whenever Plácido returned to El Cargadero, José stayed in the States.

When he was twelve, José yearned to see his mother. On his own, the prepubescent hopped trains and returned to El Cargadero, in which he hadn't stepped foot since infancy. Maria Bermudez barely acknowledged José, which broke the skinny boy's heart. He stayed in El Cargadero for a couple of months, helping his father plow distant fields and raise the few head of livestock Plácido owned. But as beautiful as El Cargadero was, and despite the mother lode in the Morenci Mine, Plácido just never made enough money. The decision to gamble and swing for Southern California wasn't hard. On the way west, Uncle Sam also made Plácido Miranda sign a registration card for World War I—saw it meself on Ancestry.com.

Others were joining the Miranda men in *el Norte*. The Mexican Revolution was just wrapping up, and troops loyal to Pancho Villa continued to terrorize villagers even though the wealthy had deserted El Cargadero long before. One of those couples fleeing the misguided revolutionaries were Bonifacia Ortiz and Sabas Fernandez.

Bonifacia was familiar with the United States. In the early 1900s, Bonifacia and four of her sisters arrived in El Paso as toddlers. Their mom, Norberta Ortiz de Martinez, traveled from El Cargadero to Texas by burro for months with her daughters, alone. A famine had stricken El Cargadero, and hundreds were dying. "I don't want to starve!" Norberta repeatedly told her husband, Benito, the son of a French soldier named Lugardo who had Hispanicized his surname to Martinez after the 1860s French occupation of Mexico to hide from the execution-happy Mexican government. Benito, however, refused to leave, insisting that if death came for him, may it arrive in the rancho of his birth. Norberta and her daughters trekked north; Benito starved to death. Norberta and the girls returned a couple of years later, but Bonifacia would have to flee yet again, this time with her husband, Sabas, for the Arizona copper mines.

In the towns of Metcalf and Morenci, hundreds of people from El Cargadero found refuge from the Revolution and a steady salary in the copper mines. The men mined; the women had children, American citizens. An entire generation of anchor babies. One was my grandmother, Marcela Fernandez, born in 1914.

My Mama Chela's childhood was like that of any American girl at the time: school, dolls, and friends. "I was completely bilingual as a child," she says, nowadays living in Anaheim and still spry in her nineties. "All the people from El Cargadero asked me to translate for them, and I would." Now, the only English phrases she knows are the nursery rhymes "The Bear Went over the Mountain," "Did You Ever See a Laddie?" and "Little Redbird in the Tree."

"People think I can't understand English, but some of the words I'm familiar with here and there," she says in Spanish. "Most of my English, I lost."

In the early 1920s, most of the *cargaderenses* in Arizona—following the optimistic words of my Papa Plácido—migrated to Anaheim's citrus groves. My grandmother's family relocated to Corona, just outside Orange County. But Mexico was improving, and in 1923, the Fernadezes returned to El Cargadero, followed by almost every other *cargaderense* in exile.

Metcalf is now a ghost town, but Morenci and its copper mine still exist. A tombstone once stood in Metcalf, marking all the people who died in this boomtown; many were from El Cargadero. The tombstone no longer exists, but a picture does—I stumbled upon it while randomly Googling one night, but can't locate it anymore. Guard your family memories with zeal, people.

❖   ❖   ❖

AREA CODES

Orange County got its first exclusive area code in 1951, and 714 ruled over the land for forty-five years. But as South County exploded during the 1990s, locals demanded their own prefix. In 1998, 949 was born and immediately became a marker of prestige—to be from a 949 meant you were from South County—rich, white, new, Newport Beach. And 714 was left to North and Central County—old, minority, poor, minority, poor minority. The equation will become further muddled next year with the addition of yet another area code to which Orange Countians can ascribe social status.

A couple of families didn't return to El Cargadero. About twenty *cargaderenses* moved to Anaheim during the 1920s, and most toiled in the city's lucrative citrus industry. While in Anaheim, my Papa Je stayed with another aunt: Maria Ramirez de Fernandez, whom everyone called Maria la Gorda (Mary the Fat Woman).

Life wasn't pleasant for José Miranda and his townspeople. Prohibited from moving into white neighborhoods, they rented houses close to citrus camps. Many restaurants barred Mexicans from entering; there were restrooms for Mexicans and whites. In the orange groves, the few white pickers always received better pay and tools than the Mexicans. Once, my grandfather and his friends tried to enter a movie theater, only to be chased out by the manager because they were Mexican.

My Papa Je learned English but rarely used it for fear white ears might burn in anger. Mexicans were expected to work, stay in their barrios, and not raise a fuss. Their neighborhoods—La Conga, La Fábrica, Colonia Independencia—were tight-knit and next to the orchards, but perpetually run-down, with shoddy plumbing or electricity, if any. If children wanted an education, they went to the segregated George Washington School and—starting in 1928—La Palma Elementary, facilities built specifically for Mexicans. But Papa Je never entered a classroom—upon arriving in Anaheim, he went straight to work alongside his dad.

Orange picking is not the fun activity depicted in high school history books. There were quotas to meet, and procedures to follow. The fruit had to be grasped, gently snipped at the navel from the twig, then tossed into a bag hanging from a strap that cut across one's chest. After about thirty pounds or so of oranges, the *naranjeros* stepped off their ladder and placed the bounty in crates. Bruised oranges weren't allowed, nor those with twigs sticking out. Two cents a box in those days. Sunrise to sunset, six days a week.

My grandfather didn't enjoy the routine, so he applied for and was accepted into the Anaheim Orange and Lemon Association Packing House, which opened in 1919 and was one of the largest in Orange County at the time. The easier schedule allowed José to make a better living, and he started assimilating. On his off days, the light-complexioned chap dressed in suits and fedoras, smoking cigarettes and palling around with other young Mexican men. They called themselves *tempranillos*—early guys—because they woke up early even after staying up long nights shooting the shit.

Around 1928, Maria Bermudez suddenly wanted to see her discarded son. Papa Plácido—who had returned to El Cargadero—had also heard his youngest son was hanging out with the wrong crowd, so he rode the tracks again from El Cargadero to El Paso to Anaheim and retrieved José. The young man was crushed. His friends pleaded with Papa Plácido to let their fellow *tempranillo* stay, but he refused. A dejected José Miranda returned to the rancho of his birth, a place about which he knew next to nothing.

The pain subsided quickly—it was marrying time. The choice of Marcela Fernandez was a formality—the Fernandezes and Mirandas knew each other—and even foretold despite the circumstances. Mama Chela had comfortably settled back in El Cargadero. Her parents had divorced due to my great-grandfather's philandering ways, leaving Mama Pacha (the nickname for her mom, Bonifacia) with a fortune and a mansion in the city of Jerez. The teenage Marcela enjoyed privilege, and her social circles didn't normally mingle with those of José Miranda.

It was in the stars, I tell you. A couple of years ago, my grandmother said she had a surprise for me. She looked through her room and showed me a picture of a young, stringy teen with a young girl. "That's a picture of me and your grandfather in Arizona, on the first day we ever met," she said, a flash of romance in her gray eyes. She was four; he was twelve and on the way to

Anaheim. We can't find the picture anymore, unfortunately—I blame one of my aunts.

In 1930, my Papa Je and Mama Chela decided to marry. They courted how any honorable Mexican couple of the time courted—he kidnapped her.

For centuries, El Cargadero's mating ritual followed a hallowed path: if a man liked a woman, he kidnapped her. The bride-to-be was in on the steal in most of the cases; other times, no. There was screaming, scandal, even murders over these abductions. No consummation of the marriage occurred during the kidnapping; instead, both families planned for a wedding. The woman had no choice—no other men dared marry her on account she was "dirty." My grandmother went willingly—so everyone says.

Yep, it's a bad custom. But the tradition continued at least into the 1960s and in the United States. One aunt's first marriage occurred this way. As a teen, a boy invited her to a liquor store, just a couple of blocks from her home, with the promise of Popsicles. Along the way, a car screeched up before the two. It was the boy's father. The two men shoved my screaming aunt into the car and sped off. The two married months later, despite her wishes. Guy turned out to be an abusive asshole.

The thought of kidnapping your future wife is inconceivable to my generation of *cargaderense* men, especially since the modern proper way is to ask the parents for their daughter's hand—still very patriarchic, but at least more advanced than whisking away your beloved. "Didn't the men of the family try to get the women back?" I asked my mom as a teen. "If a man tried that with my sister, I'd kill him or at least call the cops."

"That's just how it was then," my mom replied. *"Son costumbres de gente mensas"* (They're the customs of dummies).

◈   ◈   ◈

El Cargadero treated José and Marcela Miranda well. The anchor babies of the Mexican Revolution, those born in Arizona, had grown up and sired their own kids. The children went to school up to the sixth grade, then usually dropped out to help their parents. Almost everyone made his or her livelihood in agriculture, coaxing crops out of small plots of land handed to them by the Mexican government in the 1930s. El Cargadero had maybe three cars in those days—if people wanted to travel, a bus offered transportation, but most *cargaderenses* still preferred burros.

As a result of its isolation, the town became particularly close. Parties and the church were the focal points of the rancho—that, and the town's prized avocado trees, treasured for their buttery, oily fruit. The trees stood on the outskirts of town and lined the one road that led from El Cargadero to Jerez. The avocado trees were so big and healthy that, when the bus passed underneath, the branches brushed across the top. The town's leaders pooled money to start an export operation—El Cargadero avocados were shipped weekly to Laredo, Texas, and Mexico City. No one was wealthy, but the villagers had enough income to eat comfortably— as good as it got for peasants in those days.

Since Mexico is Mexico, all my grandmother did was have babies. There were Maria, Maria Mercedes, Maria Belen, Maria Angela, Mariana (who passed away in 1976), Alicia, and my mother, Maria de la Luz (Mary of the Light). On the boys' side were Ezequiel, Casimiro, and Jesús. In addition, my grandmother had at least three babies who passed away as infants. The Mirandas occupied a house Papa Je purchased from my grandmother's father—two stories, on a hill, with a courtyard and stables in the back.

My mom was born in 1951 but remembers little of her infancy in El Cargadero. Her first memories didn't even occur in the rancho but rather on a farm just outside El Cargadero that Papa Je purchased when she turned four. It was a beautiful estate, with a spring and well and next to grasslands where Papa Je's cows ate their fill and produced milk my grandmother squeezed out of their udders each morning. On adjacent fields, Papa Je grew peas, sweet potatoes, avocados, and peaches. He also built a machine that processed corn into masa, the cornmeal that has sustained Mexico for millennia. People from nearby villages paid my grandfather to crush their corn into the valuable foodstuff, from which they made tortillas and tamales. The house had no indoor plumbing, no electricity, and just an oil-powered stove. But the memories of my mom and her sisters paint a bucolic scene.

"I was the happiest child in Mexico," says my *tía* Angela of those days. "My entertainment was to chase chickens, playing games with the eggs."

Most of Mom's memories are tied to a creek that passed through the farm. People from the other villages went to draw water from it and fill each other in on the gossip in the valley. "It was so beautiful, so peaceful," Mami says. "So clean. One time, Angela and I were walking near the river when we heard people shouting. We were scared—it turned out to be evangelicals baptizing each other. We laughed at them and ran back home."

Despite tilling the farm to great rewards, my grandfather sold it after just a year. His older daughters were getting boyfriends, and to keep their *cargaderense* bloodline pure, my grandmother didn't want them to marry a man from outside the rancho.

"Men walked around the house at night, calling for your aunts Belen and Maria," Mama Chela said. "Every night! Around the wall, you could see the top of their sombreros. Your grandfather even bought a shotgun and fired it into the air to scare them off, but that didn't do anything."

Operating the farm wore down Papa Je. Just a couple of years after marrying, doctors operated on ulcers in his stomach but botched the procedure, leaving Papa Je with a stomach a fifth the size of a normal one. For the rest of his years, he suffered from constant malnourishment. If Papa Je consumed any more than a couple of spoonfuls for each meal, indigestion left him bedridden for days.

There was no inheritance to support the Mirandas—José's parents left little, and although Mama Chela's rich parents divorced, her parents were spendthrifts. But bad health didn't affect Papa Je's spirits or brain. He turned a nice profit selling the farm and invested the money in a massive chicken coop with five hundred hens just outside El Cargadero. He put my mother and Tía Angela in charge of collecting the eggs every morning; the girls always fought over the big ones.

All was relatively well until January 1955, when a freak frost blanketed the town. "I was six years old when people woke up and something felt strange in the air," Tía Angela recalls. "What was it? The avocado trees were very dry and hard. They split open from the frost. We had to cut the trees apart for firewood because they were destroyed."

El Cargadero's crops were ruined beyond salvage, but the avocados suffered the most. Trees split into shards; fruit froze. *Cargaderenses* tried everything to save their economy—smudge pots, water, and prayer. Nothing. They pruned the few avocado trees that hadn't immediately perished and waited. For months, men tended the surviving groves like children, praying that the coming crop would bring salvation. Instead, the first shoots of the new season were black and quickly atrophied.

Two years later, the climatic pendulum swung the other way, and a massive drought wiped out whatever had survived the frost. Many *cargaderenses* faced ruin, including my grandfather. He fell into debt on the house, and the chickens no longer operated at a profit. There was only one answer, and my mom remembers how she found out: one day, Papa Je announced to the kids, "We're going to *el Norte*," and that was that.

El Cargadero remembered a previous generation's journey to

the States. Soon, the second great exodus began. Dozens of men joined the bracero program, the initiative that imported millions of Mexican men into the United States from 1942 through 1964. During this time, the American government asked Mexico to provide its brawny, unemployed men to fill a labor shortage; Mexicans happily signed up. Two of them were my oldest uncles, Jesús and Casimiro. Buses took them to fields in Wisconsin, Michigan, California, and other states for months at a time. They sent wages back home to help their parents and siblings, but it still wasn't enough.

When the braceros returned, most *cargaderenses* headed toward Tijuana, armed with American birth certificates or sponsoring *cargaderenses* who had already spent years in Anaheim. On buses they arrived, carrying only luggage with a few changes of clothes. This wasn't a permanent move—just a couple of months, maybe even a year, to make enough money and move back to El Cargadero. Those who decided not to move were to watch over the properties of the migrants until they returned. That was the plan, at least.

On June 2, 1962, at ten in the morning, the Mirandas crossed the border. Accompanying my grandparents went the youngest children: my mom, Mercedes, Angela, Alicia, and Ezequiel. Jesús and Casimiro were already in the United States; Belen, Maria, and Mariana were married and committed to toughing it out in El Cargadero.

Before the Mirandas crossed the border, a U.S. immigration official asked my grandmother if she wanted my mom to apply for American citizenship. No. "When Luz is older, she can make the decision on her own" was Mama Chela's answer. Mami still hasn't forgiven her mother for that one.

The family's final destination was Hollister, California, a small town in Northern California. Its fame rests largely on an annual Fourth of July biker rally that inspired the Marlon Brando film *The Wild One*, rallies my family had never heard of until I mentioned them. The Mirandas moved to Hollister because my grandmother's brother José Fernandez worked there and there were garlic heads to cut, plums and pears to pick, wages to earn. The children joined in and didn't even bother with school, until an anonymous busybody alerted a social worker; she promptly threatened my grandparents with a hefty fine and deportation.

School officials put my mother in the fifth grade—on the first day of school, the bus dropped her off but no one bothered to tell Luz which was her class. Crying but not knowing any English, Mami wandered around campus for about half an hour before finding a janitor who spoke Spanish and English.

The Miranda children hated school in Hollister. Not knowing English, they found most of the classes incomprehensible. The other kids—mostly Portuguese or white—ridiculed the Mexicans mercilessly. When boys asked my *tío* Ezequiel what his name was in English, he responded, *"Igual."* The same. It's true—*Ezequiel* easily translates into *Ezekiel*. But for the rest of his time in Hollister, kids called my uncle Igual and beat him up, usually chasing Ezequiel until he climbed a tree, at which point the kids threw rocks. During gym, my mother sat to the side—my grandparents didn't have money to buy her shorts. Once, Tía Angela got in a fight with a Japanese kid, who yelled at her to go back to Mexico. "At least this land once belonged to Mexico," she shot back. "You go back to where you came from—Japan is much farther than Mexico!"

During the school year, the children picked crops on Saturday and Sunday. During the summer, it was all day, six days a week. Since they were younger, my mom and Tío Ezequiel did the easier tasks. They gathered nuts and apricots into baskets, chopping the latter fruit in half and splaying the pieces on a board.

Picking garlic and onions, on the other hand, was a task better suited for adults—for those crops, the kids had to crouch, carefully grab the vegetable from the moist soil, and cut off only the heads with special shears that caused blisters even if you wore gloves.

None of my aunts or Tío Ezequiel reminisce about those days. The only happy memory my mom has of those days were on Sundays, when a Filipino neighbor screened classic cartoons on a projector for the migrant children in the neighborhood. A couple of *cargaderenses* followed the Mirandas to Hollister, but not many. Others moved to Los Angeles or other cities in Southern California (including the father of the famous Chicana author Helena Maria Viramontes), but most who were leaving the rancho were grouping in Tijuana before proceeding to Anaheim.

One of their own had made it there: Plácido Veyna had gone from picking oranges as a child during the 1920s to owning a couple of homes and restaurants in one of the city's Mexican barrios. His brothers owned Veyna Brothers Market and participated in Anaheim's many civic parades. The Veynas gladly sponsored their fellow villagers, providing lodging and employer contacts. Another *cargaderense,* José Guerrero, also owned lots, and other men picked oranges for a couple of years before starting businesses. Even Anaheim's only Latino cop at the time, Joe Miranda, had ostensible *cargaderense* roots. His family was from Sinaloa, but a small colony of *cargaderenses* had moved to that Mexican Pacific state during the Revolution—in the minds of the new immigrants, Joe was probably from El Cargadero as well.

The Mirandas returned to Tijuana for a month until my uncle Jesús found an apartment in Anaheim. They crossed the border again on November 22, 1963, a date my mother remembers for the obvious reason. The family looked forward to living near other *cargaderenses* and to making money in the land of my Papa Je's upbringing. Just for a couple of months, of course.

Irvine: Every city wants to be Irvine, master-planned to perfection. The only slums are wherever college students from the UC Irvine, dorm, for chrissakes. Despite once being the epitome of white, wealthy, conservative Orange County, nowadays Irvine is diverse—with wealthy, conservative immigrants. Future home of the Great Park, a big mass of land that was once the El Toro Marine Air Corps and is now slated to become a park larger than Central Park—sorry for using the word *park* so much in this sentence, but a thesaurus can only do so much. **Best restaurant:** Actually, it's a grocery store: **Wholesome Choice.** Amazing buffets for Persian, Greek, and Indian food (stay away from the Chinese and the Thai). Also bakes *sangak,* a four-foot-long Persian flatbread so divine the line for a freshly baked portion is usually a minimum half-hour long. *18040 Culver Drive, Irvine, (949) 551-4111; www.wholesomechoice.com.*

"Our Climate Is Faultless":
Constructing America's
Perpetual Eden

In the early 1960s, the Anaheim City School District released a fifty-seven-page booklet titled *Living in Orange County*. School officials published it in response to the hundreds of children who were entering Anaheim elementary schools in those years, part of an American in-migration to Orange County that was turning the area from farmland and small towns to the American Dream.

Living in Orange County's protagonists were Diane and Don, siblings from Fresno who had never experienced Southern California. When Diane asked her mom if Anaheim was a big city, the mother replied she remembered Orange County from a trip long ago, when it was tiny. Now was different, however: "In fact, I think Orange County is the fastest-growing area in the country."

A brief history of the county ensued, written for children but equally relevant to their newbie parents. Diane and Don, meanwhile, zipped from one landmark to another, concluding their tour in Newport Beach. "I think Orange County is just about the best place in the whole world to live!" Don proclaimed as the book ended and the surname-less family drove home to their new Orange County lives.

The most inappropriate passage in the book, however, occurs when Diane asks her mother if Orange County continued to harvest oranges. "There are still many orange groves," replies her mother. "However, houses now cover much of the land that used to have orange trees. There are many motels and places to eat. More and more apartment houses are being built. There are many big shopping centers."

To placate any new Orange County residents who might want to see those orchards, *Living in Orange County* contained a full-page picture titled "Typical Orange Grove in Orange County." Rows and rows of orange trees spread across the frame in the photo, all the way to foothills. If you squint, you can make out the ghostly images of farmhands out in the groves, fixing an aquatic ditch.

The inclusion of such an agrarian reminder jars with the rest of the small book, which devotes itself to modern, grown-up Orange County. But the message was clear: no matter what happened to Orange County, no matter how much housing might sprout in the region, those large, fragrant trees that contributed so much to the county's status had a guaranteed, cherished place.

Forty years later, that promise is almost gone.

Consider the quarter acre or so of orange trees on the corner of Santa Ana and Helena streets in Anaheim. Every winter, their fruit hangs from the branches, bright and plump, awaiting pickers. But the grove is almost always quiet, save for pedestrians who trail their hands along the chain-link fence that keeps the trees free from trespassers. And so, the fruit falls to the ground and rots.

Nearby, in a vacant lot that was an orange grove not even five years ago, new town homes await their sale. More are on the way. Cars buzz by, oblivious to the orange grove, the fenced-off living history. Before the luxury houses came, you could walk into this orange grove, no questions asked, and pick a ripe, golden Valencia straight from a branch. Not anymore. Razor wire now tops the chain-link fence, and a gate stops people from entering at will. If you ask the men who repair cars in the factory next door if they can let you in, they run you off with a growl. Construction tools lie nearby. This was once a mere piece of a massive orange grove that covered hundreds of acres. But it won't be long before this, one of the last orange groves in Orange County, too, falls victim to Progress.

Down the street is the Sunkist Packing House, the same place where my grandfather packed oranges in the 1920s. Touted as state-of-the-art when first opened, the building is now a historical landmark, one of the last citrus packinghouses in Southern California that didn't meet the hard swing of a demolition ball. It also has no use. The last oranges were packed here in the 1950s; today, it's a furniture warehouse. The windows are broken or boarded up. The only functioning area is in the back, where the packinghouse's original icehouse served the surrounding neighborhood's beer-cooling needs decades after the last orange crates were loaded. The icehouse shut down last year.

Kitty-corner from the packinghouse stand faux New York City–style brownstones. Up the street are lofts and a new Cuban coffeehouse—never mind that few Cubans live in Anaheim. Other properties—bars, houses, used-car lots—are condemned but await gentrification.

Orange groves still exist in Orange County—the Kimberly-Clark campus in Fullerton has one fenced off, and orange trees sway just off the 5 Freeway in Irvine and near the Orange-Riverside county line. Drive around long enough anywhere in Orange County, and you'll see the irregular, waxy leaves of the tree peek out of backyards. But they're illusions: fewer than one hundred acres total from a high of more than sixty-five thousand acres in 1948.

The most prominent reminders of Orange County's past citrus dreams mock you on the 22 Freeway. A couple of years ago, county supervisors authorized billions of dollars for an expansion and beautification project. The expansion succeeded, and cars can now zoom on the 22 most hours. The beautification angle consisted of connecting soundwalls with concrete pillars every hundred yards or so, etched with bas-relief oranges, fleeting reminders of the fruit that satiated a nation and made America first notice Orange County. Those are *our* oranges—who cares if they're fake. The past must always be present here, or at least its illusion, lest the dream finally wither.

When I was a student at Chapman University in Orange during the early 2000s, hanging on the walls of Beckman Hall—a four-story glass structure that housed the school's business program—were dozens of orange-crate labels. They were collector's items and truly gorgeous, each representing a particular packinghouse, all portraying the same theme of health and heaven on the Pacific coast. The Mission Brand featured a group of befuddled monks examining oranges, with a Spanish-style home in front of acres of orange groves and Old Saddleback—the ridge made by Santiago and Modjeska peaks—in the background. Others used pretty women, genies, Indians, to sell their fruit. The labels function as artifact, as history lesson, as economic ambition. Propaganda functioning as projected dreams. Orange County as Nirvana.

To understand Orange County, you must accept the Cult of the Orange Crate. From its settlement by the Spaniards until today, residents have emphasized that they're creating a spectacular civilization, a County on the Hill: one that attracts but also inspires others to copy. The PR campaign has succeeded for over a century, even if its projected image never fit neatly into reality. Doesn't matter; if we say we're wonderful, you'd better believe it.

The mythmaking began as soon as Spanish conquistadors set the foundation for Mission San Juan Capistrano. Its caretakers deem it "the Jewel" of California's mission system and claim that a half million tourists tour the mission's grounds each year to marvel at its rose gardens, its restored golden retablo, and the ruins of Great Stone Church, the final resting place for about forty Indian converts who were unlucky enough to be praying there when a giant earthquake leveled it in the 1800s. But the mission wasn't always so revered—for a while, it served as the home of Juan Forster, an English immigrant who purchased the mission along with most of present South County from the Mexican government for $710 in 1844. Forster returned the mission to the Catholic Church in 1864, and the Church began restoring the buildings, mainly because the mission's chapel was the last existing structure where Father Junípero Serra had officiated over Mass.

Mission San Juan Capistrano's long-lost luster and relative isolation tickled the mind of Johnston McCulley, who published *The Curse of Capistrano* in 1919. This novella debuted Zorro, the mythical hero who sparked a celebration of a nonexistent California past where Spanish dons entertained guests for nights, and Manifest Destiny was applied only to the Indians. There is little mention of the actual mission in *The Curse of Capistrano*—actually, just one: the villain Pedro Gonzalez remarks he broke a sword "while fencing at San Juan Capistrano," which he occasionally guards. McCulley never fully explains why Zorro is called the Curse of Capistrano, just that the town is "where he began this wild life of his, and for that reason the Curse of Capistrano he is called."

Douglas Fairbanks filmed a version of the short story in 1920, changed the name to *The Mark of Zorro*, and the exciting Capistrano that the movie depicted became an American obsession. "The Zorro myth presented a Southern California that never existed," wrote Kevin Starr in *Material Dreams: Southern California through the 1920s*, "a material dream of chivalry, romance, swordplay, and roses rising up against a creamy white Andalusian wall."

For Fairbanks to pick this tale to film wasn't too surprising. During the silent era, filmmakers flocked to Orange County to use its diverse topography for shooting. No major film save for *The Mark of Zorro* actually set its story in Orange County, but the big names filmed here—D. W. Griffith was supposedly the first, and following were Mack Sennett, Harold Lloyd, Buster Keaton, and Santa Ana native Roscoe "Fatty" Arbuckle. Parts of Cecil B. DeMille's original *The Ten Commandments* were filmed in Seal Beach, while *All Quiet on the Western Front*'s horrific trench warfare was actually played out on the sandy slopes of Corona Del Mar. Even Fairbanks's wife, Mary Pickford, married her first husband in the Capistrano chapel, an occasion commemorated with a mission-owned painting.

The mission staff were smart—its newfound fame via Zorro grabbed people's attention, but more was needed to keep it. They found a lasting attraction in birds.

For centuries, swallows returned from their winter nesting grounds in Argentina to the Capistrano area every year around March 19. The small birds nested all around the area, not just the mission, but the annual rite intrigued outsiders. In 1930, the mission published *Capistrano Nights: Tales of a California Mission Town*. One of the stories included was "The Mission Swallows and How They Arrive Every Year for the Feast of Saint Joseph." According to the tale, a padre was walking through Capistrano near the mission when he saw a shopkeeper destroying a nest of swallows. After realizing that the shopkeeper wanted to kill them, the father announced to the birds, "Come on, swallows . . . I'll give you shelter. Come to the mission, there's room enough there for all!"

The holy man wasn't named, nor did authors Charles Francis Saunders and Father St. John O'Sullivan provide a date for the anecdote, but the idea that small birds returned every year on the same day to the mission because of a priest's goodwill struck a chord with Depression-weary America. O'Sullivan wrote, "I am safe in saying that Capistrano's charm needs no such crutch to support it." The priest wrote about the swallows, "Every month the moon blesses the ancient pile with a mystical beauty that is sufficient of itself."

Nevertheless, the mission needed money. On March 19, 1939, priests welcomed the media to record the return of the swallows. "Sure enough," wrote *Time* a week later, "sharp at 5:56 a.m., 40 minutes after sunrise, a lowering cloud appeared on the horizon, grew bigger and bigger until it all but blotted out the Mission sunlight, making the air loud with the beat of thousands of narrow wings. Suddenly, while the rest flew on to the canyons beyond, a great segment of the swallow cloud broke off, swooped down on the Mission." Tourists have flocked from across the world ever since.

It's also part of mission lore that this same broadcast inspired Leon René to pen "When the Swallows Come Back to Capistrano." As with the actual incident the song uses as a metaphor for unrequited love, the origin of its lyrics is a bit of a fib. The popular version of the story goes that René heard a broadcaster say the swallows were returning to Capistrano that morning and penned the song in admiration of the critters. But René disclosed to a Louisiana genealogical publication a couple of years ago that he got the idea for the song after his wife didn't cook breakfast fast enough. "Maybe when the swallows come back to Capistrano," he told his wife, "I'll get my breakfast." Liking the line, he wrote a couple of stanzas for it; summarily impressed, the wife made breakfast. With his appetite satiated, René finished the song's music and lyrics. "When the Swallows Come Back to Capistrano" became a WWII–era smash—Guy Lombardo, the Ink Spots, and Glenn Miller recorded it, further promoting a tranquil, appealing Orange County to an America in need of peace.

❂   ❂   ❂

San Juan Capistrano: The city that started Orange County. Mostly Mexicans live around the Mission, and the community there is slummy. The whites live farther inland, in nice places. No reason to stop in the city except the Mission, although those new houses going up in the hills are pretty nice. **Best restaurant:** Located in the oldest continuously inhabited neighborhood in California, **Ramos House Café** makes Southern-style cooking into an art form rather than some Dixie relic. *31752 Los Rios Street, San Juan Capistrano, (949) 443-1342; www.ramoshouse.com.*

While Capistrano tied Orange County to an idealized past, its booming agricultural industry promoted a profitable, appetizing present.

The region's soil had always provided fragile bounties. The families who originally owned Orange County—the Yorbas, Ontiveroses, Avilas, Rioses, and others—became rich by herding hundreds of thousands of cattle, fattening them on the nutritious grass of the county and the replenishing waters of the Santa Ana River. This industry attracted Richard Henry Dana and other Americans to Southern California in the decades before the Mexican-American War. But lethal combinations of floods and droughts largely destroyed the ranchos by the 1850s, and litigating American businessmen eager for the Californios' holdings drove many toward bankruptcy. The vintners who started Anaheim saw bumper grape and wine harvests during the 1860s, but the colony teetered on bankruptcy in the 1880s when blight destroyed nearly all the vines within a year. Over the coming decades, Orange County boasted walnut groves, sugar beet crops, lima bean fields, and sheep herds that ranked among the largest in America, only to see each collapse within years. It was to citrus, specifically the sweet, sturdy Valencia orange, that most of the county's farmers quickly tied their fortunes.

Charles C. Chapman, an orange grower and descendant of Johnny Appleseed, wrote a history of the young industry in 1911. One passage in particular embodies the determinism of that era's county leaders:

Indeed, the Divine hand has been lavish in bestowing upon all Southern California, and upon Orange County in particular, rare natural advantages, perhaps greater than those enjoyed by any other section over which the flag floats. The magnificent mountain ranges not only form picturesque scenery and giant bulwarks to guard the fertile valleys, but are our great natural reservoirs. Our coast is washed by the boundless Pacific. Our climate is faultless. In fact, it is not too much to say that as to fertility of soil, the charming climate and the scenery with its grandeur and beauty, it is not surpassed the world around.

Multiple stories purport to explain how entrepreneurs introduced oranges to Orange County, but the one endorsed by the County of Orange Archives credits Dr. William N. Hardin of Anaheim with planting the first orange tree in 1870. Hardin, the story goes, had two barrels filled with rotten Tahiti oranges from which he saved the seeds and grew trees. Sounds like yet another unverifiable fable, no? Indisputable, however, is that orange trees took well to the county. "By the blessing of nature, Orange County had the lion's share of the summer crop [of oranges] when the consumer was thirstiest," wrote UC Irvine professor Gilbert G. González in *Labor and Community: Mexican Citrus Worker Villages in a Southern California County, 1900–1950,* his 1994 history of Orange County citrus pickers.

The rise of refrigerated railroad cars in the 1880s allowed citrus farmers to ship their edible gold across the country, and California growers hawked their wares and homeland at country fairs and expos. "On crates and at garden shows, oranges were presented as pure products of nature that would provide instant contact with California's therapeutic environment," wrote Douglas Cazaux Sackman in his *Orange Empire: California and the Fruits of Eden*. But more than just provide a dreamscape, the oranges also filled national stomachs and county coffers, accounting for two-thirds of the county's agricultural profits during the 1930s and one-sixth of the country's Valencia orange crop.

Orange County groves became renowned, thanks not just to the fruits but the ornate labels on every packing box. What the labels, farmers, and civic leaders never highlighted was the means of production: Mexicans. A mix of whites, Filipinos, Chinese, Indians, and Mexicans had picked the initial harvests in the late 1800s, but by the 1920s orange growers were arranging to bring in as much Mexican labor as possible. Citrus camps sprouted across the orange groves, and the growers created Americanization programs for their wards. Men picked the crop; women sorted them at packinghouses. Even children joined in, grabbing any low-lying fruit or those that the older men dropped. The growers nick-named them *ratas*—rats.

This arrangement was generally fine until June 1936, when about twenty-five hundred *naranjeros* representing more than half of Orange County's citrus-picking force dropped their clippers, bags, and ladders to demand higher wages, better working conditions, and the right to unionize. Their demands didn't sit well with the orange growers or Sheriff Logan Jackson, himself the owner of a grove. Jackson and his fellow growers colluded with the district attorney's office, the Board of Supervisors (which had the previous year outlawed picketing in Orange County), and local police agencies to crush the strike. Freshly deputized private guards arrested Mexicans en masse and raided striker meetings with tear gas and ax handles. The growers asked the American government to repatriate the Mexican consul who sided with the strikers and asked immigration authorities to deport the same men the growers had gladly overworked just weeks earlier. After a month of virtual civil war, the strike ended—the *naranjeros* earned a small raise but not the right to unionize.

The 1936 Citrus War is ignored in most histories of American labor, largely because it's almost nonexistent in the annals of Orange County, both during the actual strike—when local newspapers ridiculed strikers and interviewed only angry police officers and growers—and in its history books. Even the most diligent researcher will be hard-pressed to find *any* mention of it in Orange County scholarly anthologies. A 1975 *Los Angeles Times* retrospective noted the paucity of information about the strike, calling it "one of the least-chronicled incidents in the history of the citrus belt." "It still is not mentioned in polite histories," an unnamed professor told the *Times*. "It was not a very pretty thing, but it tells something about where this county has been."

It's telling that the strike's best chronicler was Carey McWilliams, the great progressive journalist and longtime editor of the *Nation*. In 1939, he published *Factories in the Field*, which, alongside John Steinbeck's *Grapes of Wrath* and Dorothea Lange's Okie portraits, toppled California's carefully cultivated reputation. One of the book's sections, titled "Gunkist Oranges," was adapted from an article of the same name McWilliams wrote for *Pacific Weekly* at the height of the Citrus War. The Orange County strike, McWilliams wrote in the article, was "one of the toughest exhibitions of 'vigilantism' that California has witnessed in many a day. . . . Under the direction of Sheriff Logan Jackson, who should long be remembered for his brutality in this strike, over 400 special guards, armed to the hilt, are conducting a terroristic campaign of unparalleled ugliness."

McWilliams added in *Factories in the Field*, "No one who has visited a rural county in California under these circumstances, will deny the reality of the terror that exists. It is no exaggeration to describe this state of affairs as fascism in practice."

Even years later, McWilliams couldn't shake the strike. In his 1946 *Southern California: An Island on the Land,* he remembered being "astonish[ed] in discovering how quickly social power could crystallize into an expression of arrogant brutality in these lovely, seemingly placid, outwardly Christian communities.

"In the courtrooms of the county I met former classmates of mine in college, famous athletes of the University of Southern California, armed with revolvers and clubs, ordering Mexicans around as though they were prisoners in a Nazi concentration camp."

The Citrus War had a profound effect on McWilliams, according to his biographer, Peter Richardson. He points to a passage from his book *American Prophet: The Life & Work of Carey McWilliams,* a 1940 interview in which McWilliams said, "I hadn't believed stories of such wholesale violation of civil rights until I went down to Orange County to defend a number of farm workers held in jail for 'conspiracy.' When I announced my purpose, the judge said, 'It's no use; I'll find them guilty anyway.'"

"McWilliams saw a contrast between the fruit-crate-label version of California and ugly labor practices," Richardson told me for a 2006 story I did on the 1936 Citrus War. "It fed his notion that there was this bright, pleasant surface to California life, but it had an uglier underside. The Orange County citrus strike struck a chord for him because it was so obviously unjust."

After suppressing the strike, the growers went back to reaping millions. But the oranges didn't last. In the 1940s, a virus infected the county's groves, killing trees by the thousands within weeks. Farmers named it the Quick Decline, but the Mexican pickers called it *la tristeza*—the sadness. As more people began moving into Orange County, farmers found that their groves turned a better profit as lots to be sold and built on. Once beloved and all-powerful, King Citrus died a quiet, fragrant death.

Tract housing soon spread across these orchards and other farms in Central and North County, and cities enshrined their agricultural past with fairs and festivals—La Habra has a Corn Festival, Garden Grove celebrates the Strawberry Parade, and Tiller Days are what they hold in Tustin. But it was time to show the country a new Tree of Life.

Tract housing wasn't an Orange County invention—if anything, it copied what was happening in suburbs across the United States from Levittown to Lakewood. The idea of master-planned communities, though, reached its apotheosis both for old and young in Orange County.

Planned communities are actually old hat in Orange County. In the 1920s, while traveling from San Diego to Los Angeles, Ole Hanson passed through Orange County and was immediately enamored with the land between the Orange–San Diego county line to San Juan Capistrano—hilly, seamlessly sweeping into the Pacific or toward undeveloped wilderness. Hanson was a celebrity of sorts, having crushed a citywide strike in 1919 as mayor of Seattle and unsuccessfully sought the Republican presidential nomination in 1920.

This son of Norwegian immigrants bought the property and announced he was going to create a new city: San Clemente, named for the island within eyesight of the Orange County coast. In 1928, it incorporated as a city and pronounced itself a Spanish Village by the Sea. Drawing on the cult of Zorro and the mission already associated with the county, Hanson structured the ordinances so that all houses and businesses were built in a Spanish-revival style—whitewashed, red-tiled roofs, with flowery street names such as Avenida del Mar, Avenida Califia, and El Camino Real. The lots sold out within a year, and San Clemente opened up Orange County beachfront to the possibility of more than just sand and waves.

Twenty-eight years later, Ross W. Cortese envisioned a different kind of reverence for old times. In 1956, the developer built Rossmoor, an unincorporated area between Los Alamitos and

Seal Beach that was one of the country's first walled-off neighborhoods. Then, after a conversation with Los Angeles's Cardinal Francis McIntyre about the housing needs of the elderly, Cortese decided to create a city specifically for seniors. He opened Leisure World Seal Beach in 1962, America's first planned community for geezers. Critics accused Cortese of building a "geriatric ghetto," but the demand was there—he sold the community's six thousand houses within a couple of years.

Cortese wasn't finished. The same year he opened Leisure World Seal Beach, he bought about thirty-five hundred acres from the Moulton Ranch, pastureland that encompassed most of what today is Laguna Hills and Laguna Woods. Here, he built another Leisure World twice the size of the original. The visionary went on to build five more across the country before passing away in 1991. By then, senior housing communities were an accepted part of American aging. "The idea was so beautiful that we put it to work," Cortese told a reporter a few years before his death. "It just took off like a bomb."

Cortese chose Orange County for the experiment because he viewed it as "the new development frontier." Orange County landowners in the undeveloped south were also realizing the potential of their properties. In 1959, the University of California asked the Irvine Ranch for land to open a new university. The ranch occupied almost one-fifth of Orange County, from the Cleveland National Forest all the way to the Pacific, a swath so huge its owners set up a water system company historians claimed was "the largest private water system ever built in the United States and, possibly, ever built in the world."

By the time UC regents made their proposal to the Irvine Ranch, it was no longer in the sole possession of the Irvine family. The company's board of directors refused to part with any land, much to the anger of Joan Irvine Smith, granddaughter of the ranch's founder, James Irvine. She publicly revealed the no vote to the public, hoping to embarrass the Irvine Company into charity. In the face of public resentment, the company hired UC's architect, William Pereira, to design a model community around a planned university. He envisioned self-sufficient villages, but the housing market demanded Pereira build more than what he wanted. As it expanded, the small town incorporated as Irvine in 1971.

The same boom was happening even farther south, in Rancho Mission Viejo and Rancho Trabuco, the hilly lands in South County that weren't San Juan Capistrano or San Clemente. The family in control, the O'Neills, decided to sell ten thousand acres in the late 1950s to a group called the Mission Viejo Company, a badly mangled translation of the ranch's original name, Misión Vieja (Old Mission). One of the company's principals was Donald Bren.

If you want to blame same-look suburbanization for the downfall of America, if you hate the Orange County method of micromanaging cities down to every blade of grass and molting salamander, blame Bren, whom the *Los Angeles Times* named the most powerful person in Southern California a couple of years ago, saying, "Simply put, Orange County looks like Orange County—much of it uniformly manicured and catering to the high life and high tech—because of the influence of Bren." Imagine Gatsby combined with John Muir, Howard Hughes, and Rockefeller, and you still can't match the mysterious pomposity of the man.

Bren was the stepson of Claire Trevor, the Academy Award–winning actress who first became famous for her role as a prostitute opposite John Wayne in *Stagecoach*. After a stint in the marines, Bren returned to Southern California and began building houses in Orange County. After seeing Mission Viejo turn into a community within a couple of years, Bren sold his interest in the Mission Viejo Company and struck out on his own for a while. In 1977, he and other investors bought a one-third share in the

Irvine Company; a couple of years after that, Bren bought out all shares.

Under his watch, the Irvine Ranch turned, in just forty years, from a place to raise cattle into an ever-spreading blob of meticulously managed fiefdoms. Professors called Bren's Orange County one of America's "key laboratories of contemporary urbanism, a giant theme park," and *BusinessWeek* described Bren as "the last of the California land barons." One former employee described it thusly: "Other developers build homes. The Irvine Company builds cities." Despite such an overarching presence in shaping modern Orange County, Bren is aloof, a reclusive man who former secretary of the interior Bruce Babbitt described as "presid[ing] over his holdings like a Spanish grandee, attending to every detail, down to the placement of individual palm trees along the medians and open spaces." Don't bother trying to learn more: Irvine Company drones must sign nondisclosure statements, and Bren only agrees to interviews when guaranteed positive coverage.

Bren's success with Irvine kick-started suburbanization south of Irvine. By the 1980s, a new term entered the Orange County lexicon: *South County,* code for the newness south of the 55 Freeway where wealthier people relocated to escape their parents' decaying North and Central County neighborhoods. The county experienced a new wave of city incorporations—from 1988 until 2001, eight cities joined Orange County, almost all of them indistinguishable from one another.

The developers who transformed the county replaced the Californios of old to become modern dons. Newspapers, lifestyle magazines, and society pages hail these men as visionaries, as the area's superstars. It's not surprising that perhaps the best historian of the development of Orange County is First American Title Insurance, which has shot pictures of Orange County for almost a century.

Tens of thousands of people migrated from across the United States to the creations of Bren and others, just slightly below the hundreds of thousands who moved to Orange County during the post–WWII housing boom. The sameness of these fresh burbs—many governed by strict homeowner associations that micromanaged everything a resident could do to his abode, from the color of the paint on the door to the type of plants on the front lawn—earned widespread derision from the rest of the country. "While the wives of Orange County may not be the home-oriented drudges that Ira Levin described in his 1972 novel, the new towns could serve as model communities for the distaff side of Stepford," the *New York Times* harrumphed in 1983. No one in Orange County minded—instead, they hailed their newfound image as perfect towns governed by benevolent builders.

These new communities have spurred envy in older Orange County cities, which have strived to redevelop themselves in South County style since the rise of Irvine. Anaheim is embarking on an ambitious plan to incorporate high-rise towers for live/work purposes around Angel Stadium and the Honda Center (where the Anaheim Ducks play hockey). Santa Ana is trying similar measures—ironic, since every Orange County city is desperately trying to reinvent itself before becoming another Santa Ana, America's worst-case Mexican scenario.

The county seat had always fancied itself the center of Orange County and still does—last year, city officials spent more than $1 million to refurbish a water tower next to the 5 Freeway and paint it with a new slogan: DOWNTOWN ORANGE COUNTY. But in reality, per a 2004 study by the State University of New York's Nelson A. Rockefeller Institute of Government, the city is the toughest place to live in the United States. Santa Ana boasts other ignominious distinctions. One of the most Spanish-speaking in the United States. Youngest. Most immigrant-heavy. Most Latino. Fattest. Densest. For these reasons, Santa Ana ("SanTana," as pronounced by the city's Latino supermajority) is a dirty place in Orange County, the brown blight no one wants to discuss.

Santa Ana officials are trying their hardest to get over this Little Mexico reputation, investing millions of dollars into lofts, museums, and artists' villages in an effort to "diversify" (read *de-Mexicanize*) the city and make it "safe" for all the South County residents. But the efforts are largely for naught. Even now, with an all-Latino city council—the largest such city in the United States—the city tries to pretend it's a Bren clone, part of the Gunkist memories, not content with its reality as the Lower East Side of Orange County.

Santa Ana is lesson, warning, and code word in Orange County for cities that don't pay close attention to the folks moving in. Poverty? Can't exist in Orange County.

But one little wrinkle won't stop other people from aspiring to an OC paradise. In China, developers opened their very own Orange County in 2003, filled with town homes modeled on neighborhoods in California. "As in the case of its namesake," the *New York Times* duly noted, "Orange County (China) is mostly a haven for conservative lawyers, businesspeople and celebrities, looking for a peaceful place to rear children." The dream never withers.

Mission Viejo: Once owned by Philip Morris, now one of the slummiest cities in South County only because its housing tracts are old—and, by *old* we mean built during the 1960s. Most of the people I've met from here are absolute jerks—can't explain why, but they are. Mission Viejo High made national headlines during the 1990s because it decided to call its sports teams the Diablos, and Christian parents protested. Now, a Christian student has sued his Capistrano High School history teacher for anti-Christian remarks. Not a good town. **Best restaurant: Aloha BBQ,** a Hawaiian barbecue owned by a Korean, which means the meat is very good. *24000 Alicia Parkway, Ste. 4, Mission Viejo, (949) 581-0976.*

UNINCORPORATED COMMUNITIES

In addition to thirty-four cities, Orange County has long-standing unincorporated areas with their own charms. Sunset Beach is as close to the original Orange County bohemian surfer landscape as you can find; Midway City is a collection of dilapidated apartment complexes, a school, and a feedstore. To the east of Santa Ana and Tustin are upscale neighborhoods—Cowan Heights, Orange Park Acres, Lemon Heights—that want nothing to do with those loser cities. South County has seen the largest explosion of unincorporated communities over the last two decades, as ultra-wealthy enclaves such as Coto de Caza (to be discussed later), Las Flores, Ladera Heights, and Dove Canyon exemplify everything wrong with wealth. Special shout-out goes to the folks in canyon country: residents of Modjeska, Trabuco, and Silverado Canyons, beware of encroaching tracts!

His Fake Green Card,
Her Tomato Packing

Lorenzo Arellano first invaded the United States while holding in a major piss.

In the summer of 1968, Lorenzo told his parents he was off to Los Angeles in the footsteps of his older brothers. His father commanded Lorenzo to stay, begged that the Arellanos needed every hand possible to care for the family's meager crops and livestock. "I don't care," Lorenzo yelled while walking away from his parents' tiny house. "I'm gone."

With a change of clothes and $30 in his pockets, the seventeen-year-old hopped on a bus headed for Tijuana. The bus crawled up Mexico's Pacific coast, stopping every couple of hours to pick up more people until all the seats filled, until families sat in the aisle. Old, young, man, woman—everyone seemed headed to Tijuana in the hope of migrating to the United States illegally.

After about thirty hours, the bus finally reached its destination. Lorenzo and his cousin Gilberto spent eight days milling around the border town, selling doodads to gather the necessary funds for hiring a *coyote*—a human smuggler. At night, the two slept in a bedroom crammed with dozens of other men, all counting down the days until it was their time to play cat and mouse with *la migra*.

About a week after Lorenzo and Gilberto arrived, a white girl and a *pocho* pulled up in a Chevrolet Bel Air and called out their names. Lorenzo's brother had hired them to pick up the two young men. The couple opened the trunk. Fifty dollars. Lorenzo and Gilberto looked at each other. *"Vamos a rifárnolas,"* Gilberto told his cousin. Or, as they say in the King's English, "Fuck it."

The Arellano *primos* and another man squeezed in, bending themselves into fetal positions. Bodies touched. Warm breaths turned the trunk into a sauna—a dark, suffocating, claustrophobic sauna. The car was off to Los Angeles. It was the early afternoon.

Lorenzo heard the muffled voice of a border agent allowing the Chevy into the United States when they crossed the border. The car sped with its stock up Interstate 5. No one talked. They weren't scared, weren't nervous. Their fate was blunt: either they made it into the United States, or they didn't. Through San Diego, past Camp Pendleton. Lorenzo's limbs and body turned sore—and that Budweiser he drank before folding into the Bel Air was filtering through his kidneys.

Just one final stop before freedom: an immigration checkpoint past Camp Pendleton and before San Clemente, about halfway between Tijuana and Los Angeles. Hills are on one side; the Pacific Ocean on the other. No roads anywhere in sight except Interstate 5; if you're an illegal immigrant and the Border Patrol finds you at this point, you're heading back to Mexico.

Traffic slowed to a crawl—and then, a stop. Lorenzo's legs trembled. Damn beer!

The *gabacha* exchanged words with a Border Patrol agent. The three men held their breath—again, muffles.

And then the Bel Air sped off. The other man stirred. *"Ya lo hicimos, compa,"* he whispered excitedly to Lorenzo. *"Ya nos dieron el pase"* (We did it, buddy! They gave us the pass).

They rode for another hour or so before finally stopping in a parking lot. Lorenzo and the others stretched out. The Chevy had parked in Los Angeles's Chinatown, within walking distance of

Olvera Street, a tourist trap made to look like a Mexican village replete with strolling mariachis and vendors selling tacky trinkets. It was late—about 11 p.m. Lorenzo's brother Jesús greeted his kid brother.

"Where's the restroom?" Lorenzo asked, fidgeting.

"*No te preocupes,*" Jesús replied. "Don't worry." He drove the three to a bar called the Venus. The restrooms weren't clean.

After relieving himself, Lorenzo celebrated his successful crossing by ordering a beer. Then he noticed a disturbing image: there, in this seedy bar in a foreign country, were women. Drinking *cerveza*. And they weren't prostitutes. Lorenzo had never seen reputable ladies touch alcohol.

He walked out of the bar, shaking with fear. Lorenzo didn't blink at the thought of sneaking into the United States in a trunk, twisted like a pretzel for three hours—but this was too much.

Jesús ran after him. "*Cálmate,*" he told my father. "*Así es la vida aquí en los Estados Unidos*" (Calm down. That's how life is here in the United States).

Lorenzo marched back into the bar and drank until early in the morning. The following day, he went to work.

* * *

SAN ONOFRE

The San Onofre region is technically part of San Diego County, yet it houses important county features. Cristianitos Road starts in this area, and the immigration checkpoint here also scares legal and illegal Mexicans. San Onofre State Beach and Trestles are zealously guarded by surfers and environmentalists, who want to stop the 241 Toll Road from grazing the land. And ready to kill us all is the San Onofre Nuclear Generating Station, which every-one knows looks like a giant pair of tits.

If El Cargadero is Paradise Lost, Jomulquillo is the town that God forgot. The rancho is just down the mountain from El Cargadero, which means Jomulquillo doesn't receive the nourishing waters of the El Cargadero River until the August rainy season—and at that point, torrents split the tiny town in half. As a result, the rancho is a dusty outpost, a Sergio Leone landscape with rough men and women. Jomulquillo's houses are smaller than those in El Cargadero; the businesses in town are fewer and less varied—mostly convenience stores. For years, Jomulquillo didn't even have its own church; today, a priest conducts Mass about once a month, leaving the other weekends to laypeople entrusted with spreading God's word in His inhospitable slice of Jerez.

Little green exists in the village, whether in lucre or lushness; the dominant color is brown. And not just the streets or houses. While most of El Cargadero's residents are as light as *gabachos,* many people from Jomulquillo possess dark skin. Or so goes the myth—Jomulquillo has its fair share of *güeros,* while dark-skinned people in El Cargadero exist but tend to get shunned. Nevertheless, this misconception characterizes the relationship between the two towns. Ask El Cargadero natives to describe a *jomulquillense,* and they're likely to characterize them as violent, lazy, dark-skinned—the Mexicans of Jerez, if you will.

But the biggest difference between the two ranchos is the legacy of migration. Since El Cargadero was historically better off than Jomulquillo, its residents were more prone to aspire to a better lot and left home in pursuit of it. Jomulquillo's residents were too poor to afford a trip, too content with poverty to grumble, gamble, and leave. That changed, however, thanks to my father's family.

Lorenzo Arellano Perez was born on August 10, 1951, just fifteen days before my mother, the youngest of four boys, the sixth child of eight. The family resided in a small one-story house across the street from where my great-grandfather grew up. There was no potable water, no electricity, and the Arellanos were so poor they collected cow chips to burn for fuel.

No pictures of my father as a child exist. "We just didn't take pictures back then," my father says.

My father's childhood wasn't pleasant. At school, the teachers tied Lorenzo's left arm so that the natural southpaw was forced to write with his right hand—they said lefties were prone to mental illness. If he tried to write with the left hand, a wooden ruler smacked on his arm taught him otherwise. Lorenzo eventually learned the right way; to this day, Dad can scribble equally terribly with both hands.

The beatings soured Papi on scholastics, and after finishing fourth grade, Pepe presented young Lorenzo with a choice: go to school and I'll buy you a bike (Jomulquillo's school only went up to the fourth grade; if children wanted to continue their studies, they had to register at a school in a rancho named San Juan about twenty miles away). Or, if you don't want to study, help me with the cows. My father chose cows.

"Even young, I wanted to leave school," Papi now says. "I was playing dominoes and cards, swimming in the pools at eight. When *tu* Pepe gave me that choice to leave school, I was happy."

Lorenzo's days changed. Instead of constant schoolhouse beatings, he now watched over the family's fifteen cows. At seven in the morning, the ten-year-old and his mom, Angelita, went to the stables. His mom milked the cows to make cheese; Lorenzo shooed off the calves so they wouldn't drink too much of their mothers' milk. Afterward, he led the cows to Jomulquillo's then-grassy commons and spent the rest of the day making sure the herd stayed intact. One time, a scared cow ran into the mountains; rather than suffer a beating at the hands of his father, Lorenzo (clad in little more than sandals, pants, a shirt, and poncho) chased the cow for a day over mountains and the chill of night until finally bringing her home the following morning. As

Dad matured, Pepe also taught him how to grow corn and beans on land they owned just outside Jomulquillo.

Most of Lorenzo's peers also dropped out of school around sixth grade and helped their fathers with livestock and crops. It still wasn't enough. One by one, men left Jomulquillo to join the bracero program. My grandfather and dozens of men from his generation made the trek up north, mostly to citrus camps in Fullerton and Anaheim. From there, the men spread across Orange County's fields to pick, cut, and send money back home. One of the orchards where my grandfather picked oranges is now Thomas Jefferson Elementary, my childhood school.

"*No iban de ilegal,*" my father stresses. None of my Pepe's generation came illegally to the United States. "They came only to get ahead in life, because the dollar was always better." But they all returned; they wanted American money to invest in Jomulquillo. "There was no *Norte,*" my father remembers. "People stayed in Jomulquillo and died in Jomulquillo."

Then tragedy struck my *tío* Jesús, the second-oldest son of the Arellanos. He married a girl from El Cargadero, a beautiful woman from the García clan. But she died during childbirth, leaving a newborn son and a devastated husband. Traditionally, widowers in Jerez spend a year in mourning before taking another spouse, but Jesús was too distraught to consider another love. Just a couple of months after his wife's death, Jesús left his newborn son, Ramiro, with my grandmother and traveled to Tijuana. After cleaning stables for about a month, Jesús gathered enough money to pay for a passport that allowed him to enter the United States legally. He settled in East Los Angeles, where his maternal aunt Maria already operated a restaurant.

My uncle's bold move inspired the older sons of the bracero generation. Soon after followed Gabriel, the oldest brother, then Santos. Other young men from Jomulquillo started leaving— some with passports, others with sponsors that promised to place them in relaxed workplaces, but most illegally. Youth has no patience.

Papi was left alone in a dying rancho to help my grandfather. Many of his friends were already gone. "I should've studied," he now says. "The person who studies has many open doors. They have an easiness in speaking—he's an expert in things. The person who doesn't study has their memory in a ball—it can't be untangled, and they can't go anywhere in life.

"But what could I do? There was nothing for me in Jomulquillo. It was beautiful, but we needed to make money. And I saw how much my parents were getting from Santos, Jesús, and Gabriel. I wanted to help, too."

Shortly after my father left, my grandfather sold off his fields and animals. He entered the United States illegally in 1970; my grandmother followed a couple of years later, once all the girls were married off.

Fullerton: For a city that's been around as long as it has (since 1904), Fullerton has been refreshingly devoid of any major embarrassments—no Ku Klux Klan council like next-door Anaheim, no worshipping of cows as in Cypress or La Palma. Also smart: never bothered to level its historic (by Orange County standards, *historic* stands for anything built before the Second World War) downtown, leading to a thriving bar life and great antique shopping. Home to one of Orange County's oldest gangs, whose name we won't print so as not to draw attention to them, and we mention only because every city needs at least one bruise on its reputation. **Best restaurant: El Fortin,** makers of the best Oaxacan food in the United States. Don't know Oaxacan? Don't worry: those short Mexicans will soon invade your town and bring with them their unique Mexican food (think a combination of Indian and Mexican food, but richer). *700 E. Commonwealth Avenue, Fullerton, (714) 773-4290; also at 10444 Dale Avenue, Stanton, (714) 252-9120; www.restaurantelfortin.com.*

*　*　*

While my father set up in the States, Maria de la Luz Miranda was relearning how to live in El Cargadero.

After a couple of years in Northern California, the Mirandas headed back to Anaheim, where my uncles Casimiro and Jesús had relocated. The two brothers found their parents and siblings a small house in an Anaheim neighborhood filled mostly with old white people.

Although Anaheim was one of the main cities transformed by the housing boom in Orange County, many orange groves and agricultural fields still existed during the 1960s. Toward the eastern part of the city, in what's now ritzy Anaheim Hills, orange trees dominated the landscape. They also encircled Disneyland and prettied the cities directly north and west of Anaheim. The area was slowly industrializing, but the need for cheap immigrant labor hadn't lessened.

Just down the street from the Mirandas were the Ureños. A Saldivar, a Casas here and there. On the other side of town were the Veynas, who owned a restaurant, a grocery store, and houses that served the area's braceros, and had served as El Cargadero's unofficial consulate to the United States for decades. The majority of *cargaderenses* didn't want to leave the rancho, were determined to make it—but their resolve was breaking down. As the years passed, more of them moved to Anaheim, either around the Veynas or Mirandas.

The Mirandas didn't own a car, so their view of Anaheim was limited to church, work, and school. Purchases were made in only two stores—El Zacatecano, a small market in an Anaheim barrio known as La Fábrica because it was next to a factory, and Northgate Supermarket. Nowadays, Northgate Supermarket is one of the country's largest Latino-owned supermarkets, but an Asian couple ran the place when the Mirandas arrived. The two marts were the only markets they knew of in Anaheim that sold tortillas and other Mexican products. They preferred Northgate over El Zacatecano, because the *pochos* in La Fábrica always gave them a hard time for being Mexican. "They'd try to speak to us in English, and when we didn't know, they'd laugh," my mom said. "One time, I told them, '*Ustedes son mexicanos—¿porqué no hablan español?*' When they didn't say anything, we laughed and they shut up."

Opportunities for fun were rare—Sunday Mass at St. Boniface, youth activities through the Legion of Mary, trips to Santa Ana with their older brothers to see Spanish-language movies. The focus was still on earning enough money to return home. If a *cargaderense* celebrated a birthday, the exiles marked the occasion with a party at his or her house or a picnic at the park. The children played in the backyard; the adults talked about El Cargadero, which wasn't improving as evidenced by the increasing attendance every time there was a party.

A sadness seeped into the Mirandas. El Cargadero was too devastated to support them, and the United States demanded too much—they couldn't enjoy either place. Papa Je tried to pick oranges but had to stop on account of his deteriorating health. Whenever he put on the bags orange pickers use to collect oranges, it cut through my grandfather's skin, leaving permanent scars on his shoulders. He applied for and received welfare, but it wasn't enough to maintain a family of five. And there was still the house in El Cargadero to pay off.

To keep the family solvent, Angela, my mom, and Ezequiel returned to the fields. They were supposed to toil full-time, until a social worker reminded my grandparents that the kids were required to enter school. My mom enrolled in Horace Mann Elementary. Although she was twelve years old and should have been in sixth grade, the teachers sent her to the first-grade classes to learn English. "I couldn't learn because I didn't know anything," she says. Mom slept through her classes because she was tired from the fields.

On weekends during the school year, Maria de la Luz picked strawberries in Placentia. During the summer, she picked tomatoes down south in El Toro six days a week. "I had to wake up at three in the morning to catch a bus," she remembers. "Since it picked up a lot of people, I was the first one on. We'd show up in El Toro around seven in the morning. The hours would go until five or six. I wouldn't return until eight at night, the last person off the bus."

Asked if she was happy at that age to work and study at the same time, my mom shrugs. "I thought that's how we had to live in this country. I didn't pay much attention—I just did what I was told."

She wasn't at Horace Mann even a year before teachers advanced Luz to Fremont Junior High—not because of passing grades, but because Mami was simply too old to continue in elementary school. Fremont administrators grouped all the Mexican kids in one classroom, where they received instruction for three periods under a Mr. Peralta, the only Spanish-speaking adult in the school. Eleven Latino students were at Fremont in 1965—all of them Mexicans, eight from El Cargadero. In the elementary schools that fed into Fremont—Benjamin Franklin next door, Thomas Jefferson about a mile away, and Horace Mann—were even more *cargaderense* kids.

My mom claims no one ever discriminated against her, but that probably owes more to her natural shyness and reticence to talk about uncomfortable subjects rather than to enlightened white students. My *tía* Angela and my *tío* Ezequiel are much more open. "I've never been hurt so much in my life as I was hurt in school," Angela recalls. She was at Anaheim High, just down the street from Fremont, best known in Orange County for its powerhouse football squads. Daily, Angela and the other Mexican students faced harassment from their white counterparts—never mind that they were usually fairer-skinned than the *gabachos*. One time, Angela and her Mexican friends sat down in the cafeteria at the only table available. Within seconds, the white students at that table left. Then the students at the tables around that table left, and the next ones, until the crowded cafeteria was suddenly empty.

Anaheim High School's teachers weren't much more tolerant. "In gym class, we would get F's because we didn't want to change our clothes; it wasn't proper in our culture to wear shorts," Angela said. "They advanced us along, even though we didn't speak English. They wouldn't let us use the typewriters or anything. It was so horrible. In homemaking class, our job was to clean the entire school like janitors."

My *tío* Ezequiel suffered more than anyone else. Horace Mann was a repeat of Hollister for him: boys chased my uncle during recess until he climbed the monkey bars or trees, whereupon his antagonizers aimed rocks at his head. At Fremont, white boys frequently knocked Ezequiel's books out of his hands and kicked them away. Threatening notes were left in lockers. And more beatings. One boy in particular kept bullying him every day. Ezequiel changed the route he walked to and from home; the boy discovered it and punched him up harder. "You won't escape us," the boy often snarled at Ezequiel. "We're going to get you."

The beatings continued for months until the boy presented Ezequiel with an ultimatum: meet him after school alone, in a garage, or else. Ezequiel debated ditching school, but feared what "else" meant. So one afternoon after school, Ezequiel entered the boy's garage, where other previous harassers had gathered. No referee, no school administrators, no adults to intervene. Last man standing. The garage door closed. The boy's older brother announced the fight was on.

All the pent-up rage in Ezequiel poured out of his fists. Then the kicks. The bully went down, and Ezequiel straddled his shoulders and began pummeling the punk. *Thwunk. Thwunk.* Crunch after punishing crunch. All landing on the kid's face. A bloody nose followed, then knocked-out teeth. The onlookers cringed in a mix of horror and amazement—but Ezequiel was even more scared.

"I'm not going to get out of here alive," Ezequiel thought to himself. "I'm going to have to kill this kid, because there's no way I'll ever be able to show up at school again."

Ezequiel didn't kill him. For reasons he still doesn't understand, the boys allowed Ezequiel to escape. His face was scratched; his chest, bruised. That day, my uncle went to my Papa Je and announced he didn't like school. After that, Ezequiel never bothered with it again. This time, no social workers bothered my grandparents for letting Ezequiel drop out.

Papa Je was accepting welfare, but it hurt his pride deeply. Shortly after Ezequiel dropped out, Papa Je decided to return the family to El Cargadero—though the house still wasn't paid off, hopefully God might provide. The misery of the United States wasn't worth its higher wages. The year was 1967.

My mom had frequently dreamed of returning to El Cargadero, but she discovered an alien world when they repatriated. "There wasn't any electricity," she says. "Only dirt and bricks, and no running water. And you had to make *everything*. If you wanted to cook, you'd have to chop wood and use it. If I wanted to wash clothes or dirty dishes, go to the well, get water, and take it back home. Wash yourself? Go to the river."

Although the Mirandas had subsisted in the United States for only about five years, life in El Cargadero hadn't evolved past the Third World. Electricity wouldn't arrive until 1970; running water in the 1980s. My mom and her sisters were so clueless about how to live on the rancho that my Mama Chela hired a local girl to do chores for the family.

Mami spent only a month in El Cargadero before my Papa Je sent her and Tío Ezequiel back to Anaheim. El Cargadero's agriculture had never recovered from that fatal frost more than a decade ago—my Papa Je thought there wasn't a future in El Cargadero for his children. More important, he needed a reliable income source since doctors told him to retire young or die. My mother didn't complain. "I never protested about anything," she says. "I thought everything was right, whatever they told me. I didn't know any other type of life—for me, whatever people said to do was right."

Ezequiel and Maria de la Luz moved in with my *tía* Belen, who'd left El Cargadero around 1964. Times had been tough on her—for a while, Belen's family slept in a car as her husband found odd jobs. Sympathetic to her situation, a family friend invited Belen and her children to live in a boardinghouse. One day, immigration raided the place and deported everyone except my aunt and her family—they were legal on account of my Mama Chela's American citizenship. Belen stayed with the house.

My grandfather didn't allow Maria de la Luz to return to Fremont Junior High, where she had just started ninth grade before leaving. Mami began picking strawberries from February to June—$1.25 an hour, twenty-five cents for a box that usually filled with fifteen strawberries. She wasn't the best of pickers until one day the teen noticed she lagged behind the other ladies from El Cargadero. "That day, I told myself, 'I'm not going to fail anymore,'" she says. "I started picking like I never picked before"—twist the stem gently so the star wouldn't tear off and pull, again and again, until she finally caught up to the ladies. She never lagged after that.

Strawberry picking isn't the most excruciating agricultural work, but that's like saying lethal injection isn't the most painful method of execution. Unlike with other crops, gathering the tart, luscious fruit was an all-weather task. When it rained, *freseros* donned coats and boots to save the strawberries from rotting on the vine. In the searing heat, they picked faster in hopes of nabbing the strawberries before they shriveled. One day, the sun beat down so brightly that the small baskets in which the farmworkers packed the strawberries melted, negating an entire day's salary. My mother's knees are permanently stained a light black from kneeling in dirt so much during those years.

Work was all my mother lived for as a young woman. On days off, she usually washed her clothes or cleaned the house. She couldn't leave the house without Belen or another adult as a chaperone. Although more people from El Cargadero were moving into Anaheim, there still weren't enough to re-create a community—no children that married, no babies to baptize, no young women to commemorate with a quinceañera.

There were few opportunities for a woman like Maria de la Luz—no English, no education, no husband. But after a couple of months in the strawberry fields, Tía Angela told her about Hunt-Wesson, one of the largest canners in the country. They operated a multi-acre factory in Fullerton, where hundreds of workers juiced oranges, canned tomatoes, even squeezed pudding into plastic cups for school lunches. If you put in enough years and hours, even the lowliest Mexican could gain benefits and a working-class salary.

Mami lied about her age and started sorting tomatoes from eleven at night until seven in the morning, six days a week, from June until October. Hunt-Wesson didn't guarantee anything to newcomers—they had to wait outside Hunt's until their number was called, much like a day laborer. One night, my mother huddled throughout the night along with dozens of women, most from El Cargadero. No one entered Hunt's. That was an aberration, though, and Mami proved her worth to company brass and was continually selected.

The Hunt's factory slowed down in the autumn, so from October until February, Mami returned to El Cargadero with my *tío* Ezequiel to relax. They drove nonstop, from California to El Paso to El Cargadero, the same route my grandfather had followed so many years ago, but in a sturdy Dodge Ram instead of hopping railroads. There, El Cargadero's Anaheim contingent partied almost every day, brought back gifts to their poorer relatives, and rested until early spring. And every spring, more *cargaderenses* joined in the trek back to Anaheim.

SHOPPING

One can tell what area of Orange County one is in by the style of shopping available. The much derided strip mall is actually where you'll find the most vibrant businesses—independent stores, hole-in-the-wall restaurants, managed by entrepreneurs with little capital other than their savings and a high-interest business loan. Most operate in North and Central County; South County is the king of the shopping plaza, acres of chain stores and the occasional higher-end operation. There will invariably be a Barnes & Noble/Borders as an anchor, midlevel national restaurants such as the Cheesecake Factory, and a lot of tutorial centers. Malls dot the county and vary in glamour, from the opulent South Coast Plaza and Newport Beach's Fashion Island to the prole MainPlace Mall in Santa Ana and the Block in Orange. Mom-and-pops? Only in the slummiest barrios.

My father first stayed in the United States at the house of his *tía* Maria in East Los Angeles, along with about fifteen other men from Jomulquillo. He spent a couple of months at the flophouse before moving in with Gabriel to live closer to the carpet mill where Gabriel put him on the payroll. Papi's role was straightforward—he walked around with a glue gun and patched tears in carpet rolls. *La migra* frequently raided the plant, so on most days Gabriel—in the country on a legal visa—went to the factory early, asked the bosses whether immigration planned to raid that day, and fetched my father if everything was clear.

Hours were long—from three in the afternoon until eleven at night—but the *jale* paid well: Papi made more in an hour than he hoped to make in a week back in Jomulquillo, and English wasn't necessary. Too bad Lorenzo wasted all the money on the vice—billiards, concerts, and especially alcohol (I'm sure women as well, but my father will never own up to that—maybe in twenty years, but not now. Sorry!). He began drinking and smoking at age thirteen, breaking into his father's room to steal beer and cigarettes. "What the dad does, the son copies," he now says. "And the way a man is, that's how the family comes out." It didn't help that all the Arellano brothers were alcoholics, and they'd frequently spend weekends drinking on the front porch, arguing, crying, and singing loudly to songs on Lorenzo's record player.

In late 1971, Lorenzo became homesick. He asked for time off from carpets and bought a fake green card for $300—his new name was Jorge Alberto Bastida Orozco. Confident the fake green card was enough to guarantee reentry to the United States, Lorenzo returned to his rancho for two weeks. He enjoyed the stay—drank and partied mostly—but realized there was no future in Jomulquillo. Many of his friends from Jomulquillo already moved to the United States, most to the San Fernando Valley or Los Angeles.

Before he left, a couple of friends from Jomulquillo who planned to sneak into the United States asked Lorenzo to help them drive a truck to Los Angeles. Since everyone in the pickup had fake papers, they assumed driving into the United States wasn't going to be a problem. But just to be cautious, the *jomulquillenses* decided to try crossing from Mexicali into Calexico, a less dangerous crossing than the Tijuana–San Ysidro line my father had successfully navigated two years earlier.

After waiting in line for about an hour, the truck approached a U.S. border agent. He asked the young men for their papers. He glanced at the first three guys and their fake documents. No problem. Next was my father. Although all the fake green cards looked identical, the border agent allowed everyone to pass except Dad—not only did *la migra* rip up the green card on the spot, but they sent Jorge Alberto Bastida Orozco to prison for a month.

Just as they show in B-list crime movies, the warden allowed Lorenzo to make one phone call. He dialed the number of his sister Mela, who had illegally immigrated to East Los Angeles the year before. The family expected Lorenzo to return from Mexico that night.

"Mela, es Lorenzo—no me esperen" (don't wait for me). And with those words, there was no trace of Lorenzo Arellano for a month.

Not only did Lorenzo try to get into the States under a fake name, but when the border guards asked Jorge Alberto Bastida Orozco what his real name was, he replied Carlos Arellano, knowing a jail term for trying to enter the United States illegally prohibited him from ever entering the country legally again. When Lorenzo entered prison, he still used the Carlos pseudonym, so immigration officials didn't uncover his real identity. By the time Jesús hired a lawyer to get Lorenzo out of prison, there was no way to locate him. And since the guards didn't let Papi make any more phone calls, and he didn't want to draw too much attention, his family frantically searched the California prison system for a month for any sign of their Lencho (a nickname of my dad).

Pen time was uneventful for Carlos—mostly sleep. "I've always been very lucky," Papi says. "In prison, I made friends with the cook, and he'd always give me extra helpings of beans and bread. There were a lot of criminals and a prison gang, but one day, the head of the gang told me, 'We don't have any problems with you, *chavalo* [young man].' And they left me alone."

After the month passed, immigration officials arranged for a one-way bus ride to Mexicali. Lorenzo entered prison with $250 but left with just $20. In addition to a fine, the prison guards shook Dad down. He knew no one in Mexicali, but managed to hitch a ride to Tijuana. There, my father finally called Jesús. *"¿Donde has estado?"* Jesús said, on the verge of tears. "Where have you been?" My father was unfazed. He asked Jesús to drive down to Tijuana with Lorenzo's belongings: a change of clothes, his record player, and two uncashed checks. Possessions in hand, my father returned to Jomulquillo, unsure of what was to follow. Was there any choice, though? A month after returning to Jomulquillo, he decided to try to sneak into the United States one final time.

This time, he ended up at Colonia Libertad, a run-down Tijuana neighborhood known as the Tierra de Nadie—No-Man's-Land. For $125, smugglers allowed Lorenzo to crawl through a sewer tunnel the coyotes swore emptied out into the United States. Lorenzo didn't bother to verify—he had no choice.

For forty-five minutes, Lorenzo crawled in total darkness. He couldn't lift his head, couldn't turn back, couldn't stop—dozens followed behind, dozens were ahead. Sewage formed a shallow pool at the bottom of the sewage pipe. Thighs ached, clothes stank, fingers became raw scraping against wet metal.

The tunnel emptied out next to a 7-Eleven. From there, Lorenzo and others behind him ran across an intersection into a safe house, where they hid until a truck transported him to another safe house. After about an hour of sitting in a dark room, Jesús picked up his baby brother and dropped him off at Gabriel's house.

The following day, Lorenzo returned to the carpet factory. "Where have you been?" the boss demanded.

"I was deported," Lorenzo replied, and was about to continue when the boss cut him off.

"We gave you a two-week vacation, but you've been gone three months. We replaced you. We can't employ you anymore—they're cracking down on illegal immigrants harder." With that, Lorenzo Arellano was fired.

A couple of days later, he ran into a former coworker who owned a carpet-cutting business. "Hey, Trino!" the guy called out to my father. My father had used his uncle Trino's Social Security number and identity at the carpet factory that fired him. "Want to work for me?"

Lorenzo joined the man's factory—same responsibilities as his previous position, but with better pay. The company transferred to Irvine, where it's now a multimillion-dollar business. At first, Lorenzo commuted between Los Angeles and Irvine, having applied for and received his driver's license and Social Security number in 1970 even though he hadn't bothered to remedy his illegal status. In 1975, Dad moved into an apartment complex in Santa Ana to cut the commute. The Armenian who owned the apartments liked Lorenzo so much he made my dad an apartment manager for four of his properties and even offered to sell them to him at a low price. My father refused.

"I've never had the ambition to be rich," he says. "I'm just a conformist. So instead, I wasted all my money on beer and cantinas."

In one of those cantinas, around 1973, he overheard six guys talk about El Cargadero. Lorenzo Arellano was incredulous. Of all the bars in the world, people from his region were in this one. Lorenzo pondered this while slugging back another beer. "*¿Y que hacen ustedes de El Cargadero aquí?*" he asked them. "And what are you people from El Cargadero doing here?"

"*Vivimos aquí en Anaheim,*" one replied. "We live here in Anaheim. And there's a lot of us—even people from Jomulquillo."

The illegal immigrants drank for hours. Meanwhile, just a block away from the bar, Maria de la Luz Miranda returned from another day at Hunt's, with no idea of what the future was bringing, and no aspirations except a restful sleep.

COUNTYWIDE GOVERNMENT

Countywide government agencies still play a large role. The Orange County Board of Supervisors used to be a developers' puppet show that sold off county land for cheap; nowadays, it's almost a ceremonial post only good for trying to slash the pensions of the county unions. The district attorney's office was racked by cronyism in its earlier years under current DA Tony Rackauckas but forever redeemed itself with the 2005 prosecution of Greg Haidl, an eighteen-year-old who led his two friends through the gang rape of an unconscious teenager with a Snapple bottle, pool cue, and lit cigarette, while they filmed it. Haidl is the son of former deputy Don Haidl, currently a canary for the government as it prepares to prosecute former sheriff Mike Carona on felony conspiracy charges. If you can tell me what the Board of Education does besides grandstand for conservatives, I'll buy some textbooks.

Where All the Good Idiot
Republicans Go to Die

Conservatism: Orange County's greatest stereotype. The one that has dominated the American psyche for decades. Wealthy, white Republicans. Of the nastiest kind. Kind of wacky. Where the wackiest of the wackiest not only find a forgiving audience, but the audience elects them to office again and again. "Liberal becomes synonymous with idleness, sedition, youth, homosexuality, dirty feet, amphetamines, and New York City," *Harper's* wrote in 1973. "Conservative implies office hours, clean shoes, hypocrisy, old age, foreclosure, drill sergeant, and Orange County, California." *Fortune* wasn't much kinder, calling us "nut country" in 1968. But forget what the pundits tell you about this place—get to know just a few of our teddy bears for yourself:

- **Congressman William Dannemeyer, 1979–93:** Once suggested people with AIDS emit "spores" and insisted that a combination of garlic and cod-liver oil "deserves serious consideration" as a cure for the disease, which he claimed was "God's way of punishing gays." Dannemeyer also read the following into the *Congressional Record*:

    Activities peculiar to homosexuality include: Rimming, or one man using his tongue to lick the rectum of another man; golden showers, having one man or men urinate on another man or men; fisting or handballing, which has one man insert his hand and/or part of his arm into another man's rectum; and using what are euphemistically termed "toys" such as one man inserting dildoes, certain vegetables, or lightbulbs up another man's rectum.

Gracias, Congressman, for making us all aware.

- **State Assemblyman Nolan Frizzelle, 1980–92:** "Apartheid is the device by which the white government in South Africa seeks to gradually educate the black people so they can govern themselves adequately. If the people understand that is what apartheid is, rather than the systematic discrimination that has been painted to them, then they might have a different attitude."

- **State Senator John Seymour, 1982–91:** Called a law that sought to make it easier for refugees to enroll at California community colleges "discriminatory" against American citizens.

- **State Senator John Briggs, 1974–81:** Author of the Briggs Amendment, which sought to ban homosexuals from teaching in California public schools. Said of San Francisco's gay teachers, "I assume most of them are seducing young boys in toilets," and called the city "the moral garbage dump of homosexuality in this country." To that, gay rights martyr Harvey Milk replied, "Nobody likes garbage 'cause it smells. Yet 8 million tourists visited San Francisco last year. I wonder how many visited Fullerton?"

- **Congressman James Utt, 1953–70:** In 1963, published a newsletter warning that the United Nations was training "a large contingent of barefoot Africans" in Georgia to invade the United States. Also stated, "The federal government is like the child molester who offers candy before his evil act."

- **Congressman John Schmitz, 1970–72:** Most famous for being the father of Mary Kay Letourneau, the former Seattle schoolteacher who had an affair with a sixth-grade boy, but infamous even before that for his sound bites: once described pro-choice advocates as "a sea of hard, Jewish, and (arguably) female faces." Also quipped, "I may not be Hispanic, but I'm close. I'm Catholic with a mustache." Okay, at least he was funny. The John Birch Society kicked him out for being *too* extremist, and he kept a second family on the side.

- **State Assemblyman Mickey Conroy, 1991–96:** Proposed paddling as a way to discipline teens who graffitied, arguing, "Paddling will command respect, if not fear." Also settled a sexual harassment suit—was ass-slap happy, allegedly.

- **Congressman Dana Rohrabacher, 1989–present:** Buddy of disgraced Jack Abramoff. Attributed past global warming to dinosaur farts. Also palled around with the Taliban before 9/11.

- **Congressman Bob Dornan, 1976–96:** Such a legend among foot-in-mouth fans that I urge you to buy *"Shut up, Fag!" Quotations from the Files of Congressman Bob Dornan* at www.nathancallahan.com. It was his wife that yelled "Shut up, fag!" at an AIDS activist; Dornan, meanwhile, once cracked, "Don't use the word *gay* unless it's an acronym for 'Got AIDS Yet?'"

I can go on, but hopefully you get why Orange County's caveman image is so powerful. Professors, journalists, and even entertainers relish propagating OC's conservative chops. In 1978, the Henry Fonda–starring play *First Monday in October* imagined that the first female member of the U.S. Supreme Court was an Orange Countian to the right of Dick Cheney. A couple of years ago, *The West Wing* featured an episode where the liberal administration of Martin Sheen's character, Josiah Bartlett, planned to stop by Orange County.

"What kind of a reception are you expecting?" a staffer asked Bartlett's press secretary, worried about the natives.

"Don't be fooled," she responded. "They love us. . . . I think they really like it when we come to town. When we were there last month, we were working the crowd and some young boys worried, possibly, that I couldn't afford fruits and vegetables on a government salary tossed me some of their own."

But the most famous lines about Orange County's conservatism came from the Great Communicator. In 1967, while presiding over the opening of what's now John Wayne Airport, then California governor Ronald Reagan quipped, "Now that I've seen this wonderful new airport, I know it's easy to get to Orange County if I ever need political sanctuary."

That isn't his most famous Orange County hosanna, however. In 1984, President Reagan flew to El Toro Marine Corps Air Station. The Gipper was in the county to kick off his reelection campaign at Mile Square Park on Labor Day, an event that attracted at least sixty-five thousand people—to this day, one of America's largest-ever campaign rallies. Before the shindig, he had a welcome message for the locals.

"It's nice to be in Orange County," Reagan told a small gathering of reporters, "where the good Republicans go to die." He paused. "I guess good Democrats, too."

Reagan repeated the same statement sans the afterthought for the rest of his career until it became gospel. It was genius rhetoric, since all parties win: liberals get to deride Orange County for its ever-Paleo ways, while conservatives consider it an enshrinement of truth.

Rather than run from its backward reputation, the local GOP propagates it to the point of parody: during the 1990s, a group of Orange County Republicans in the California legislature actually referred to themselves as the Cavemen. The headline on the Orange County Republican Party's Web site states it represents "America's Most Republican County!" (exclamation point in the original!). In her 2001 book *The Big Orange: The History of Republican Politics in Orange County: 1950–2000,* former GOP chair Lois Lundberg didn't bother with such humility:

> *Probably no one area outside of Washington, D.C. so leads the country in political importance. Candidates flock here to raise money, get support, test their chances to political success, and in some way associate themselves with the magic that is Orange County politics. When I travel in the United States or in other countries, I am so frequently asked how did Orange County become so important, how does it work, and how did it happen.*

All of this is bullshit. Yes, the most committed Republicans in the United States operate here—and by *committed,* I mean people who deserve a permanent trip to the sanitarium (kidding!). Sure, politicians peregrinate by the dozens to raise millions here— during this year's presidential race alone, John McCain, Rudolph Giuliani, Mitt Romney, but even Barack Obama and Hillary Clinton each raised more than $1 million from our fat cats, and each received more votes in the 2008 Democratic primary than any of the GOP candidates did in their primaries. And Republicans make up all members of the Board of Supervisors; have all but one congressional, State Senate, and State Assembly seats; and the supermajority of the council and mayoral seats in Orange County. However, despite all the media attention, despite the deep-

pocketed patrons and autoeroticism, the Orange County Republican days are numbered. See, our Republicans have displayed a
Shakespearean propensity to fuck everything up for everyone,
but especially themselves—and as Orange does, so will the rest of
the Republicans. Hope endures, Señor and Señora American.

> **Yorba Linda:** Known worldwide for being the birthplace
> of Richard Nixon and home to his library; otherwise, mostly huge
> houses on acres of land and private roads. Rather boring place,
> but who needs excitement when you have prosperity like this?
> **Best restaurant: Supatra's Thai Bistro,** with as many curries as
> there are black people in Orange County: seven. *21560 Yorba
> Linda Boulevard, Yorba Linda, (714) 693-2888.*

In 1974, University of California, Santa Cruz, professor Karl
Lamb made a bold statement. Noting Orange County's traditional
conservatism and the country's Watergate fatigue, he claimed
Orange County was politically seceding from the GOP—and "as
Orange goes" (the title of his book on the subject), so would the
United States. "In the post-Watergate era, these new forces do not
necessarily lead to a Republican majority," Lamb wrote. "National
voting patterns will be more like those of Orange County in the
future than they were in the past. Orange County is not so much
joining in the mainstream as charting its new direction."

Lamb's prediction was accurate, but he got the politics wrong.
As Orange County went more conservative, so did the United
States. So *is* there truth to the hype? How did such a small region
assume such an influential stereotype? Was it what the sociolo-
gists say, a confluence of WWII veterans fearful of liberalism
destroying their government-subsidized slice of the proverbial
dream? Does it even go back to the Civil War veterans (both

Union and Confederate) who migrated to Orange County and became many of its first elected officials? Was a researcher right when he wrote, "This basic conservatism, which has endured in the face of change and transition, seems to be an intrinsic facet of Orange County character, a faith that even outsiders adopt once they set foot in the area"? After all, there must be a reason why those fools get elected to office, no? How long can a paragraph run with only questions?*

Conservatism's stranglehold over Orange County ain't a mystery: it's the money, stupid. The county's old guard, its ranchers and farmers, paradoxically, perhaps hypocritically, wanted the government out of their lives, except when it meant protecting their livelihood or jailing minorities. The 1936 Citrus War set a template in which businessmen used government to achieve their goals at the expense of everyone else.

During the 1950s, immigration authorities rounded up four elderly Latinos at the behest of Orange County farmers because they organized during the 1936 struggle. The case, known as the Santa Ana Four, drew national attention, but it didn't matter— three of the men were shipped to Mexico. One wife went to Washington and testified before the House Un-American Activities Committee, pleading clemency for her husband. She went as far as meeting with Congressman Utt, himself the son of an orange grower. A private letter housed in the collections of the Southern California Public Library in Los Angeles stated, "Mrs. Espinoza quoted Congressman Utt as saying that he would like to do something about the McCarran-Walter Act but that the Associated Farmers [a confederation of OC growers] wouldn't let him." Another private letter disclosed that Utt "intimated that he had received many requests from his constituency asking him to

---

*Hey, as a writer who has patiently answered *preguntas* for the past three years in my *¡Ask a Mexican!* column, I'm entitled to ask a few myself.

do something for Mr. Espinoza, but he regretted that at this moment he could do very little because the Associated Farmers of Orange County did not approve of Mr. Espinoza. He advised Mrs. Espinoza to see if she couldn't convince the Associated Farmers to change their minds about Mr. Espinoza."

The 1950s housing boom ended the days of powerful farmers, but a new crop of civic leaders—developers, businessmen, church leaders, and politicians—effortlessly assumed power. In those early days, Orange County conservatives wrote the guidebook for the GOP's modern success—rich benefactors, rabid activists, and an obsequious press. They wanted good, God-fearing white people in the "new" Orange County, and those folks gladly moved in and decided to change what they didn't like. In Anaheim, voters organized to get rid of a sex-education program and recalled a school district trustee in 1962 because he *hosted* an ACLU meeting at his house. Parents complained to school boards if high schools displayed any United Nations logos. Prominent county conservatives promoted the Francis Amendment, a 1962 ballot measure that sought to require public employees to disclose any ties to communism or other leftist causes. Adults organized anticommunism "schools" where students of all grades heard lectures on the evils of the Red Menace; one such assembly, at Anaheim's Glover Stadium, attracted seven thousand students. And thousands joined the notorious John Birch Society.

Primary among the early movers were Walter Knott and Carl Karcher. If these men are known nationally at all—and my inflated sense of Orange County's relevance insists you must've heard of them—it's as the respective eponymous owners of the Knott's Berry Farm amusement park in Buena Park and Carl's Jr., one of the country's first hamburger chains (a 2007 *Portfolio* spread skewered Carl's thousand-calorie hamburgers and television commercials featuring a leather-wearing Paris Hilton washing a car). Both men made their millions pleasing the masses—Karcher through burgers, Knott with his cultivation of the tart boysenberry (originally created in the 1920s by Rudolph Boysen, an Anaheim parks superintendent) and by creating the nation's first theme park after he reconstructed old California ghost towns on his Buena Park farm to please the hours-long lines wishing to eat his wife Cordelia's chicken dinners.

The two used their wealth to promote conservative causes— Karcher organized anticommunist schools for children and was the principal donor for California's Briggs Initiative. Knott used his wealth to set up a publishing company that distributed free pamphlets titled "The Socialist Plan for Conquest" and "Communism on the Map." He even built an exact replica of Independence Hall across the street from his berry farm, one so precise that it mimicked fingerprints set in the original's bricks and housed a Liberty Bell that weighed just five pounds less than the original.

Karcher and Knott set an example embraced by the county's nouveau riche. In 1963, a group of Orange County businessmen founded the Lincoln Club, a PAC-cum-kingmaker with the express purpose of uniting conservatives around Republican candidates. With typical Orange County conservative humility, it calls itself "the largest and most active political club in the United States." The group originated after California's 1962 gubernatorial election, when local activists became furious when moderate Richard Nixon entered the GOP nomination race at the last moment and stole the Republican nomination from firebrand Bakersfield assemblyman Joe Shell. In protest, many Shell supporters sat out the general election, leading to Nixon's humiliating defeat.

Not all conservatives enjoyed the principled seppuku committed by Republican activists. "Licking our wounds," recounted Arnold Beckman, a founding member and one of the principal funders behind the invention of the silicon semiconductor (which powers virtually every electronic device), in a 1993 speech to conservative activists, "a group of us resolved to try and do something about the sad situation. We would not repeat these mistakes and we would try to take constructive action that would lead not only to unity within the Republican Party, but to the development and election of superior candidates to public office."

The nation was noticing—on February 20, 1963, the Pulitzer Prize–winning political cartoonist Herblock inked a panel titled "Birchhead." Dead soldiers litter a palm-tree-strewn beach, as a caveman climbs a flagpole behind mission walls to hang a flag with a mastodon and the legend RIGHT-WING EXTREMISM. The setting wasn't specified, but obvious.

Orange County's brand of conservativism faced its first test at the 1964 convention for the California Republican Assembly, one of the state GOP's principal organizations for grassroots conservative activists. The GOP leadership favored a Nelson Rockefeller–type leader, a Republican in Name Only, and the Orange County delegation gnashed its teeth. After a hard fight, the CRA elected Nolan "Apartheid Isn't Bad" Frizzelle to the group's presidency.

Frizzelle and his faction united behind Barry Goldwater, the Arizona senator who went on in 1964 to lose to Lyndon Johnson by one of the largest margins in an American presidential race. But that election trained thousands of activists, who transferred their enthusiasm to actor Ronald Reagan, who gave a speech at the GOP National Convention that year in one of his first forays into politics. Decades later, Goldwater boasted that he carried "five states and Orange County."

Through these years, conservatives found a forgiving, sympathetic public bulletin board in *The Santa Ana Register,* which continues today as the *Orange County Register* and is the county's only major homegrown daily. The *Register's* past is not particularly celebrated by the paper today, but it's a guilty pleasure for fans of antiquated bigotry—reporters were instructed to refer to public schools in their stories as "tax-supported" and "gun-run" and were required to study libertarianism at paper-funded "freedom" academies. Reporters were just following the mandates of publisher R. C. Hoiles, a wiry, perpetually frowning man whom *Time* once described as "slightly to the right of Herod" and "terrible-tempered."

Not everything was wrong about Hoiles. His was one of the few newspapers in the United States to publicly oppose the internment of Japanese during World War II. But an avowed conservatism and anticommunist stance ensured Hoiles ran just about anything that jibed with his worldview—attacks on liberalism, attacks on liberalism, and the occasional puppy story. Conservative activists used the *Register's* pages to advocate their positions and advertise their causes. Nowadays, the *Register* no longer is such an organ, except in its letters section.

After Goldwater's defeat, county conservatives built for the future. In 1966, they helped Reagan secure the GOP nomination for California governor and mobilized to have him win the general election. Two years later, this unassuming machine helped Orange County's wayward son Richard Nixon become president in 1968. Nixon was born in Yorba Linda, a tiny farming town in northeastern Orange County that nowadays is a wealthy enclave. He only spent a couple of years as an adult in Orange County, mostly to open up a law practice in La Habra and propose to his future wife, Pat, in the cliffs overlooking Doheney State Beach in Dana Point. Orange County voters couldn't do much to help him in his prepresidential elections, as he was outside the district, but supported him in 1968. Later, Nixon opened his Western White House in San Clemente and enlisted marines to wipe the city's beaches clean of surfers whenever he went for a seaside stroll.

No comment about Watergate needed in this book (buy Rick

Perlstein's *Nixonland* for that), except that the disgraced Nixon returned to adoring crowds at El Toro Marine Air Corps Base. But his debacle signaled a seeming denouement for the Republican Party, seized upon by *As Orange Goes* and others as proof the evil OC GOP was faltering. The Briggs Amendment failed spectacularly in 1978, inspiring the formation of the Log Cabin Republicans (the gay wing of the GOP) and even a reprimand from Ronald Reagan. County Democrats made inroads during the 1970s, capturing three of the five seats on the Board of Supervisors and even a congressional district. In 1981, former conservative hero John Schmitz was discovered to have kept a second family for years.

The Republican Party trudged on, gaining seats after most of the Democrats elected during the 1970s were convicted of felonies. After that, the Lincoln Club and other rich Republicans reinvested in their grass roots, tapping into the Young Americans for Freedom on Southern California campuses to cultivate future party leaders—many of today's congressmen and state senators entered county politics that way. With the ascendancy of Reagan, the Orange County GOP again became a nationally known and feared force.

But the party's arrogance frequently got the best of it. In 1989, the Orange County Republican Party paid a $400,000 fine for stationing security guards outside voting booths in Latino-heavy precincts during a California State Assembly election for Curt Pringle (currently Anaheim's mayor). The head of the party was Tom Fuentes, a native of East Los Angeles who forsook the priesthood to become communications director for the Catholic Diocese of Orange before parlaying that into a leadership role with the GOP. Fuentes and Pringle claimed they were merely trying to remind people that illegal immigrants couldn't vote, but no one bought the excuse. Pringle won that election but lost two years later to Tom Umberg.

More embarrassing was 1994, when Orange County declared bankruptcy—the largest such municipal bankruptcy in American history. Everyone involved was a Republican—all five county supervisors. Even the ordeal's biggest critic, John Moorlach (currently on the Board of Supervisors), was a Republican, dismissed as a Chicken Little by the party. Moorlach had run for the treasurer's seat that year, warning anyone who would listen that the county's investments were leading it toward ruin, but no one paid the staunch conservative much thought—remember why the Lincoln Club formed. Party unity above all.

Nothing prepared the Republicans, however, for the 1996 congressional race between Dornan and Loretta Sanchez. Dornan was a ten-time incumbent, a brilliant politician and absolute ass of a man. He represented Orange County's only lower-income district, which consisted of swaths of the cities of Anaheim, Santa Ana, and Garden Grove. Dornan's anticommunist fervor placated Vietnamese voters; appeals to Catholicism kept Latinos happy. And his all-American image guaranteed that white voters in his district—who kept getting reduced and older every year—reelected him. In reality, Dornan rented a house in Garden Grove but hung out on a five-acre estate with a twelve-room house in Fairfax, Virginia. Sanchez, on the other hand, was an Orange County native—the child of Mexican immigrants. In 1994, she unsuccessfully ran for a seat on the Anaheim City Council as a registered Republican with the surname Brixey, that of her then husband. For the race against Dornan, she switched parties and used her maiden name.

"She can't beat me," Dornan told the OC Weekly. "Bob Dornan is a father of five, grandfather of ten, military man, been married forty-one years. She has no kids, no military, no track record. I win."

He didn't. Sanchez pulled out a nine-hundred-vote victory. The shocker earned national coverage, and the ire of Orange

County's Republican establishment. Dornan called upon the Newt Gingrich–led Congress to launch an investigation, alleging Sanchez and other Latino activists registered illegal immigrants to vote. They even subpoenaed my *OC Weekly* colleague R. Scott Moxley for records regarding stories he investigated for our paper. Nevertheless, the election stuck. Dornan ran again in 1998 but lost even more decisively. And ever since, Sanchez has become the queen of Democratic politics. Republicans absolutely despise her, consistently calling her a slut and more for risqué Christmas cards featuring her MILFy body and her cat, Gretzky. The poor Republican Party has been reduced to running token candidates against her—and Sanchez slays them every two years.

Sanchez isn't the best of Democrats—not even close. She held a fund-raiser at the Playboy Mansion but dropped it after criticism from other Latino leaders. Listen to her, and it's as if Reese Witherspoon's character in *Legally Blonde* became reality. But with her Hispanic surname and war stories—the Latina who slew the Dragon Dornan!—she'll reign over Central Orange County until she decides to run for senator or governor. Republicans view her as a Moby-Dick, but even they've learned from her a valuable lesson: don't piss off Latinos.

In 2003, Newport Beach council member Dick Nichols told a newspaper reporter he didn't favor installing more grassland in picturesque Corona Del Mar State Beach, because too many Mexicans sat on it. It was classic Orange County looniness— crotchety white man spouting off insanities. Latino activists asked for his resignation, but he refused. The Republican Party unleashed its revenge, however; when it came time for reelection, they declined to endorse Nichols, effectively kicking him out of office. The last time he was seen at a political event, it was for a fund-raiser for the Minuteman mayor, Costa Mesa's Allan Mansoor.

Then came Sanchez's 2006 opponent, Tan Nguyen. Nguyen

would've been an ideal candidate for the Republican Party to promote just five years earlier—self-made, a refugee, and Vietnamese, the one minority group in Orange County committed to vote Republican. He was running on an anti-illegal-immigration platform, with inventive campaign signs—a yellow-and-red placard in the colors of South Vietnam that read STOP ILLEGAL IMMIGRATION, followed by a green stoplight reading GO WITH TAN. However, the GOP did little to support Nguyen, probably because he ran for a different congressional seat two years earlier as a Democrat.

But the Republican Party was forced to pay attention after thousands of letters were sent out to Latino voters stating immigrants couldn't vote. The letter was signed "Sergio Ramirez" and purported to have been sent by the California Coalition for Immigration Reform, a Huntington Beach group discussed further in a couple of chapters. Nguyen at first denied any involvement, yet curiously defended the letter, saying it wasn't anti-immigrant at all.

Unlike the 1988 poll-guard incident, the Republican leadership moved quickly to quash the controversy. Current OC GOP head Scott Baugh called the letter "reprehensible and stupid," asked Nguyen to resign, and stressed to a disbelieving public that the Orange County Republican Party had nothing to do with his actions. California governor Arnold Schwarzenegger called Nguyen's actions a "despicable act of political intimidation and a hate crime." Such Republican rebukes against their own had not been seen since the days Nixon successfully ran Orange County tax assessor Andrew J. Hinshaw against John Schmitz in 1972 after Schmitz quipped, "I don't have anything against Richard Nixon visiting China; I only have something against him coming back." (Hinshaw was later convicted of accepting bribes during that race.) The Nguyen debacle received national attention, especially after he refused to resign, and the old stereotypes about Orange County's rock-ribbed lunatic Republicanism sprung anew.

You might have noticed a pattern—for all its vaunted power, with the exception of Nixon, all the major Orange County Republicans never were elected beyond the local level. Truthfully, Orange County has released just a couple of figures onto the nation, and all of them are disasters.

In 2002, President Bush appointed George Argyros—an Orange County slumlord whom sports fans remember as the penny-pinching owner of the Seattle Mariners during the 1980s—as ambassador to Spain. Argyros's only real talent was raising money, and the man did it well, helping raise about $30 million for Bush's failed California campaign. Argyros proved hugely unpopular in Spain since he convinced then prime minister José Maria Aznar to enlist his country in our War on Terror despite mass opposition by the citizens; and his position was not helped by the March 11, 2004, Madrid bombings that killed hundreds. The American government recalled Argyros at the end of 2004. Another choice appointment was Roland Arnell, the chair of Orange-based Ameriquest Mortgage. Bush made him ambassador to the Netherlands even as his mortgage company was ruining homeowners and pushing the American economy toward a recession. The only Orange County figure to even somewhat properly serve the American people is Securities and Exchange commissioner Christopher Cox—and frankly, I'm just waiting for the man to side with big business. He always did in his sixteen years in Congress serving Orange County's richest areas.

Be glad our conservative influence is limited. You don't want these dolts screwing over anyone but us. Consider the case of a dead little girl and a power-hungry marshal.

Samantha Runnion was the type of little girl that once sparked film series: wide smile with tiny teeth, shiny cheeks, and curls to rival a double helix. It was impossible to dislike her:

only cretins were capable of hurting little Samantha. On July 15, 2002, as Samantha played outside her Stanton apartment, a heavyset Hispanic man asked her about a Chihuahua. After a brief conversation, the man shoved the screaming five-year-old into a car and drove off. Police found Samantha's naked body on the side of Ortega Highway the next day—coroners determined Runnion was sexually and physically assaulted before dying of asphyxiation.

While detectives investigated the crime, Orange County sheriff Michael Carona prepared for reporters' questions. At a press conference aired live in Southern California and on cable channels nationwide, Carona warned Runnion's abductor, "Don't sleep. Don't eat. Because we're coming after you. We will take every resource that's available to us to bring you to justice." Deputies arrested a suspect shortly after, and a nation sighed in starry-eyed relief that a badged man kept his word.

Carona's fifteen minutes didn't end there. He gave the eulogy at Runnion's funeral—or tried, before breaking down in tears. The capacity audience at Garden Grove's Crystal Cathedral stood up and applauded, but Carona shook his head no. The national media treated the sheriff as the new Duke—Greta Van Susteren gushed, "We're all rooting for you," while Larry King crowned him "America's sheriff" and went on to ponder in his *USA Today* column, "Sheriff Mike Carona of Orange County, California, is a new national media hero, and deservedly so. Wouldn't shock me if somebody tried to get him to run for president."

With the goodwill toward Carona in mind, the lords of Orange County sprang into action. A month earlier, Arnold Schwarzenegger received an honorary doctorate from tiny Chapman University in Orange for . . . it's still a mystery. Or is it? Chapman University's board of trustees and donor rolls include Orange County's richest and most powerful men, guys with deep pockets and Napoleonic complexes. Chapman's then chairman of the board of trustees,

George Argyros, was away in Spain. Schwarzenegger used many of those same donors to catapult himself into California's governorship the following year.

Carona represented a limitless future to these donors. He was perfect for higher office—a Patrick Stewart type of sexy bald, with great teeth, cerulean eyes, a tattooed smile. Christian. Married. Devotee of Reagan. Ran unopposed for a second term. Andy Griffith, but hotter. And now, national hero. As the years passed—as Schwarzenegger assumed office, and President Bush won his own reelection—speculation increased about Carona's future. Lieutenant governor alongside Schwarzenegger in the 2006 election was feasible—maybe even senator. State assemblyman at the least.

But Carona wasn't any choirboy example of Republicanism. One of his first actions when originally elected in 1998 was to ask the Board of Supervisors to loosen rules regarding the appointment of assistant sheriffs. He wanted to deputize many of his donors, despite their having no experience in law enforcement, as a reward for their money. The board agreed. That bit of rule-bending begat more. He palled around with mobsters, sexual harassers, convicted felons. Nevertheless, the Republican Party stuck by their man, and the county at large looked the other way—after all, he'd caught Runnion's killer. Even when Carona proposed in 2005 to give his deputies immigration powers, allowing them to identify criminals as illegal immigrants in violation of federal law, Latino opponents respectfully disagreed with him instead of screaming racism.

Thankfully, Carona's ascent ended before it began.

In October of 2007, Orange County—even the nation— looked on in disbelief as a federal judge indicted Carona on ten felonies. Broadcast around the world were images of Carona in shackles, his wife and mistress (Deborah and Debra, respectively) beside him. Subsequent media reports painted a portrait of a man who habitually cheated on his wife, allegedly profited from the deaths of Orange County deputies, and allowed campaign contributors to breach federal regulations and film top-secret Homeland Security locations for a proposed television show called *DHS*.

By then, the Republican Party was already in disarray. The sheriff's department was in shambles: most of Carona's cronies (Caronies, per badass *Orange County Register* columnist Steve Greenhut) were long gone after abusing their positions—best example was Raymond Yi, who left after he was accused of flashing his badge and pulling his gun at golfers who refused to grab his lost ball. (He claimed that it was self-defense.) Carona's right-hand man, Don Haidl, resigned while unsuccessfully fighting to keep his son Greg from jail after young Haidl participated in a gang rape of an unconscious girl with a Snapple bottle, pool cue, and lit cigarette. Carona had barely won reelection in 2006, winning just 50.1 percent of the vote to avoid a runoff. Just a couple of days after his victory, he suspended his main rival, Deputy Bill Hunt, because he dared accuse Carona of corruption. Hunt was demoted from being in charge of operations in San Clemente to patrolling the streets of Stanton, the town in which Samantha Runnion had been abducted. Hunt instead resigned.

Carona expected conservative support to continue after his indictment—his consigliere, after all, was Michael Schroeder, the former head of the California Republican Party and also the adviser to Orange County district attorney Tony Rackauckus. But it wasn't enough. The sheriff's deputies union, county supervisors, even the county's once-conservative *Orange County Register,* called on Carona to resign and save the GOP face. The party leadership stayed quiet, too shocked to go against Schroeder, too scared to cross Carona, fearful their reputations in American politics were going to get turned from keepers of the Reagan flame to a bunch of Ollie Norths. The truth. Party unity above all.

Newport Beach: Whenever you say *The O.C.* or *Newport Harbor: The Real Orange County,* you are in fact discussing this old, wealthy, deeply Republican seaside community, where old money meets nouveau riche for margaritas, marriage, then divorce. No ghettos here, but a lot of recovering-addict homes in the city's Balboa Peninsula, where Orange Countians flock during the summer to see pretty women whose fake breasts cost more than most people's Camrys. Its Corona Del Mar neighborhood is a playground for rich women seeking to snatch younger men. Be careful, boys: though these cougars have a lot of cash, they're packing so much silicone that any heavy friction might set them ablaze. **Best restaurant:** Anywhere that sells Balboa bars, a slab of vanilla ice cream dunked in chocolate, then sprinkled with different candied ingredients. That's the one culinary noncrop contribution Orange County has given America. *Man,* is Orange County lame!

The Philadelphia Story

For the Freudians, here are my first four memories:

- Mami cradling a two-year-old me as she sobbed, having just suffered another fight with my father. Papi—wild-eyed, furious, undoubtedly drunk—yelled at us and slammed the door as he stumbled off into the night. Mom and I sit in the kitchen of our crumbling home. I cry as well, fearing the monster who abandoned us isn't done with his abuse.

- Chewing gum. Crouching in a closet. Hiding from my father. He's angry. Mami is missing. Scared. Save me!

- My mother bathes me. I'm happy. I'm about three.

- It's a big blur from the bath until this: Papi enters my kindergarten classroom, holding my three-year-old sister's hand while confessing to the teacher in mangled English I forgot my vitamins. He's happy. I'm try to look cool in front of the other kids while chewing Flintstones vitamins. The pretty schoolteacher laughs.

Life turned from misery to happiness for me between those two years thanks to the restorative powers of Alcoholics Anonymous and assimilation. And it's only been uphill from there.

❖   ❖   ❖

But before I discuss the weepy-moany early years and the subsequent rise, I need to explain how Maria de la Luz Miranda and Lorenzo Arellano married in the first place. Just after Christmas 1975. Just outside El Cargadero. Hundreds of people from the rancho enjoying themselves during an all-day picnic near the town reservoir. Lots of food. A baseball game. All-day music. Polkas and waltzes blurted out via a brass band, with a booming bass drum providing a powerful beat that echoes through the picturesque, barren mountains.

Maria de la Luz is there. She, Ezequiel, and dozens of other *cargaderenses* had returned from another long year picking oranges, canning tomatoes, and other blue-collar vocations for a couple of months in the *patria*. Joining them was my father, who was spending a couple of weeks in Mexico before readying to sneak into the United States *yet again*. Lorenzo couldn't shake Mexico despite his stint in jail for breaking into the United States and had returned to Jomulquillo that winter—he knew a couple of guys from El Cargadero who invited him to the fiesta, promising pretty girls and liquor. Mostly liquor.

Lorenzo danced with a few girls before eyeing my mother, wearing a dress and all alone. The lanky twenty-four-year-old sauntered up to Maria de la Luz, sporting cowboy boots, a long shirt, and a weathered Stetson. "*¿Bailamos, no?*" he asked confidently. "Let's dance, no?"

"No," my mom replied. "I don't know you."

He stomped back to his friends. "*¿Entonces pa' quien viene si no viene a bailar?*" he angrily remarked out loud. "In that case, why does she come here if she doesn't come to dance?" The friend relayed Lorenzo's frustration to another friend, who relayed it to another, until his words reached my *tía* Angela.

"Let that guy dance with you, no?" Angela told my mom. "He's the brother of my friend Nacha." The two knew each other because Nacha (my dad's sister, Ignacia) helped raise my *tío* Jesús's son, Ramiro, whose late mother was from El Cargadero. On trips to El Cargadero so Ramiro could know that side of his family, Nacha befriended Angela.

The connection didn't matter to my mother. "I don't know him," she repeated. And that was that. She danced with other guys that night; Lorenzo mostly sulked.

A couple of months later in Anaheim, my mom went to a wedding reception for an El Cargadero couple at an Elks lodge. It was one of the first El Cargadero parties ever held in a hall instead of a home. The change of venue was necessary; in less than a decade, Anaheim's *cargaderense* enclave had grown from a couple of families to dozens—Gamboas, Fernandezes, Saldivars, Guerreros, Casases, Viramonteses, Garcias, and many more Mirandas. And this didn't include other people from Jerez and its outlying ranchos, whose numbers were growing each month. Mexico's economy wasn't recovering, and Anaheim's *cargaderense* web not only welcomed their *paisanos*, they found them employment and lodging.

The increased number of families meant more occasions to celebrate—and more opportunities for young adults to find mates. That's one of the reasons my mom dropped by that wedding—a guy had asked her to become his girlfriend, and she planned to say *sí* that night.

She claims not to remember the guy's name anymore, which I don't believe since she also asked me not to retell this anecdote as to not provoke my father's jealousy. Turns out the guy wasn't allowed to enter the party because he didn't have an invitation. Tía Angela and Mami went outside to try to sneak him in, with no luck. As Maria de la Luz descended the stairs back to the dance floor, she saw Lorenzo standing against the wall. He had sneaked back into the United States by climbing a fence and running. Fast.

Without missing a beat, Lorenzo cracked at Maria de la Luz, "Okay, *now* do you want to dance?"

They danced all night—hours. It was an awkward pairing, as my father was uncoordinated even when sober, and my mother— ever the stickler for perfection—insisted on leading during dancing. Nevertheless, the two hit it off, and Lorenzo asked Maria for her phone number—or, rather, a friend did. Just as Maria was preparing to leave, her sister Mercedes's brother-in-law went up to her. "Uh, Luz, Lorenzo wants your phone number—do you mind giving it to me?" After a couple of phone calls, Lorenzo and Maria de la Luz became *novio y novia*.

Mom roamed with her sister Belen at the time, so it was difficult for Lorenzo and Luz to spend time together. Dates consisted of talking outside Belen's house while sitting on the porch, or meeting during El Cargadero dances, where my *tía*'s Victorian eyes kept them honest. Papi surprised Mami with a day at Disneyland on one of their few nonchaperoned dates, but Lorenzo promptly threw up after exiting Space Mountain.

It was a yin-and-yang pull. Maria: white, calm, orderly, from El Cargadero. Lorenzo: brown as wood, prone to violent outbursts, from Jomulquillo. Love bloomed. The twenty-six-year-olds married at St. Boniface Church in Anaheim on September 16, 1977. Shortly after their honeymoon in Las Vegas, my parents moved their few belongings into an apartment not far from where my father had managed apartments in Santa Ana. They hadn't even unwrapped their wedding presents before Papa Je and Mama Chela—who'd moved back to Anaheim after a couple of years in El Cargadero—announced they'd had enough of Anaheim. My grandfather suggested that the young couple move into the house he was vacating.

The euphemism for the house on 832½ S. Philadelphia Street in Anaheim is *granny flat*, but "substandard, virtually illegal housing" is more apt. One bedroom, one bath, one living room, a kitchen, and a garage next to an alley where neighboring apartment dwellers left hypodermic needles. Made of wood, with tar paper as a roof, linoleum flooring in the kitchen, and a gravel driveway. Its only redeeming quality were the avocado trees next to the driveway, which neighboring families frequently picked clean. Once, when the toilet became clogged, one of my mother's coworkers at Hunt's walked in to fix it.

"What are *you* doing here?" Mami asked, incredulous.

"Your landlord? He's my brother," the friend replied. She walked around for a bit. "I'm so sorry," she told my mom. "No one should ever live somewhere with exposed wires. I'll make sure to yell at my brother."

The house once stood on the edge of orange groves, and though the trees were gone, King Citrus still lingered. West on Santa Ana Street was the abandoned Sunkist Packing House. East on Santa Ana Street was a cannery, and the scent of oranges being squeezed into OJ blanketed the neighborhood with a sweet, sticky scent. Trains rumbled by daily to pick up lumber from yards about two hundred feet from the house. And a block away was one of the last orange groves in the city, right next to the spot where the 1936 Citrus War started. Mexicans—many of them descendants of orange pickers, many new immigrants—ruled this neighborhood, packed into apartments, converted garages, or old homes.

One reason my parents liked living in this shack was its proximity to *cargaderenses*. Two blocks down Philadelphia was my *tía* Mercedes, whom everyone called Meme and who married a man from Jomulquillo. Within walking distance of Meme was my *tía* Belen—she also married a *jomulquillense*. This was the neighborhood where the Veynas had housed braceros decades earlier. A couple of minutes away to the east was my *tío* Ezequiel, who stayed in a granny flat with his wife and children; my *tío* Casimiro and *tía* Maria moved into the houses in front of his. To the west, next to Anaheim High, lived my *tía* Angela. Sprinkled—hell, smeared—

between these points were others from El Cargadero. Even the
next-door neighbor, a third-generation Mexican-American named
Jose Rodarte, whose grandson spoke no Spanish and idolized *Fast
Times at Ridgemont High*, had roots in El Cargadero—his ancestor
Lino Rodarte was a prerevolutionary Robin Hood immortalized in
a corrido written by my maternal great-great-grandfather Sabas
Fernandez.

The first years of marriage were rough for Mom and Dad.
Mami worked fewer hours after I was born in 1979 but continued
to hit the graveyard shift at Hunt's. My father, meanwhile, became
a supervisor at his carpet company. Though still an illegal immigrant, he now commanded four weeks of vacation and a good
salary.

All of it went to waste.

Papi was an unrepentant alcoholic. After a day cutting carpets, a beer and tequila. Weekends? Alcohol until he collapsed,
leaving my mother to drag him back home—literally—from wherever in Anaheim he had passed out. He started skipping Mon-
days at the factory regularly. And woe if there was a party.
"Uh-oh, there's going to be a fight—Lorenzo Arellano is here"
was the warning whispered whenever he showed up. As a toddler,
my father even served me beer in a cup, which I lapped up happily. Like father, like son.

My mom pleaded with him to stop drinking, hoped that the
birth of my sister Elsa in 1981 might tame him; instead, he
abused Mami. Neither admits to this point, but those years forever chilled the relationship between my maternal aunts and
Dad. They told me horrible stories—beatings, humiliations,
fights. Propaganda or reality, I'll never know—no one wants to
talk about it. Even when I confronted my mom recently, she
replied coolly, "Your father never hit me—he only yelled. If he hit
me . . ." She trailed off into false bravado.

What I can verify are the DUIs—multiple. For the last offense, a judge ordered Papi sign up with Alcoholics Anonymous or face prison. He went on the bender of all benders—eight straight days at home, at bars, everywhere. Papi's eyes became bloodshot; his gut more bloated than ever. When my father entered the United States, he wore size 20 pants. Now, he was lucky to slip into size 36 jeans. "My stomach hurt," he says. "I could feel ulcers forming inside of me. Gastritis. My liver stung." He couldn't sleep, didn't want to eat. Just drink.

"And then I saw you and Elsa," he continues. "Alone. Just little kids. Your faces were so sad. Your faces showed that *ustedes* wished that your dad was around more often. I felt ashamed. I didn't want to live this life anymore. I never drank another drop of alcohol again."

Mom-vouched version: My dad got in a fight with a drunk from Jomulquillo. Got his ass whipped. Stopped drinking so that the next time they met, Lorenzo would be sober enough to kick the guy's ass. A quarter century later, he's still waiting for his revenge.

The toll of those years will probably emerge if I undergo therapy— but, right now, the childhood memories between kindergarten and second grade are peachy.* Most photos of me from those years show me smiling, with ruby cheeks, crooked teeth, and a mop top. On weekends, my father walked Elsa and me to the orange juice plant, where they sold us freshly squeezed ambrosia from tin cans. Dad also let us tag along to *la cafeteria,* where he chatted with dozens of men from El Cargadero while Elsa and I played video games. The days he left before we woke up, Papi brought back doughnuts—four sugar, four glazed, four chocolate.

Mom watched over us in a different way. Despite slaving away at Hunt-Wesson from five in the morning until three in the after-

---

*Orange you glad I used a different fruit metaphor?

noon, she still cooked dinner every day. There were no such things as leftovers or microwaved food—the only meals she refrigerated were pinto beans and pink-hued rice, the staples of every Mexican meal, which Mami cooked in pots large enough to bathe an infant. Although she had dropped out of school early and knew no English, Mami tried as much as possible to prepare her children for elementary school. At home, she played songs from Cri-Cri (the Mexican version of Dr. Seuss sans the surrealism and with many more animals) on an eight-track player and led us in sing-alongs. Mom always tuned the television to *Sesame Street* and *Mister Rogers' Neighborhood* to expose us to English before entering school. While she washed clothes at the Laundromat, Mami taught me the alphabet, colors, and numbers in both English and Spanish. By the age of three, she reminds me proudly, I knew the fundamentals in two languages.

It was an impressive undertaking for this woman with an eighth-grade education—to prepare her children for the opportunities available in this country but denied to her by circumstances and the ways of the old world. Remember how I said Mami dropped out of school to help my Papa Je with the bills? That's only part of the story. All the younger girls—Angela, Maria de la Luz, Mercedes, and Alicia—wanted to get high school diplomas in the United States, but my uncles told Papa Je school wasn't for women. Though loving his daughters, Papa Je respected his sons first, and none of the Miranda girls advanced past tenth grade.

Rancho customs weren't going to influence Maria de la Luz's children, though—at least not *too* much. On my first day of school, administrators asked my mother whether she wanted me in English-only or bilingual classes.

"English," she replied. "Because I never learned English, and I want him to learn."

By second grade, I spoke mostly in English. I've gradually lost my Spanish since.

Buena Park: One of our many cities with a stupid Spanglish name. Calls itself "The Center of the Southland" despite not being center to anything except Knott's Berry Farm. One interesting personal note: the United Food and Commercial Workers labor hall hosted many El Cargadero quinceañeras and weddings until someone was supposedly killed at a non-*cargaderense* party. Damn Mexicans with their shooting guns . . . **Best Restaurant: Chung Ki Wa Tofu Restaurant,** located in the northern parts of Buena Park's emerging Koreatown. Best *soon tofu* ("boiling tofu soup"—tastes better than it sounds) in Orange County. *5238 Beach Boulevard, Buena Park, (714) 562-8989.*

❋   ❋   ❋

Many Latino authors and pundits wax with pathos about their tribulations learning English, about the shame they felt in not knowing the language or being brown in an all-white world. I've read melodramatic essays by grown men and women nearly weeping at the memory of bringing tortillas to school, only to face the taunts of their classmates. A precious few make a name for themselves out of it—how's English treating you now, Richard Rodriguez? But there's no gnostic mystery to my conversion from Spanish-only to bilingualism. It just happened. No growing pains, at least none I can remember. Just happened. And the burritos? Please. From kindergarten through sixth grade, my mother always packed the same lunch: peanut-butter-and-grape-jelly sandwich with apple juice. Never burritos—not because I was embarrassed to eat them at school, but because I loved peanut butter too much. Still do.

I'm being harsh. Unlike that of my parents and aunts and older generations of Mexican-Americans, my school experience through those early years was *muy* Mexican. Thomas Jefferson Elementary—built on orange groves that my Pepe once picked—was in the midst of a demographic change by the time I entered kindergarten in 1985. The kids in my classes were almost all Mexicans—only the upper grades had white students, and more kept leaving every year. I don't recall experiencing racism during my elementary years—at Thomas Jefferson, the minority were whites, and us Mexican kids delighted in teaching them bad words. Besides, ethnicity wasn't a big deal for us—we were just children who liked playing marbles and soccer during recess and daring each other to combine different drinks during lunch and swig.

The only time my *mexicanidad* was an issue happened during playtime. Once in a while, we rounded up as many kids—boys and girls—as possible and played a game called *la migra*. The premise was brilliant: teams split up into Mexicans and *la migra*—immigration officers. A kid would yell *"¡La migra!"* and the Mexicans ran, while *la migra* chased us. It was a glorified version of tag, combined with a dash of hide-and-seek and red rover (did I forget to mention other kids assumed the role of the U.S.-Mexico border?). Playing a Mexican was more fun, but being a border agent had its charms.

At Thomas Jefferson, I apparently blossomed. I add the sense of false humility only because teachers consistently bumped me to a higher grade, starting in first grade. Every morning, I reported to homeroom but went to the next grade level the rest of the day for every subject except math. I'm not sure why they didn't just advance me another grade—had to be the math. Was terrible at it—still am. Mami encouraged my studies by dropping off Elsa, me, and my best friend at the time—a son of a family from Jerez—at the Anaheim Public Library every Saturday, where we spent hours. My favorite books were biographies—one series focused on famous people who suffered greatly as young children—and Uncle Scrooge comics. I was one of the few kids in my class who ordered from Troll books, usually *The Guinness Book of World Records*. I still have the first book I bought with my own money, the 1987 edition.

My peers in those years thought I was cool for being smart. I won an award in second grade for reading fifty books in one year. Reading became my raison d'etre, mostly because I was a weakling with a noodle arm and toothpick legs. My aunt gave me an encyclopedia for the letter *A* for my eighth birthday, and my mom bought me a World Book encyclopedia volume spanning the letters *N* and *O*. I asked my parents to buy me an entire edition, but they refused—they were too poor, but the excuse they always gave was they were waiting for a sale. Until high school, any report I had to do for school came out of those two encyclopedias. For my president's report in fifth grade, I examined—who else?—Richard Nixon; for countries, I wrote about Nepal and Norway. I know more about Kathmandu than any non-Sherpa ever needs to.

> **La Palma:** Orange County's smallest city, and the most Asian by percentage—more than half of its fifteen thousand residents are Celestials. Originally known as Dairyland, because Dutch cow farmers incorporated during the 1950s to protect their livelihood from encroaching tract housing. A couple of years later, these Farmer Jans got their heads out of the manure and converted the dairy farms into tract housing unparalleled in North County. **Best restaurant: Ellen's Pinoy Grill,** a Filipino place frequented by nurses and the occasional white man. *7971 Valley View Street, La Palma, (714) 522-8866.*

While I was becoming a nerd, my father went through his own positive metamorphosis. In 1986, he suffered two herniated disks trying to lift a carpet. Dad went on disability for two years and never returned to the company. "When I started at that carpet company, it was really small," he says. "Now, it has hundreds of workers. I was going places. I could've been something great."

Papi could easily have relapsed to alcohol to ease his crippling pain. But give the man credit—he didn't. Was never even tempted, he says—and I believe him. While recuperating, Papi began taking me to Alcoholics Anonymous meetings—or, as he called them, *la junta*. The meeting.

"I didn't like it at first," he admits. "But after going a couple of times, I found that it was helping me mentally, the experiences. The medicine is to listen." Soon, he began volunteering to organize parties, clean up, and to tell other *borrachos* about Alcoholics Anonymous. By his count, my father has weaned dozens of men off booze over the years, including his three brothers.

We attended meetings at least three times a week. They were in an old, large home in Anaheim converted by Alcoholics Anonymous into their meetinghouse. What was once the main living room became a dance-hall-cum-meeting-room complete with beer glasses engraved with the names of recovering alcoholics. It was nice—and the Spanish-speaking recovering alcoholics weren't allowed in. The Mexicans entered through the back of the house. The three or four times my dad entered from the front or side, the *gabachos* always shot us dirty looks. The Mexicans had access to a pool table in the rec room, but only for an hour before their meetings. And those meetings were relegated to a tiny room upstairs, or a slightly larger one in the back—never mind that more and more Latinos sat in the meetings every week.

The Latinos and the *gabachos* rarely interacted, not even on the great equalizer of the pool table. One time, a white man did play alongside my dad and his friends; afterward, I remember the guy leaving the rec room and another man snickering, "Why did you play with those Mexicans? How did you understand them?" The pool player—who was minutes earlier laughing it up with Dad over last bets and trick shots—said nothing.

Alcoholics Anonymous was the only real father-son time I spent with Dad in those early years, and I'm not sure why he dragged me along. I went willingly, but only because Papi gave me quarters to

play video games. During the actual meetings, I mostly slept or read
MAD magazine. Over the years, however, through involuntary
immersion (and only in retrospect), I learned to appreciate the
experience. A.A. was a wonderful way to sober up (pardon the
expression) to the harshness of excess, and the beauty of austerity.
Every meeting began the same way. We repeated the Twelve
Steps—a litany of admissions, apologies, and aspirations regarding each alcoholic's shattered persona—and followed with the
Serenity Prayer, one of the most honest, beautiful sayings I know:

> *Lord, grant me the serenity to accept the things I cannot change,*
> *Courage to change the things I can,*
> *And the wisdom to know the difference.*

After that, men—and it was almost always men—spoke about
their alcoholic experiences. Of fortunes and families lost. Humiliations. Beatings. Their stories scared me straight. Even today, I try
not to touch alcohol for fear that my genes might get the best of me.
Whenever my father spoke, everyone listened. He wasn't necessarily a charismatic speaker, nor was he bad. He was just a regular guy, with a quick smile and serious eyes. He wasn't a natural
leader—he never led any of the meetings, but everyone paid attention. He still frequents Alcoholics Anonymous meetings and
hasn't touched a bottle in twenty-four years.
The invocation of the Serenity Prayer went beyond alcoholism.
Despite having spent years in this country, my parents didn't feel
prosperous. Not for a lack of trying—during his time on disability, Papi took English classes nightly. He knew how to speak the
language—just with a terrible accent, and not beyond a junior
high comprehension. My parents lodged long hours for small
wages, and the children kept coming—the third, Alejandrina, was
born in 1986. We shopped mostly at thrift stores and swap meets,
with the occasional splurge at Kmart or Target.

About once a month, we traveled to Tijuana—Dad had applied for legal residency through marrying my mother and was now able to cross the border legally—and stocked up on Mexican goodies: candies, detergent strong enough to clean the Augean stables, and other miscellany. I loved those trips—Tijuana and its allure of candies and illegal firecrackers will please any American boy, but even better was our habitual stop at the Surfin' Chicken, a restaurant in San Clemente that makes the best charbroiled chicken in the world. Its burly owner is a childhood friend of my dad's, from another rancho in Jerez. While my dad and the man—nicknamed El Cuatro (The Four) for reasons I've yet to determine—talked about life in the old country, I enjoyed El Cuatro's tacos and admired the autographed photos of various football teams who'd dined at the Surfin' Chicken while stopping by the county to beat the Los Angeles Rams.

With no money for vacations or fancy toys, Mom and Dad compensated by allowing Elsa and me to hang out with as many kids of our age as possible—that is, as long as they were from families they knew. Our weekends alternated between paying house calls to people from Jomulquillo and from El Cargadero. Due to proximity, I grew closest to the sons of my *tío* Ezequiel, Victor and Plácido, two mischievous brats who lived and breathed Joe Montana. But I equally enjoyed kicking it with the cousins from my dad's side, most of whom had relocated in East Los Angeles or Montebello. They were all a couple of years older than me, better versed in street smarts than your sheltered hero. With them, I tasted my first wine cooler and watched my first porno, pleasures for which I owe them deeply.

If we didn't swing by the home of folks from the old country, we caught up at labor halls or the many parties that went on every weekend across Southern California. And when we had nothing to do, Mom and Dad rented the blood-soaked escapades of Charles Bronson and Chuck Norris. Interestingly, whenever there was even a *chance* for nudity, my parents covered my eyes. See, *that* might warp a child's mind.

Except for Bronson's stilted dialogue, English wasn't part of the adult world, which I found odd. At school, all the kids spoke it. Among cousins, we only used English. But when addressing adults, we always addressed in Spanish—and they didn't like it when we tried to speak back to them in English. More than one adult yelled *"¡Habla español!"* whenever I spoke English in front of them—yet, they ridiculed my Spanish. See, I was speaking more Spanglish than Spanish by second grade and couldn't even pronounce letters—for instance, the double *r*, that rolling *r*, got lost somewhere between the roof of my mouth and the tip of my tongue. Out came a gurgle that sounded more like a Chinese trying to pronounce *rice rocket renegade*. I frequently wondered out loud why the scolding adults didn't bother learning English—this was America, after all. In whispered tones, those offended adults told my parents I was becoming too Americanized, that I wasn't Mexican enough. I didn't get it.

It also didn't help that I wasn't spending as much time in Mexico as everyone wanted me to. Every winter, Anaheim *cargaderenses* continued the long tradition of returning to the rancho. Since many of those immigrants now had American-born children who couldn't miss school, the trips lasted weeks, instead of months. My dad went every year to relive his youth. But while every other kid spent Decembers in their parents' home villages, my mother insisted we not miss school, at least until Christmas vacation. The two argued about the virtues of missing school—Dad insisted my sisters and I needed to keep in touch with our Mexican roots, while Mom maintained school was more important than spending time in abandoned villages. There really was no reason for her to be in Mexico—all her brothers and sisters were in the States, and while Papa Je and Mama Chela were in El Cargadero, they were planning to move back to Anaheim and give up on El Cargadero for good. Mom won.

I only remember three trips to Mexico as a child—as a toddler, as a small kid, and in second grade—and I only remember the last trip vividly. A week before the start of Christmas vacation in 1987, Papi pulled Elsa and me out of school. We left Anaheim at six in the morning and drove until reaching El Paso at midnight. From there, it was a straight shot down to Zacatecas. Dad followed the same roundabout route so many *cargaderenses* had followed in the early days. We reached El Cargadero the following night, Dad having driven nonstop for about forty hours, save for bathroom breaks and to throw away a plastic bag in which I vomited due to car sickness.

For three weeks, I played with the kids in the rancho, all of whom migrated to Anaheim within a couple of years. Old men and women, adults I had never seen, doted on me—most of them moved to Anaheim within a couple of years. I saw my grand-parents—old but incredibly kind and ever fascinated with me—they left that year for Anaheim and never returned. Papa Je took me into the mountains ringing El Cargadero on his burro, showed me the shack he'd erected as a shelter to rest. Accompanying me that day was my cousin Marcelo, two years older than me. When I told them I had to go to the restroom, Marcelo handed me a rock. "Go around the hill and wipe with this," he said. I never knew rocks scraped so smoothly—better than public-restroom toilet paper, it was.

By that point, both Jomulquillo and El Cargadero were a bit more developed, but each village still had only one telephone, and the streets turned into impassable swamps whenever it rained. What I found most odd was that almost everyone we met in El Cargadero either rented in Anaheim or had relatives in Anaheim. And just as at home, there were parties to patronize, girls to chase, guys who liked my sister to beat up.

During that trip, Mom and Dad drove to Jerez to buy a house— my parents spoke of moving back within a couple of years. *"¿Quieres vivir en México?"* Dad asked when we were returning to Anaheim, now on a plane since the truck we'd driven from Anaheim to Jomulquillo was to be our transportation in Mexico. The idea was intriguing enough—what kid doesn't like to run around for three weeks?—and everyone was nice, but I didn't answer. It didn't sit well with me—Mexico didn't compare to the United States, so why would my parents bother to return?

My parents bought the house, but we never moved into it. They've been renting it out all these years to a couple. At the time, however, my parents were serious—enough to ship my toys and books to that house. They're still at that house in boxes, twenty years later, waiting for me to tear them open. Scooby-Doo action figure, where are you?

> **Fountain Valley:** An anomaly, as farmland is still tilled in this bedroom community, and its city seal features an emblem of a fountain that looks more like the ass of a thong-wearing woman bending down. Home to Coastline Community College, a place of higher learning so obscure most people don't know it exists. I mention this only because I nearly left them out of this book—and if I did, betcha eight bucks no one would raise a fuss. **Best restaurant:** Millions of people obsess over ramen—not me. Nevertheless, a plug for **Shin-Sen Gumi Ramen,** for fast, delicious noodles and a publike atmosphere that will remind you of *Kill Bill: Vol. 1* sans the 5-6-7-8s and blood. *18315 Brookhurst Street, Ste. 1, Fountain Valley, (714) 962-8952.*

Upon returning from Mexico in the New Year, tragedy struck young Gustavo.

Everyone has a seminal moment, an event that taught him or her how cruel the world could be. Talk to many Mexicans, and they'll point to racism—real or perceived—that made them feel ashamed. For me, it was glasses.

Before we left for Mexico, an eye doctor told my mom I needed specs. When we returned, my mom bought them. Everything changed. Suddenly, girls who thought I was cute stayed away; boys didn't pick me for teams. And everyone used the first slurs ever directed my way: four-eyes. Geek. And nerd.

It was crushing. My glasses were Coke-bottle thick, wider than a coffee mug, virtual sombreros on my beady second-grade eyes. I begged Mami not to make me wear them, but she insisted. So I "broke" my glasses at the beginning of third grade. When my mom bought new ones, I didn't wear them, swearing to my teacher we were too poor to replace them—which was probably true.

For one final, glorious year, I was cool. My peers quickly forgot the glasses, and everyone liked me again. In fourth grade, however, the doctors insisted I wear glasses. Thankfully, I was about to move. A one-bedroom shack simply wasn't enough to house a family of five. Dad didn't want to leave, though. He had just started learning how to drive a big-rig truck and wasn't sure if anyone would hire a novice. But my mom had made sure he didn't spend any of the disability money he earned from the carpet-cutting injury. She saved their money in empty Hunt's tomato cans, storing them among the other foodstuffs in the house, because Philadelphia Street was sketchy. Our house was broken into a couple of times; they stole my mother's jewelry, but never her savings.

My mom wanted more. Without informing my father, she scoped out houses throughout Anaheim (only Anaheim: anywhere else in Orange County would've been betraying El Cargadero). We settled on a house in a gang-infested Anaheim neighborhood— even worse than the previous one. I didn't argue—it had a pool! Besides, my maternal cousins were going to occupy the shack on Philadelphia. It would remain in the *familia*.

I didn't even spend a year at my new school, Patrick Henry Elementary, located a street away from our front lawn, before teachers bused me to Sunkist Elementary. School psychologists determined that I was gifted and talented, and Patrick Henry only offered advanced classes up to the fourth grade. At my new school, I was one of two Mexicans in my classes. But I never experienced racism—far from it. Everyone was a nerd—our entire class was filled with outcasts. My best friends were an Indian, a Korean, a Jew, and a Taiwanese. But because I was bused, and my parents were too busy to drive me to other kids' homes, I didn't have many friends around my new neighborhood. I was again forced to find solace in books. The vicious nerd cycle continued.

Everyone else in the Miranda clan was improving as well. All my aunts and uncles in Anaheim bought bigger houses, and my *tío* Jesús (my mother's brother, not my dad's) moved into the house once occupied by my *tío* Ezequiel. Ezequiel transitioned from orange picking to construction, quickly becoming a foreman who oversaw massive projects across California. Both my aunts Angela and Alicia opened up their own store, and Tía Alicia (call her Licha, *por favor*) bought a house next to my *tío* Ezequiel's. That's where my Papa Je moved in and spent his last years.

Papa Je had endured potato peltings, a limited stomach, and poverty and beat them all. But mortality was catching up. He walked with a cane and stayed a couple of weeks at our new house in 1989, recuperating in bed from a broken hip. It was the only extended time I ever spent with him. I just remember his gravelly voice, forged by years of chain-smoking, and a warm smile that never left his face whenever we were together. Old age prevented Papa Je from moving around too much, so we spent most of the time watching news in Spanish and Warner Bros. cartoons. He didn't regale me with tales of his youth because they weren't necessary—spending time together was enough.

Papa Je never truly recovered from his bum hip, and successive bouts with pneumonia weakened José Miranda's health but never his mind. He passed away at the age of eighty-four in late 1990. The funeral was at our home parish of St. Boniface in Anaheim, which easily holds over a thousand people. More than that filled the pews and spilled outside. My grandfather wasn't a rich man, wasn't flashy, never involved himself in anything more than his family, yet the turnout shocked me. How did he know so many people? I thought. Where did all these mourners come from?

During the wake, funeral, and a month of rosaries we chanted afterward at my *tía* Licha's house per Mexican Catholic tradition, my mom introduced me to hundreds of people. "This is so-and-so, she's your third cousin twice removed," she'd start. "He's the son of my cousin's daughter. That old man was your Papa Je's godson." *Son del Cargadero.* They're all from El Cargadero.

"Where do they live?" I always asked.

"Anaheim," Mami almost always responded.

For the first time, I realized that there were a *chingo* of Mexicans in my world.

La Habra: Although crossed by Beach Boulevard and Imperial Highway, two important Southern California thoroughfares, La Habra is one of the most isolated cities in Orange County because no major freeways pass through it. Its most apt story is that of Glenn Allison. In 1982, he became the first person ever to roll three consecutive 300 bowling games in a sanctioned league when he accomplished the feat at La Habra 300 Bowl. But the sport's governing body disqualified Allison's achievement because the lanes were polished with too much wax. So sad, so La Habra. **Best restaurant: Chicken Box,** a converted house where the love of broasted chicken didn't fade away with the Eisenhower years. *330 E. Whittier Boulevard, La Habra, (714) 525-1345.*

Gimme That OC Religion

In Lake Forest, a city with neither a natural forest nor a lake, thousands of cars inch every Sunday toward Saddleback Church, the 120-acre compound built by the mega-million-selling *The Purpose Driven Life*. No frustration, no road rage: everyone smiles thanks to the bliss of the Lord's parking attendants, who guide the SUVs, the Lexii, and the humble Toyotas to their proper spots. Where you park depends on how you seek salvation this morning. Spread out across Saddleback's campus are buildings of various ages and styles, but more impressive are the tents—honest-to-goodness gleaming white canopies that hearken to the Christian revivalists of the past, each able to hold hundreds of Christ's well-tanned children.

Wanna rock? Head to Venue Tent 2, home of Saddleback OverDrive—but if you're in more of an emo mode, then Saddleback Elevation does great things on Saturday nights (plus this is the singles' service). *Habla español?* No tent for you—¡*El Encuentro!* The Encounter! is in the Plaza Room (even in religion, Mexicans get short shrift 'round here). Hawaiian-themed services, gospel Gospel, kiddie salvation, Saddleback has it all—and if you want a glimpse of the Golden Child, Saddleback founding pastor and Hawaiian-T-shirt-sporting Rick Warren, stick around the Worship Center, a simple auditorium sitting on a hill that oversees the rest of Saddleback Church. Ask ahead to know when Rick's there—he's usually jet-setting to Africa or North Korea trying to save the world. And when a different hunger sets in, the Terrace Café sells a killer breakfast burrito that you can munch on while viewing four different Saddleback services.

Saddleback represents the "new" Orange County—remember that Lake Forest is in South County—but its true heart roars half an hour away in a campus that looks like a former school, on the border between Costa Mesa and Santa Ana. Fire! Brimstone! Bad gays! The End Times are here! From this pulsing abscess springs forth the Calvary Chapel doctrine of accepting the world's rejects, then transforming them into homo-hating zealots—if one of their thousand or so branches aren't in your town soon, expect them next fall.

Or, is this land's soul inside the fake-antebellum mansion that serves as the headquarters for the Trinity Broadcasting Network, the world's largest televangelism network? HAPPY BIRTHDAY, JESUS! a Christmas-light display proclaims every Christmas, next to the 405 Freeway. What's more godly than wealth, especially when all you have to do is call 1-888-731-1000, donate money, and the Lord will return it one hundred–fold? What person epitomizes Orange County Christianity—hell, Orange County—more than Jan Crouch, the pants-wearing half of the TBN empire, a woman with a giant shock of pink hair and whose use of makeup relegates Tammy Faye Bakker to Carmelite-nun humility?

Probably Robert Schuller. You know the lovable gramp—he's the guy with snow-white hair, big glasses, a wide, permanent smile, and a gray-and-burgundy robe that looks more appropriate on a college provost than on the man behind *The Hour of Power,* the Sunday-morning church show, which you've surely flipped through on the way to *Meet the Press,* that is the world's most-viewed church service. You know the *Hour*: happiness spewing from an unusual church of glass—hence the nickname Crystal Cathedral. Warren and TBN heads Paul and Jan Crouch, even crotchety Calvary

Chapel founder Chuck Smith, are whippersnappers compared to Schuller—plus, you can buy cool Divinity® ties and Crystal Cathedral teddy bears after Schuller's Good News. Consumerist and Christian—can't get more Orange County than that!

Perhaps you believe in the Virgin Mary, that she was free of sin and conceived immaculately. Then follow to the one true faith, the denomination that created this big mess called Orange County. Here is the second-largest Catholic diocese west of the Mississippi. Hang out with the geniuses who manufactured a priestly sex-abuse settlement larger than Boston's, who plan to build a cathedral right up the street from a mega-mall at the same time they shutter parochial schools in an effort to save silver.

Or maybe you don't care for Jesus. Maybe you believe in Allah, the most merciful and compassionate—peace be upon him. Mosques are sprouting across Orange County at the rate of one a year, but the most prominent remains the Islamic Society of Orange County, located with Garden Grove's section of Little Saigon. The head imam is Muzammil Siddiqi, who prayed alongside President Bush in the National Cathedral just after 9/11. A good man—so how did the American Al Qaeda Adam Gadahn get radicalized in Siddiqi's mosque, where great Indian food can be had for five bucks every Friday night? And why does UC Irvine's Muslim Student Union attract so much attention from right-wingers? Maybe because they wear green graduation sashes critics claim are an endorsement of Hezbollah and hold seminars about Palestine entitled "Holocaust in the Holy Land"?

Pondering the Islamic question is Robert Morey, head of Faith Community Church in Irvine and the self-proclaimed world's foremost expert on Islam. He claims to have predicted the 1993 World Trade Center attack two weeks before it happened, to have been the first to identify Osama bin Laden as the mastermind behind the 1998 bombings of American embassies in Africa, and continues to urge the American government to drop nuclear bombs over the Islamic holy city of Mecca in an effort to end the War on Terror. Plus, he cooks great Texas-style chili!

So many more influential godly men and women roam the county. Remember the near schism between the American Episcopal Church and the Anglican Council over the ordination of a homosexual bishop? Blame St. James in Newport Beach for starting the schism—I'd say blame their former pastor, Praveen Bunyan, but he quit last year after admitting to shtupping a parishioner. Santa Ana is home to the largest bilingual church in *los Estados States,* Templo Calvario. One of the world's largest libraries on Zoroastrianism is down the street from Westminster's best Vietnamese sandwich shops. Sarang Community Church ranks among the biggest churches in the country, period—and its services are in Korean. One of radical Christendom's top donors, Howard F. Ahmanson Jr., hides his Tourette's in Newport Beach. And you know those folks who insist gays and lesbians can learn to leave their sodomite ways? Yep—Orange County started that movement as well. Even Buddhists can enjoy the Pao Fa Temple, one of the largest Buddhist temples in America.

Lake Forest: One of the oldest communities in Orange County, and also one of the youngest. Was known as El Toro from the late 1800s up until the 1990s, when residents decided to incorporate as Lake Forest in honor of trees next to a man-made lake. The old-timers had a fit but were outnumbered by newbies who only knew they didn't want any Spanish in their hometown's name. Best known to the world as the home of Saddleback "Purpose Driven Life" Church. City lost a lawsuit against the ACLU when it tried to run day laborers out of the city. **Best restaurant: Abel's Bakery** was once a Jewish bakery run by a Mexican Mormon; Mexicans still run the best Jewish bakery in Orange County and can fill all your mandelbrot, hamantaschen, and challah needs. *24601 Raymond Way, Ste. 7, Lake Forest, (949) 699-0930.*

This is truly God's country. And if you don't believe, get the hell out.

A 2005 *Harper's* article named Orange County the country's second hotbed of evangelical Christianity after Colorado Springs. *Outreach* magazine lists four Orange County churches in its 2007 list of the one hundred churches with the largest congregations in America—Saddleback is number four, Calvary Chapel Costa Mesa is thirty-nine, Mariners Church in Irvine is number forty-eight, Sarang is forty-nine—and if you add in the ten other Calvary Chapel churches on the list not based in Orange County, Orange County notches fourteen, far more than any other U.S. metropolitan area. And my calculations don't include the dozens of mega-movements—Harvest Crusades, Promise Keepers, Kenneth Copeland Ministries, and other roving caravans of Christ—that set up camp at the Anaheim Convention Center, the Honda Center, and all of Orange County's major arenas, stadiums, and warehouses every year to audiences of thousands and millions of dollars in donations.

Religion is Orange County's saving grace—we redeem our vicious, ugly traits by repenting on Sunday. It drives politics—many elected officials use faith to bolster their voting drives and inform their policies. When the Santa Ana Unified School District debated in 2004 whether to allow domestic partner benefits, trustee Rosemarie Avila shared the news with her pastor, Calvary Chapel's Chuck Smith; he promptly told congregants to protest. More than three hundred people showed up at the SAUSD board meeting two days later, ranting about gay conspiracies and railing against Hollyweird. The speeches that night made the Scopes Monkey Trial a paragon of erudition by comparison.

For a county that prides itself on Progress, the adherence by natives to such conservative strains of religion appears counter-intuitive. But Orange County's pioneers frequently let faith influence their actions, and not just in the obvious example of Mission San Juan Capistrano. As Orange County transferred to American hands, as the Mission fell into disrepair and St. Boniface Church opened in 1860 to serve the Germans in Anaheim, other true believers founded competing communes and cults. The settlers came from across America and brought various denominations—Methodists, Presbyterians, Lutherans, and Episcopalians can all boast Orange County's oldest congregations. Westminster began as a Presbyterian temperance colony in 1870 founded by the Reverend Lemuel Webber, who purchased sixty-five hundred acres for the purpose of creating a "settlement of persons whose religious faith, notions of morals, and education, should be so nearly alike, that they might cordially cooperate from the first in the maintenance of a Christian Church and a superior school." Webber's legacy was such that Westminster farmers refused to grow grapes for decades after the pastor's death because they associated grapes with alcohol. In the area near what's now Fountain Valley, so many passing preachers put up their revival tents in the messy terrain that residents nicknamed it Gospel Swamp.

But Orange County's first religious celebrities weren't Christians. It's hip nowadays to eat organic, but the eco movement is actually old hat in Orange County. In 1876, Englishman George Risdale Hinde told friends that "spirits" commanded him to move to what's now Placentia with his family, build a ten-room mansion in which the rooms had no corners, and import trees from across the globe. Two years later, Dr. Louis Schlesinger moved in with the Hindes, and the men created the Societas Fraternia, which they claimed "would grow to great proportions and which would be superior to any society or sect in the world."

The Societas became the talk of Orange County for its peculiar beliefs. Members were restricted to a fruit-and-vegetable diet, and that food couldn't be cooked, as Hinde claimed "cooking destroys the spirit essence which prevades everything in nature." Work was frowned upon because "as nature has provided everything actually necessary for man's existence, the necessity of continual toil does not exist." Sprinkle with a little socialism and free love, and it wasn't long before the county fathers wanted the Societas Fraternia out.

Deliverance came in the form of a dead one-year-old girl, whom Societas members reputedly only fed apple shavings. Hinde and Schlesinger were tried in court for the child's murder. The trial drew national media coverage, but a jury dismissed the charges, according to Orange County historian emeritus Jim Sleeper, because "the publicity was detrimental to [Orange County's] claim as a haven of health."

This didn't stop the local press from dubbing the Societas the Placentia Grass Eaters and constantly haranguing them; the *Santa Ana Standard* opined in 1890, "A little wholesome hanging would be good for the entire community of frauds and fanatics." As a result, the Societas largely retreated from the public eye and became even more orthodox under the leadership of a new member: Walter Lockwood, who changed his name to Thales. Thales did finally permit members to cook food, but he forbade them to seek an education, leave the mansion's premises, or even talk to outsiders when selling produce grown on the Societas's twenty-four-acre property. The cult survived until Thales's death in 1921; their mansion was torn down about a decade later, at which time the corpses of dead members were found on the property.

Nevertheless, the Societas Fraternia lives on. Placentia residents insist that ghosts still inhabit the former Societas property, which was on what's now located on the corner of Placentia

Avenue and Palm Drive. Thales and Hinde introduced the maca-
damia tree to the mainland United States and developed varieties
of walnuts and loquats—known as the Placentia Perfection and
Thales, respectively—that growers and gourmands still prize.
"Their example encouraged [early Orange County] settlers to
experiment with adding new foods to their diet," wrote a contributor in the 1967 collection *Rawhide and Orange Blossoms: Stories
and Sketches of Early Orange County,* "and through their contributions to subtropical fruit culture, the Thales Colony helped pave
the way for the vast subtropical fruit and vegetables industries of
Orange County."

After the Grass Eaters and Gospel Swampers, Orange County
theology lay low for about a half century with the exception of one
key individual: Charles E. Fuller. His father grew oranges, but a
freak frost in 1913 forced Charles to seek a position as a manager
for an orange-packing house in Placentia. Fuller went on to purchase twenty acres of orange groves in the city and became president of the Southern California Citrus Packing Association. But
he longed to serve God. Living off the profits of his fruits while
studying to become a preacher, Fuller created Calvary Church
(not to be confused with the Calvary Chapel movement), after
elders at his previous church, Placentia Presbyterian, showed the
young man out because his Sunday Bible classes attracted more
congregants than the church's regular services. Fuller, for his part,
didn't appreciate that Placentia Presbyterian Church assisted
Mexican citrus workers. "My mother used to recall how the Placentia church had a project of caring for the babies of the Mexicans who picked oranges for the growers," wrote Fuller's son,
Daniel, in his 1972 biography of his dad, *Give the Winds a Mighty
Voice.* "She remembered, regretfully, that in those days she and my
father felt that the church should simply preach the Gospel and
leave to other organizations the task of caring for people's physical needs."

Fuller began airing his Sunday-evening sermons for Calvary on a local radio station as an experiment, and he immediately discovered an untapped market for Jesus. The young preacher urged listeners to donate money to his radio show. "Your investments will pay large dividends for time and eternity. Help to bring cheer, inspiration, and heavenly manna to thousands" read one such fund-raising plea in 1930. It worked: Calvary Church elders booted Fuller because he was spending more time on his radio show than preaching to the Calvary faithful. Soon after, Fuller launched the *Old Fashioned Revival Hour*. Rather than allow his program to consist solely of a church service and his sermons, Fuller put a special focus on music to teach Christianity. This approach made his show a global phenomenon—at the height of its popularity, the *Old Fashioned Revival Hour* aired in 182 countries, a feat so impressive that the *Encyclopedia of American Gospel Music* wrote it "holds a special place in gospel music history because of its enormous global impact in spreading the melodies and spiritual songs of Western Christianity around the world." With its success, Fuller founded the Gospel Broadcasting Association and also created the Fuller Theological Seminary in Pasadena, one of America's premier institutions for Christian thought and the largest multidenominational Christian seminary in the world.

Though he continued to live in Orange County and kept his orange groves, Fuller broadcast the *Old Fashioned Revival Hour* from Long Beach, just across the county line. The county was still too small to support megachurches—smaller congregations dotted the cities. All of that changed with the arrival of a succession of migrant couples who married Fuller's tinkering with technology with their own unique spins on the Nazarene to create new Christianities.

❀   ❀   ❀

Garden Grove: Along with neighboring Westminster, one of two cities that include most of Little Saigon. Also home to Little Seoul, one of the largest Korean population centers in the United States. Despite such significance, the city suffers from Disneyland envy, as the amusement park is just over the city limits in Anaheim. Garden Grove allowed hotels to flourish near Disneyland in an effort to siphon revenue off it, but the city always wants more. Proposals to transform the streets near the Mouse House have ranged from allowing Indian casinos to flooding neighborhoods with water for an amusement park to building a floating museum sponsored by an oil sheikh. Also worth noting is that the city can host the California Coalition for Immigration Reform, the Crystal Cathedral, its Asian communities, *muchos* Latinos, *and* a monthly gay orgy and not erupt in flames. **Best restaurant:** Undoubtedly **Regina's Restaurant,** which specializes in the meat-heavy meals of Argentina and is one of the best places in America to watch a soccer game—if you're Argentine. Others, eat your great meals and don't utter a peep. *11025 Westminster Avenue, Garden Grove, (714) 638-9595; www.reginaargentina.com.*

When Robert Schuller arrived in Orange County in 1955, he wanted to impress his wife with Southern California's beauty, but the Iowa natives drove up to their brand-new Garden Grove home and were nonplussed. "We turned down an unfinished road that wound through a hundred and fifty look-alike, brand-new houses waiting to be painted," Schuller wrote in his 2001 autobiography. "There were no orange trees, not even green lawns. Only bare dirt and bare stucco-framed structures." And then poor Schuller bit into an avocado, mistaking its gnarled skin for an edible husk.

The couple were joining the waves of migrants to Orange County in those years. Schuller—a pastor in the Dutch Reformed Church—was entrusted by his denomination's elders with creating a small outpost in Garden Grove, but found it difficult to attract a congregation: in an area brimming with Christians, few were Dutch Reformed. In his first couple of days, Schuller noticed thousands of people like him—new to the area, yearning for spiritual guidance. He found inspiration (and a venue) in the Orange Drive-In, a multiscreen open theater just off Interstate 5 in the city of Orange (it's presently being turned into condos). Schuller had once prayed at a drive-in service in his native Iowa and noticed how accessibility could persuade otherwise dispassionate people to attend church. He placed a notice in the *Santa Ana Register* and other papers, advertising his new church with the tagline "Come as you are in the family car!"

His Garden Grove Community Church became a national curiosity, as Schuller preached the Word standing on top of the Orange Drive-In concession stand. Rival pastors quickly blasted their young peer for holding church on unholy ground where sin frequently happened the night before in the backseats of cars, but Schuller didn't stop. From this only-in-Eisenhower-America beginning, Schuller sparked a Christian revolution, creating a new approach that combined Scripture with the teachings of his mentor Norman Vincent Peale, author of *The Power of Positive Thinking*. Unlike other pastors, Schuller crafted his message to be as positive as a smiley face—"possibility thinking," he deemed it. Such a philosophy was perfect for 1960s Orange County—uneasy with its wealth. Nowhere was this better expressed than in Schuller's first book, 1963's *God's Way to the Good Life*. The young pastor wrote:

> *You have a God-ordained right to be wealthy. You're a steward of the goods, the golds, the gifts that God has allowed to come into your hands. Having riches is no sin, wealth is no crime. Christ did not praise poverty. The profit motive is not necessarily un-Christian.*

Merely comforting the comforted wasn't enough for Schuller to succeed. According to his *Prayer: My Soul's Adventure with God,*

Schuller was "politically neutral but quite possibly a liberal, at least in spirit," when he began in California. The young man's ideology changed, however, after hearing a lecture by Fred Schwartz, a self-proclaimed expert on communism who headed the Long Beach–based Christian Anti-Communist Crusade.

"I had no inkling," Schuller recounted in *Prayer,* "that many leaders in mainline Protestantism were sympathetic to Marxism as an alternative to capitalism, which they saw as systematically evil." As a result, Schuller pulled his Orange County congregation out of the mainstream National Council of Churches of Christ.

"I was now tempted for the first and last time to accept an invitation to go full-time into anti-communism and join [Schwartz]," Schuller wrote. Then, according to *Prayer,* God spoke to Schuller, saying, "Watch out for communism, and watch out for anti-communism, and watch out for anti-anti-communism." Schuller's God and my God might be the same Savior, but mine has a better editor.

After his revelation, Schuller claims in his autobiography to have forsaken politics. The truth, however, is more complex. According to Lisa McGirr's excellent 2001 examination of 1960s Orange County politics, *Suburban Warriors: The Origins of the New American Right,* Schuller was active in anticommunist activities despite claims to the contrary. *Suburban Warriors* revealed that Schuller served on the religious committee of the Orange County School of Anti-Communism, a five-day celebration held in 1961 to lecture people on the Red Menace, culminating with a midday rally held in Anaheim's Glover Stadium, where more than seven thousand elementary school students heard speaker after speaker.

Members of Schuller's congregation at the time, McGirr wrote, were part of Orange County's nutty conservatives and included Congressman James "Barefoot Africans" Utt. In addition, Schuller joined the Californians' Committee to Combat

Communism in 1962, a group formed to help pass the Francis Amendment, which sought to ban the hiring of people with communist "leanings" in the state. After the legislation's defeat, McGirr says, Schuller left "controversial political activities." By then, Schuller helped set a new template for Orange County religion. John Birch conservatism, while popular in Orange County, didn't appeal to the nation at large, so Schuller quickly ditched the polarizing views and embraced the gospel of prosperity—"God wants you to succeed!"

The church expanded exponentially shortly after Schuller's dabbles in McCarthyism. By 1961, he'd raised enough money to commission a Richard Neutra building that formalized his drive-in ministerial approach: while he preached inside a chapel, a glass door separated Schuller from his drive-in congregation hearing Schuller's sermon on tinny radios, allowing him to walk toward them. In 1970, he started airing his church's services on *The Hour of Power*, and the world was now privy to Schuller. Millions liked what they saw: a relentlessly optimistic man who ignored man's Fall to emphasize one's potential. It's broadcast to this day from the Crystal Cathedral (opened in 1980), a playground for Christianity with a stream running through the worship area, a huge American flag inside the chapel, and topped by its namesake, a ten-thousand-glass-panes bell tower rising to the sky. Tacky yet godly, and hard to hate—the epitome of Schuller.

Schuller set a precedent—an outsider arrives and taps into the restless Orange County masses, spawning a new Christianity that reflected the Orange County of the moment. After Schuller came Chuck Smith. In 1962, Smith received an invitation from a Costa Mesa ministry named Calvary Chapel to save its floundering church. His wife opposed a move from Corona (just across the Orange County line, where they had just started a church) until receiving what Smith described in an official church history as a revelation:

*One night I came home from a Bible study and my wife met me
at the door. She had been crying. She said, "Honey I've been in
prayer and God has really spoken to my heart. The Lord has
made it clear that I'm to submit to you. You're the pastor, you're
my husband. Wherever you feel God wants you to minister, I must
submit to you . . . though I think you're crazy to even think about
it. Surely, you've forgotten about it by now. But even if you
decided to go, I would have to submit to you."*

Smith attempted to tell his wife that the Calvary Chapel board
wanted a decision the following day before she interrupted him,
"Don't tell me! Don't talk to me about it. I'm not ready to move,
I'm only to submit at this point."

Submission to Smith and his proxy Jesus would become the
trademark of Calvary Chapel. Smartly, Smith knew that to draw
adherents to his fundamentalist message in the liberal 1960s, he
had to offer more than rigidity. At that time, Orange County was
becoming a haven for the counterculture, much to the consterna-
tion of the county fathers. In Laguna Beach, acolytes of Timothy
Leary's created a nonprofit church called the Brotherhood of Eternal Love, which quickly expanded from teaching Eastern religious
principles into running one of the largest drug cartels in the United
States. (I could continue, but this is where I'll shamelessly plug my
colleague Nick Schou, who wrote an amazing article about this a
couple of years ago and is currently writing a book on the subject.
E-mail him at nschou@ocweekly.com). The hippie movement also
created the creepy cult known as the Children of God, but nowadays called the Family International, best known for introducing
the concept of "flirty fishing" (enticing converts through sex) to
Christendom—it began in Huntington Beach in 1969.

"These long-haired, bearded, dirty kids going around the streets
repulsed me," Smith admitted in his Calvary Chapel history. "They
stood for everything I stood against. We were miles apart in our

thinking, philosophies, everything." But Smith's wife felt the call of God to reach out to these kids. And the boyfriend of Smith's daughter—a hippie-turned-Christian identified in church narratives only as John—regaled the couple with talk of his successful conversion efforts.

Smith asked John to bring him a hippie. John drove down Fairview Road in Costa Mesa and picked up Lonnie Frisbee, a Costa Mesa native who had spent the previous years wandering through California on one long acid trip. When John asked Frisbee if he needed a ride, the hippie refused. "Hey, I'm not going anywhere, man," Frisbee replied. "I'm a Christian and I'm just hitchhiking to witness to whoever picks me up."

Smith was pleased. "I wasn't prepared for the love that came forth from this kid," he wrote in Calvary Chapel's 1981 history. "His love for Jesus Christ was infectious. The anointing of the Spirit was upon his life, so we invited Lonnie to stay with us for a few days."

With Frisbee's flowing hair and beard, bona fide bells in his bell-bottoms, and flowers in his hair, it's logical that *The Encyclopedia of Evangelicalism* described him as "the quintessential Jesus freak." Frisbee and Smith began baptizing en masse on the picturesque beaches of Corona Del Mar State Beach. The Jesus Movement was born, fascinating the nation, receiving prominent play in *Time* and network news. The Calvary Chapel movement became one of the largest Christian ministries on earth and birthed other megamovements such as the Vineyard Movement and the Harvest Crusades. Smith also revolutionized Christian music through Maranatha! music, a record label that allowed non-traditional Christian singers—rock bands, folksingers, etc.—to record their songs and mass-distribute to churches. Equally influential was *The Word for Today,* a radio program Smith began in the 1970s that he also recorded on cassette tapes and distributed across the globe—podcasts before iPods.

But Frisbee and Smith split just a couple of years into their hippie ministry over doctrinal reasons; it also didn't help that Frisbee was a homosexual. Frisbee never returned to the Calvary Chapel fold, yet Smith gave the eulogy at Frisbee's 1993 funeral, held at Crystal Cathedral. Before thousands, Smith compared Frisbee with a well-known, long-haired biblical figure, "Samson— a man who knew the powerful anointing of God's light. What could have been . . . a man who never experienced the ultimate of the potential. I often wondered what could have been."

As Calvary Chapel helped spark the rise of New Wave evangelicalism in the United States, the Trinity Broadcasting Network built on the efforts of Fuller and Schuller to evangelize worldwide via mass media. In 1973, Paul and Jan Crouch joined with Jim and Tammy Bakker to start broadcasting Christian-themed television shows in Southern California. Their talk show about Christianity lasted but three days before the couples launched a fund-raiser to save the station. Viewers responded immediately— even if they couldn't see the Crouches on their television, which in the early days aired on a low-power UHF station. "Telephone calls came in from all over Southern California," wrote Crouch in his 2003 *Hello World!: A Personal Letter to the Body of Christ.* "How they even knew we were on is a mystery and a miracle all its own. . . . Many said, 'All we can see is a snowstorm, but we can hear you just fine! Keep up the good work; we are praying for you!'" Shortly after, a friend donated a Santa Ana studio to the Crouches, from which they began *Praise the Lord.* The show transformed into an entire network, the Trinity Broadcasting Network. The Bakkers left shortly after its incorporation over direction. Jim and Tammy wanted to invest in programming; Paul and Jan felt infrastructure was more important. The Crouches' vision turned out to be best for Christian televangelism.

Unlike with other Orange County Christian movements, the Crouches didn't concentrate on preaching to a congregation;

instead, they offered a venue for others who wanted to use television for outreach. The plan worked: pastors from across America—even Robert Schuller—bought airtime on TBN. Today, it is the largest televangelism network in the world. Though possessing a global reach, the Crouches are better appreciated in Orange County as camp classics, each dressing like the Missouri hicks they were, frequently crying on the air and admonishing viewers to send in more money to fund their multimillion-dollar lifestyle, which includes mansions across the globe and private chefs. Their youngest son, Matthew, has followed their parents in a different kitsch path: his Christian-themed movie thrillers, *The Omega Code* and *Megiddo: The Omega Code 2,* are the *Left Behind* series combined with Roger Corman.

The 1970s saw Orange County birth another crucial Christian development. Across the street from Disneyland in Anaheim was Melodyland Christian Center, a former musical theater that was transformed into a Pentecostal church. From here sprang Exodus International, the country's first ex-gay movement. Founder Michael Bussee started it to wean homosexuals from their longings via the power of Christ. But Bussee fell out of the organization in 1982 when he and a fellow "ex-gay" realized they loved each other on a flight home from a conference. Exodus International continues as one of the largest ex-gay ministries in the world.

Also, in the 1970s, a young newlywed couple drove to Orange County, this time to study at Schuller's Institute for Church Growth. Southern Baptists by denomination, Kay and Rick Warren had concerns about learning from Schuller, whom they considered little better than an apostate for his unconventional ways. Schuller had decided to teach his megachurch secrets to anyone who was interested, regardless of denomination. "An indisputed fact is that I am the founder, really, of the church-growth movement in this country. . . . I advocated and launched what has become known as the marketing approach in Christianity," Schuller once remarked. Rick Warren would become one of Schuller's most successful students.

Inspired by Schuller's charisma, the Warrens returned to Orange County in 1979 with a U-Haul, a young daughter, and little else, not even an apartment. Immediately, Warren began proselytizing—the Realtor who helped the Warrens find their first apartment in Lake Forest became Rick's first saved soul in Orange County. Within a couple of years, Warren graduated from holding services inside his condo to hosting them at the gym of Laguna Hills High School, starting in 1982.

During his first gym service, Warren displayed the bravado that puts off some traditional Christians but enthralls millions. He told the small crowd that the congregation would one day build a church with twenty thousand members, operate out of a campus with multiple buildings, and spark a rekindling of the Holy Spirit not seen since the Great Awakening.

"I stand before you today and state in confident assurance that these dreams will become reality," he told an unbelieving audience. "Why? Because they are inspired by God!"

Like Schuller and Smith before him, Warren tapped into a wave of new arrivals numbering in the tens of thousands, now populating South County, richer than ever but still in need of salvation. It was with and among these people that he created the philosophy of Purpose Driven®, the idea of administering a ministry through a biblically based strategic plan. Using diagrams, charts, and seminars similar to what he'd learned from Schuller, Warren traveled the country to teach churches how to grow, eventually publishing *The Purpose Driven Church* in 1995 and developing a thousands-strong global network of pastors. As he spread his mantra, Saddleback Church grew—his boast from so long ago became a reality after he purchased property in Lake Forest near the 261 Toll Road to better connect with his parishioners. In 2002, he published *The Purpose Driven Life,* which started with words anathema to Orange Countians: "It's not about you."

Yet this wasn't enough for Warren. In the years since *The Purpose Driven Life*'s publication (it's now the top-selling religion book in history that's not the Bible, with more than 40 million copies in print), Warren has continued to tutor church leaders. More surprising, Warren has focused on eradicating AIDS and poverty in Africa, a worldwide view rare for county Christianity, which always focused on saving itself but staying away from terrestrial concerns. He's also tried to play world mediator to the chagrin of some conservatives, meeting with Syria and vowing to introduce Christ to North Korea. Warren's church is a member in good standing with the Southern Baptist Convention, but it's a gentler kind of evangelical Christianity, fusing Schuller's possibility approach with Smith's caring fundamentalism, all with little of the Crouches' excess.

Catholicism in Orange County, by contrast, assumes humbler airs than its Christian brethren despite being the cagiest of the bunch. From the days of the Mission, the Catholic priests have concerned themselves with assisting the poor. Through the 1960s, Church leaders frequently set up missions in Latino neighborhoods, simple wooden structures devoted mostly to liturgy and social services. With a rise in migrants, the Diocese of Orange was spun off from the Archdiocese of Los Angeles in 1976 to oversee the growing Catholic population. Upon assuming the new diocese's bishopric, Los Angeles auxiliary bishop William Johnson remarked, "The very name, Orange, suggests a golden treasure, and the new diocese is all that in its physical characteristics, its people, and its traditions."

Upon its founding, the diocese did everything possible to tarnish its golden shine. Unlike the Crouches, Schuller, Smith, Warren, and other Christian movements, the Catholic hierarchy mastered the art of ingratiating themselves with local politicians to grow in power and protect the Church from prosecution. The Catholic hierarchy learned that to succeed in the county, they needed connections in the corridors of power. Its first communications director was Tom Fuentes, a longtime Republican Party activist who went on to lead the Orange County Republican Party for many years. This connection to the lords of Orange County, Catholic or not, ensured that the Church largely avoided justice in the most horrific crime perpetuated in Orange County's history, even more disgusting than Taco Bell: the rape of innocents.

Almost from the beginning of the Orange Diocese, officials colluded with law enforcement to hide boy-buggering priests. In a confidential memo dated March 27, 1975, Monsignor Joseph Rawden, chancellor for the Los Angeles Archdiocese, wrote that Father Eleuterio Ramos, who had just started at St. Joseph in Placentia, would start psychological care. The suggestion came from the Orange County district attorney's office, citing "a recent incident." Ramos went on to become the most prolific child rapist in Orange County's history, admitting to at least twenty-five molestations in his fifteen years of terrorizing Catholic parishes. His reign of terror ended in 1987 only because Church officials shipped him to Tijuana, after he admitted to violating *another* boy.

Ramos is one of many examples. In 1985, Michael Driscoll— then chancellor for the Orange Diocese, now bishop of the Diocese of Boise—wrote a letter to a priest in Liverpool, England, begging him to accept Father Robert Foley. Foley had just admitted to molesting an eight-year-old boy during a camping trip organized by St. Justin Martyr in Anaheim. The boy's mother, Driscoll wrote, "has threatened to go to the police," and Foley "is in jeopardy of arrest and possible imprisonment if he remains here." Foley left the United States for England; he never faced prosecution for his crime. The following year, Huntington Beach police tried to interrogate Father Andrew Christian Andersen after parents filed a police report alleging the popular priest grabbed their son's crotch during a film. In confidential police reports, detectives described how the Church hierarchy whisked Andersen away and refused to answer their questions. Andersen received a suspended sentence after receiving hundreds of supportive letters from parishioners.

Even worse was the case of Michael Harris. He was the former principal of Mater Dei High in Santa Ana, an athletic powerhouse and the largest Catholic high school in the western United States. In 1986, Harris became the first principal of Santa Margarita High in Rancho Santa Margarita, a Catholic school in South County built through tapping into the area's developers who no longer wanted their children to attend Mater Dei, as the city around it was becoming increasingly Mexican. But Harris—nicknamed Father Hollywood for his charisma—abruptly resigned in 1994 after Church officials asked him to undergo counseling for his attraction to teenage boys. Harris never admitted any wrongdoing, even though the Church has paid out millions of dollars to settle lawsuits filed by his alleged victims. He now runs a lucrative nonprofit in Southern California and even bunked for a while in the Newport Beach home of William Lyon, one of Orange County's many megadevelopers.

Most of these horrid stories have been exposed in this millennium, when lawyers began suing the Orange Diocese for millions and also to release confidential personnel files that proved Church leaders' complicity in covering up the sex crimes within their parishes. A class-action settlement was finalized in November of 2004—$100 million for ninety victims, at the time the largest settlement in the history of the Catholic Church, larger even than Boston's.

Admittedly, I write with anger about the Catholic Church, but for purely selfish reasons. I was born into the Catholic Church, even had aspirations of becoming a priest until puberty taught me

I'd never be able to keep priestly vows. St. Boniface in Anaheim was my parish, and the pastor through the 1980s up until the mid-1990s was John Lenihan. Everyone knew the Irish priest had admitted to sexually molesting teenage girls, but no one ever bothered to raise a fuss about it. Even as a young boy, I remember being bothered that Lenihan's admission was widely known among my family and our friends, but that no one did anything about it. Instead, our parents had a simple answer: "Father John has a problem." I continued with my sacraments, but this excuse gnawed at me through early adulthood.

In early 2004 (sorry for jumping ahead—I'll explain my journalism career in better depth in a couple of chapters), I began digging into the Orange Diocese sex-abuse scandal. Priests attacked me from the pulpit as I exposed coverup after coverup. In the St. Boniface Church bulletin, a pastor blasted me for daring to criticize the diocese's continued purchase of million-dollar homes to house their priests instead of letting them live in a rectory as in the old days. Last year, Church officials hired a lawyer to threaten me with lawsuits after I began investigating Mater Dei boys' basketball coach Gary McKnight, a massive (both figuratively and literally—the man is as fat as Curly of the Three Stooges, but without the warmth) presence in prep hoops nationwide. McKnight had allowed his former assistant coach Jeff Andrade to return to campus despite school officials testifying under oath they had ordered McKnight to ban him after they let him go for having sex with a fifteen-year-old girl. Nothing ever came of the legal threats, and the Orange Diocese paid Andrade's victim over a million dollars in a settlement. McKnight just won his second-straight California State prep hoops championship; Andrade organizes high school fund-raisers in California.

Despite these sins, church pews fill every Sunday with the faithful; Orange County has over 1.3 million Catholics, and its future—like the county's—is Mexican. Every year the Orange

Diocese holds a Red Mass at Holy Family Cathedral in Orange. The Red Mass is a Catholic tradition in which a region's law enforcement officials attend Mass to receive a blessing from the bishop or cardinal. Judges wear their robes, law enforcement their uniforms, lawyers their suits—the very men entrusted to uphold God's laws in the secular world. They enter the humble cathedral in a procession through the aisle. Following them is the Church hierarchy, buttressed with the relief that no one can catch them. None of the other major Orange County Christian movements are so bold, so vile. So lucky.

But their time will slip, as well. Bishop Tod D. Brown recently published *Diocese of Orange: Learning, Loving, Living Our Faith,* a history written by two diocesan administrators. On page 95 is a picture of Brown signing an agreement for the opening of JSerra Catholic High School. Have some fun: visit blogs.ocweekly.com/navelgazing/ex-cathedra and look for the entry titled "Stalinism, Sex Abuse, and the Catholic Diocese of Orange." Ain't it funny? Orange County Christianity can try to wipe its tawdry pasts clean, but Truth prevails.

Stanton: You know your city is in bad shape when most Orange County residents only know the tiny town for being the home of Samantha Runnion, the murdered five-year-old girl who earned former Orange County sheriff Mike Carona his first national exposure. But don't overlook the great baseball batting cages! **Best restaurant:** Not only is Peruvian food stellar at **Nory's,** but its rotisserie chicken—crispy on the outside, juicy on the inside with a marinade created from soy sauce and garlic—is a religious experience that makes you forget you're eating in Stanton. *6959–63 Cerritos Avenue, Stanton, (714) 761-3332; also at 933½ S. Euclid, Anaheim, (714) 774-9115.*

Costa Mesa: The city that wished it were like neighboring Newport Beach but is condemned to be known as the place where a Mexican-bashing mayor came into office. Working class at its core, and home to South Coast Plaza only because the mall didn't incorporate in Santa Ana, for which city officials thank Jehovah by the hour. **Best restaurant: Pupusería San Sivar,** a Salvadoran restaurant that specializes in the pupusa, a half-gordita, half-quesadilla that's nothing but yummy goodness. *1940 Harbor Boulevard, Costa Mesa, (949) 650-2952.*

Genesis and the Stetson

When my father dies, I'm going to decorate the mortuary with hats. Giant sombreros and trucker's *cachuchas*. Baseball lids stitched with the interlocked *L* and *A* of the Dodgers. Cheap, smelly corduroy caps bought from swap meets and yard sales for fifty cents. Wide-brimmed. In lieu of flowers, I'll ask mourners to donate *tejanas*—what Mexicans call Stetson ten-gallons—to their favorite Tijuana orphanage.

My dad loves hats. There's a practical component to his infatuation: male-pattern baldness cruelly afflicts the Arellanos at a young age (which reminds me: anyone know a good hatter? E-mail me at themexican@askamexican.net). But the main reason he keeps more chapeaus than the average film-noir tough guy is to keep up with the Mirandas. See, all the *hombres* from Jerez in the United States sport hats at least once a day—and probably sleep in them as well. The most popular choice is the *tejana,* and Papi kept at least four at any given time while I was growing up, and to this day. Each has a particular purpose. The sweat-stained one made of straw is for leisure time or to wear while maintaining his beloved lawn and palm trees; black means it's time to play billiards; creamy white signifies he's going to visit family. And if society calls, Dad dons a magnificent gray Stetson softer than cotton candy, a monument to machismo worth every peso of its $500 price.

That glorious Stetson is just the (pun intended) capper to my father's regular outfit. As important are the boots: pointy and sturdy enough to survive more than two decades. Jeans are a given for any male in America, but only the Mexican men are fabulous enough to pull off elaborately embroidered belts called *cintos piti-ados* with bits of glitter sewn into arabesque curves made from the delicate threads of the agave plant (the same botanical Swiss Army knife of Mexico that produces tequila). A silver belt buckle holds the *cinto pitiado* together; in a pinch, the buckle can double as a shovel.

When I was growing up in the early 1990s, Papi wasn't the only overdressed Mexican in our Anaheim *jerezano* colony, which had expanded from his native Jomulquillo and Mom's El Car-gadero to include other ranchos—San Juan, El Porvenir, Rio Florido, Los Morales. Anthropologists have noted that individuals in poor societies spend inordinate wealth on ludicrous, unnecessary items, and the men of Jerez practiced conspicuous consumption like hedge-fund investors. These immigrants earned enough money to move from apartments into Anaheim's cornucopia of tract housing, then transformed the neighborhoods into mini-haciendas featuring imported tile, exotic trees, and fountains worthy of Tivoli; any remaining *gabachos* white-flighted away. The typical *jerezano* truck, meanwhile, rumbled through streets like a mastodon and tended to feature a decal that read JEREZ, whether as a dignified bumper sticker or in individual Old English lettering.

The ultimate peacock feathers for Papi's generation, however, were clothes: who boasted the biggest belt buckle, which feet slipped into the most exotic animal leather (I remember armadillo, alligator, ostrich, even fetal cows), whose *cinto pitiado* featured the most threading, and whose *tejana* featured the largest number of X's (Stetson ranks the quality of their cowboy hats with X's, on the inside rim. My father only had a 10X hat; to be a big man, you

started at 100X. Hey, we were working class). With such a sartor-
ial fixation, you'd swear these machos were auditioning for *Project
Runway*.

Such attention to appearance didn't exist in the rancho—
poverty eliminates vanity quickly—but it was essential to surviving
el Norte. Not only did my father and his peers have to spend
money like *gabachos* to prove they were well-off and succeeding to
everyone else, but a *jerezano* in the States needed to dress Mexican or face rancho gossipers bandying around that most devastating insult: *pocho*. A Mexican who has lost his heritage. Me.

Most of the boys from Jerez dressed like their daddies whenever there was a social occasion for the ranchos. I hated the style,
not because I didn't appreciate the look but because I couldn't
pull it off. No cowboy I knew, Mexican or American, ever wore
glasses—only city slickers needed specs in John Ford's films. But
my dad didn't care—Lorenzo Arellano's primary goal in his new
country was to make his son dress like a Mexican.

Our Stetson standoff didn't start until junior high school.
That's when the dozens of parties we haunted every month suddenly transformed into more than an excuse to eat free food and
hang out with friends. I learned this the mature way. While standing outside a seedy downtown Los Angeles nightclub with a friend
of the same age, I suggested we ditch the wedding reception
inside and go play arcade games at a nearby liquor store, just as
we'd done during boring parties since elementary school. "Nah, I
want to dance with girls," he replied.

"Aren't you a bit too young for that?" I asked. We were both
fourteen.

"What are you—gay?"

"Fuck you," I argued. "I felt my girlfriend's tit already." I lied—
the girl whom I had a crush on at the time was as flat as a surfboard.

"If you don't dance, you're gay," he responded, and off he
went, leaving me to ponder this Mexican Truth.

Cypress: La Palma, but bigger. First called Waterville because of its many wells, then changed to Dairy City upon incorporation in 1956 for the same reason as La Palma. Its only redeeming feature is Cypress Community College, and only because its weekend swap meets are the county's best. **Best restaurant: Señor Big Ed,** the county's only Puerto Rican restaurant. *5490 Lincoln Avenue, Cypress, (714) 821-1290.*

*   *   *

The teenage years are momentous in any culture, and *jerezanos* have a creative way of ushering their children into this vital epoch: dances. And not just any type of writhing and grinding—our shimmying involves holding each other and swaying to polkas and waltzes, the stuff most Americans only see during Oktoberfest or Milwaukee Brewers games. These are the dances of rural Mexico. (Want to know why Mexicans dance like Polacks and Krauts? Go buy my first book, *¡Ask a Mexican!*)

I'm sure jaded *gabachos* see Mexican dances as another nod to culture and tradition, but it's actually a brilliant initiation ritual. Dancing incorporates the same philosophies and intricacies that bind civil society. You first ask a girl for permission to share a dance; if she refuses, you respect her decision and move on. If the request is accepted, you quickly negotiate points—how close you can hold each other, the duration of the dance, even the opportunity to dance again—as you proceed to the floor.

Then you actually dance. Cooperation is not an option but a mandate if the dance is to be enjoyable or repeated in the future. Steps must be in unison; the enjoyment of the other person is integral to the fulfillment of the contract. The best dancers are not those who are the most handsome or beautiful or even polished, but those who understand the need for unselfishness, as each person entrusts the other with his or her body, safety, and pleasure.

Mexicans know that dancing holds communities and families together. Once children are eligible to dance, they're eligible to take care of their community, too. It's Hobbes's social contract personified, a person-to-person treaty involving negotiation, compromise, trust, and adherence to the agreement. Mostly, though, it's a great way to cop cheap ass-grabs.

Jerezanos throw dances for the flimsiest of reasons—a birthday, quinceañera, or maybe a fund-raiser for a *club social,* the Mexican term for hometown benefit associations that sprang up during the 1990s to raise money for the lazy Mexicans who lingered in the rancho. These organizations transformed Mexico by initiating a program called *tres por uno* (three for one): for every dollar that participating *clubes sociales* raised, the Mexican government matched their contributions on a federal, state, and local level. Decades of graft were replaced with asphalt, potable water, electricity. It's because of *tres por uno* that Mexico is teetering into the Second World, instead of being mired in the Third. Hundreds of *clubes sociales* sprang up across Southern California in the 1990s, but El Cargadero's was among the most powerful; from the group came Andres Bermudez, who was the first Mexican migrant ever to run for office back in Mexico when he unsuccessfully sought Jerez's mayoral seat in 2001. *Cargaderenses* valued the group primarily because the fund-raising dances were da *bomba.*

We even throw dances at baseball games, for chrissakes. Every major holiday, the Jerez ranchos with residents in Southern California gather in the city of Norwalk to hold all-day tournaments at a municipal park. The tournaments began in the 1980s, organized by the immigrants themselves, and each team was composed solely of men from one rancho. As the years progressed, their sons joined the teams, usually playing in their Little League or high school baseball jerseys. Hundreds of people cheer from the sidelines each holiday, and the games feature *bandas,* torta sellers, announcers. Attendance has dwindled in recent years, but the tournament goes on. And, yes, between games, the baseball diamond transforms into an impromptu dance floor, and everyone dances—even players in their cleats.

It isn't enough to throw a dance, however. Whoever holds the dance also has to impress everyone by providing a prime location—depending on how rich or important the family is, either a backyard, community center, church community room, or giant labor halls that easily house a thousand people. Just to give you an idea of how grandiose these parties were in my youth, one thousand people showed up for my brother Gabriel's baptism reception in 1992. A B-list celebrity—Juan Zaizar, the John Denver of *ranchera* music—stopped by to serenade my cousin Angie during her fifteenth birthday party. *My Super Sweet 16* has nothing on us.

No matter what the occasion, each dance follows a preset format. There is a church service that people skip; photos in a public park because no one can afford a studio; a limousine to carry the person or couple or family of honor around, followed by a flank of lowriders or trucks. Guests trickle in to the party around 6 p.m., and the dinner never changes: refried beans, Spanish rice, clammy macaroni salad, and *birria,* a soupy shredded beef or goat stew native to the state of Jalisco that somehow became the official wedding dish of *cargaderenses.* Rarely tortillas—usually *bolillos,* small French rolls that people stash in their handbags and pockets because they're so yummy. The meal isn't catered but rather a labor of love lorded over by a small army of aunts, mothers, and pubescent girls who begin cooking the night before and don't stop until the party is almost over, at which point they dance.

A mariachi band performs during dinner, and the most musically gifted member of the host family joins them at some point to belt out a song. From my dad's side, the vocalist was always my cousin Leti; from my mom's, my *tío* Ezequiel. Everyone listens respectfully but fidgets, eager for the band that follows—a *conjunto norteño*, composed of a drummer, guitarist, bassist, and accordionist fingering out polkas, or—better yet—a mighty eighteen-member *banda sinaloense* brass orchestra that blasts out fast-paced oom-pah-pah rhythms with enough decibels so that speakers aren't necessary. A concert follows for the next five hours, interrupted only by a DJ who plays the same kind of music along with the occasional English-language song to placate the increasing number of Americanized young *cargaderenses*.

These hoedowns are breathtaking—hundreds of couples merge into a giant, swirling organism; they mimic electrons by swarming around an ever-churning nucleus. The music heals: clumsy folks suddenly sway or twirl with facility (unless the song is a *zapateado*, a furious stomp that resembles fighting cocks prepping to rumble). Even the nondancers play a role. Single men stand alongside the walls eyeing the single women; single women huddle together dressed in conservative skirts or gowns, usually chaperoned by an older *mujer*. Children run around creating havoc, sleeping underneath tables or on chairs once they tire. It is community, lovely for everyone.

For me, it was hell.

I loved these dances—the great music, the *bolillos*, the spectacle of it all. I just didn't want to dance. Or, rather, I did—but it was impossible. Besides having no coordination, I was a terribly shy nerd, and Mexican teenage girls simply can't stand dorks. No matter: every Mexican male older than fifteen was expected to ask women to dance. Cousins didn't count; platonic pals, worse. You had to ask strangers, or girls you wanted to *pretender*—not Chrissie Hynde's old group, but the Mexican term for courting. Something was terribly wrong if someone wouldn't dance. No excuses: if you were older than fifteen and Mexican, you *had* to dance.

My turn as Fred Astaire was doomed at the bud. Women had the right to refuse anyone, and guys didn't argue the point unless they wanted the girl's father to respond with a Budweiser bottle. The señoritas all wanted to dance with older boys—and they *always* wanted to dance with the guys from Mexico who didn't speak a lick of English. They had no use for me—I was their classmate, their friend. I was shit out of luck.

I only danced with a girl I didn't already know twice. One was a married woman whom I didn't realize was married until my cousin told me that her husband wanted to meet me outside, alone. The other chick was ugly. Beyond that, I scored sympathy dances with girls who I knew had pity on me. They all urged me to just ask a stranger, and I always tried—and they always said no. Excuses ranged from "I'm tired" to "The next one" to "*Now* I'm tired" to "I'm on my period." Meanwhile, I watched with envy as my friends, assisted by their cowboy boots, jeans, and Stetsons, notched dances and dates with ease.

Maybe it wasn't me, I theorized; maybe it was my clothes. When I went to parties, I dressed in plaid shirts, khakis, and Doc Martens, a combination of cholo and Poindexter. Maybe I had a better chance if I dressed like my father, I reasoned. It helped my friends; why not me?

Maybe my father might finally shut up. Every weekend, as we loaded into his blue Ford Ranger for another dance, my father asked, "When are you going to wear a *tejana?*"

"Next party, I promise." I kept promising for a good two years.

He bribed me with money. He questioned my manhood. He wondered if I was a real Mexican. I enlisted my mom in the battle to keep me Stetson-free. Her argument used my Papa Je as thesis and conclusion: he never dressed like a poor Mexican; he always wore a suit or a cardigan sweater, a pocket watch, loafers, slacks, and a fedora, a carryover from his days growing up in Anaheim; and he was more Mexican than a cactus. Therefore, Gustavo can wear whatever he wants. "So why don't the rest of Gustavo's cousins dress like their grandfather?" Papi replied. My dad might have dropped out of school in the fourth grade, but he's a sharp one.

Finally, my father found a weakness. For my thirteenth birthday, I asked for a one-day rental of a Sega Genesis system from the local video store. I played *John Madden Football* for hours and repeated the ritual every birthday for the next two years. My Nintendo was fine, but I only owned four games: *Gyromite* (with R.O.B.!), *Duck Hunt*, *The Legend of Zelda*, and *Popeye*, and I beat of all of them quickly.

We were getting ready for yet another party one weekend when my father climbed into the Ranger. I was fifteen. "Will you wear a *tejana* if I buy you the Genesis?" he asked through the small window connecting the cabin to the camper. He pronounced *Genesis* as *Yenesees*. I agreed.

Enter the Stetson.

A couple of weeks after Papi and I made our deal, a group of young people stood in the driveway of my cousin Erica's house in East Los Angeles. No photographs exist of this day, and thank God for that, so let me *attempt* to describe the phony I was, dressed like a Mexican in front of a group of them. Imagine a skinny kid—five feet eight inches, no more than 130 pounds, with glasses as thick as a bank teller's window. Stuff him into supertight blue jeans, cuffs slightly frayed. Hang a bandanna in the right back pocket with ARELLANO printed in Old English font. Add cheap black cowboy boots, a knockoff Stetson, and an itchy long-sleeved shirt. Make sure the boots or jeans have not been broken in. Refry with insecurity. Voilà! We have a laughingstock.

Various cousins and friends had gathered at Erica's house because her quinceañera was coming up and we had to practice her waltz. When they're teens, most Mexican kids get invited by peers to join quinceañeras. Americans know them as the brown version of a debutante ball, but it's better than that: it's a coming-of-age ritual, an excuse to party, a cattle call, a proper Austro-Hungarian event. Teenage Mexicans usually look forward to performing in quinceañeras because it's a way for them to hook up. I always ended up with the ugly friend or cousin of the quinceañera girl. Bitches abused my friendship, I tell you—still can't get over it.

Families spend months in preparation for the quinceañeras—bands, halls, food, poofy dress, deciding who will be in the girl's processional court—but all concerns bow down to the *vals,* the waltz. Yep: Mexicans stage productions worthy of a Merchant-Ivory film. Any respectable quinceañera features one between the dinner and the *banda,* the more traditional the better. Most girls stick to the canon of Strauss, Verdi, and Tchaikovsky for their dance, and damn if it ain't off-putting to see an old Mexican woman who has probably never seen a cello performance in her life hum the crescendo of the "Triumphal March" from *Aida.*

The cool kids modernized *valses* with hip-hop, R&B, anything but an actual waltz. Erica was a cool kid, the youngest daughter of my *tío* Jesús. She was, like me and my siblings, one of the "good" Arellanos, one of the cousins who never joined gangs, did drugs, or sparked gossip among the aunts. Erica wanted to do a cowboy-themed waltz for her quinceañera. One of the hot songs of the moment was a line step that Nashville amazingly never discovered, so she made the girls in her court dress like damsels out of *Petticoat Junction,* while the guys wore Stetsons and tuxes.

I argued with my dad that this fulfilled our agreement—just wear a Stetson and the Genesis was mine, right? "No, you have to wear it to a party before Erica's quinceañera," he said. "*And* you have to ask a girl to dance."

I figured debuting my cowboy style among kith and kin at dance practice might numb the sting. Fifteen years later, those bastards—meaning my family, meaning mostly my sister Elsa, my dance partner for that quinceañera—who were at Erica's house still rib me. Remember that scene in *The Graduate* when Benjamin Braddock walked through his parents' house in a scuba suit to the delight of the adults? Welcome to the presentation of Mexican Gustavo.

Worse yet, there was still a *chica* to ask for a dance, if I wanted the Genesis. It happened the following week, at a union hall in East Los Angeles. At the party, a proud Papi introduced me to his friends. A dozen straight conversations began, "Oh, so your son finally decided to start dressing like a Mexican!"

When my father wasn't looking, I made a quick dash to the Ranger and hid inside for the rest of the night. I never asked a girl to dance. But my father was satisfied. And true to his word, he bought a Sega Genesis.

After Erica's quinceañera, I never wore a Stetson again. (The *vals*, by the way, was a riot. I can still remember the guy who taught it to us. *Point-step, point-step, point-step, kick. Move forward! Now, back in the closet!*) I threw the boots away and began dressing for parties in slacks, long-sleeved white shirt, skinny red tie, and suspenders—just like my Papa Je. I wanted to dress any way but Mexican.

To this day, my father reminds me about the Genesis and the Stetson. "You promised you would start wearing *tejanas!*" he grumbles. But he's not angry. Deep down in his heart, I'm sure he knew I looked like a dork. And I'm glad he learned from my example. When my brother Gabriel came of age, he never forced any of the rancho costume customs on the boy.

The Genesis? Lasted a long time. Good system.

❖   ❖   ❖

Los Alamitos: Seems like a bigger version of La Palma and Cypress, but further scrutiny reveals it's a *much* bigger version of La Palma and Cypress. Birthplace of Olympic gymnast Cathy Rigby. Los Alamitos High's football program is consistently among the best in Southern California. And Los Alamitos Race Course features the fastest quarter-horse races in the United States—too bad the track is actually in Cypress. **Best restaurant:** Keeping with its all-American image, the pick is **Volcano Burgers,** which makes a chili dog worthy of Texas. *3652 Cerritos Avenue, Los Alamitos, (562) 430-6004.*

The Stetson experience soured me on the Jerez social scene, and I pleaded with my parents to leave me at home whenever there was a party. They refused. The only people who didn't pay their respects to Jerez's various celebrations were *pochos* who disavowed their *mexicanidad* and cholos who were too busy getting stoned (as opposed to smashed on Budweiser like the men at the parties). Again, if you were normal and Mexican, you had to dance—end of discussion. I offered Mom and Dad a compromise: only parties for El Cargadero. That meant four dances a month instead of six. Fine.

That was the biggest error of their American experience—more than Papi's alcoholism, Mom's lack of assimilation. My initial thought was a better idea, since going to these parties meant I soon discovered the hotness of my cousins.

When I entered ninth grade at Anaheim High School, I noticed that many of the girls who went to the El Cargadero parties were my new classmates. The typical *cargaderensa* is one of Mexico's finest lasses: long hair, eyes like the moon, modest curves, yet a demon on the dance floor. I was too much of a pussy to ask them to dance, let alone date, so I just talked to them at school and fell into the relentless vortex of the Friend Zone.

I fell hard for an alabaster beauty with brains to match her ass.
I talked to my mom about her; she frowned. "You can't go out
with her," she snapped. "That's your second cousin."

It was more of the same with almost every other *chica*. That
one? Yep. How about those twins? *Sí*. And those *cargaderense* girls
who were on vacation, the ones I shared guacamole with at the
baptism of my cousin's son? She's the daughter of my aunt's
grandchild, my mom said of almost any El Cargadero girl I mentioned.

It turned out that almost everyone from El Cargadero was
related to one another in some way. Through further research, I
discovered that people from El Cargadero didn't look *too* down on
second cousins marrying each other. Far from it, a couple of my
young loves' siblings and uncles were married to their second
cousins.

Taking into consideration our town's proud incestuous tradition, I reasoned in my desperately horny mind that if I didn't find
out a girl was my second cousin until after I began liking her, then
lusting after her was okay. Convoluted logic is swell, right?

The point was moot—few girls liked me, not because we were
second cousins, but because I wasn't Mexican enough. They
swooned over pubescent cowboys, not twerpy pseudo-hipsters. I
thought about sporting the Stetson again, but I saw myself in the
mirror and thought better of it.

Nevertheless, one second cousin was kind enough to invite me
to her quinceañera court. In her infinite kindness, the girl said she
wanted to set me up with a pretty cousin of hers I had never heard
of. The cousin and I talked on the phone before seeing each other,
and we hit it off immediately. Then I actually met her—I'm not
going to describe the gal since she's very much a sweetheart, but
let's just say she wasn't my type. She was also my second cousin—
and the product of a marriage of second cousins.

While trying to court one second cousin and evading another,

I began confiding my feelings in *their* younger cousin. We hit it off and started dating after about a month of flirting. Just a year younger than me, she had impossibly curly hair. When I told my mom about this, she frowned again. "That's your second cousin. Her dad is my cousin."

I used my knew-no-evil card, and our relationship lasted two years. Did I mention her parents were second cousins as well? After she cheated on me, I swore off second cousins for good. Most of them are married now, to guys from El Cargadero who aren't their second cousins. Assimilation wins again.

*   *   *

SPORTS

Though we have a recent Stanley Cup winner in the Anaheim Ducks and a World Series champ with the Los Angeles Angels of Anaheim, the county is a graveyard for teams who joined ill-fated leagues: the American Basketball Association, World Football League, North American Soccer League, and who even remembers the International Roller Hockey League? We hosted the Los Angeles Rams for a couple of years, and the Los Angeles Clippers love to dick with us every year by playing a couple of games at the Honda Center, which has hosted many NCAA basketball tournament rounds. We've skipped surfing and skateboarding here, but only because they're not real sports. Prep team powerhouses such as Mater Dei, Los Alamitos, Mission Viejo, and Santa Margarita football and basketball teams consistently slay their opposition but rarely win on a national level—much like the Republican Party. Newport Beach businessman Paul Salata is the founder of Mr. Irrelevant, the "award" given each year to the last player of the NFL draft—once a tongue-in-cheek ceremony, now overblown like everything else ESPN grasps its tentacles on. We've skipped surfing and skateboarding here, but only because they're not real sports. Tiger Woods is ours, Florida!

My identity issues weren't limited to Mexican dances. Anaheim's school boundaries meant my friends from Sunkist Elementary went to a different junior high from me, and the friends I made at Sycamore Junior High enrolled in a different high school from Anaheim High. The cousins I grew up with moved away or were in different grades from me. By the time I entered high school, I was left with just one real friend: Juan Arturo Marmolejo, otherwise known as Art. He lived across the street from my *tío* Ezequiel and was as much of a loser as me. More on him later—all I'll say about him now is that the first time we met, he tried to steal my hat.

Since I didn't succeed at being a good Mexican, I tried becoming a cool American. That failed, too. In eighth grade, all the popular boys—Mexican, white, black, not Asian—began painting or etching graffiti because that was the fad at the time. I didn't have the guts to graffiti anything except my home. Our walls are stucco white, so I bought an aerosol can of white paint and sprayed DO!NK on the walls, a take on a wrestling clown. All was fine until one day my mom wet the walls with the hose. DO!NK emerged to laugh at my poser ambitions. "What is that?" my mom screamed. "Maybe it came with the house," I offered. God bless my mom—she bought the lie, despite Elsa's protestations. My vandalism is intact to this day, forgotten by everyone until now.

I wasn't a bad teen, but I kept getting into serious trouble. Sycamore Junior High had historically been one of Anaheim's humbler junior highs, but it was poor by the time I entered in 1991. Three-quarters of the student body were Mexican, and the white kids segregated themselves from us. I endured all the horrors a nerd faces in junior high: bullies demanded my lunch money, jocks pantsed me during PE class, girls cracked jokes at my stench. (I didn't discover this until three years ago, when I looked through my seventh-grade Sycamore Junior High yearbook. Scribbled multiple times, by different students: *You smell. You stink. Try a shower. P.U.* Those comments had perplexed me a good decade until I remembered that during seventh grade, I took one shower a week. Back then, I was petrified of slipping in the shower and dying after watching too many Life Alert commercials. Oh, young Gustavo!) The harassment affected me because I failed algebra, earned multiple detentions for talking too much, even socked a Korean kid once because I was bored. But it was my writing that continually damned me.

A short story I wrote led to a meeting with the school psychologist because it involved a school bully killing a nerd. (I plagiarized the beginning of the story, by the way, from a look back at the first meeting between the Cleveland Browns and Philadelphia Eagles penned by genius sports columnist Rick Reilly. The only time I've ever tried to pass off another writer's words as my own. Best to flush out the Jayson Blair in you when no one's reading.) Even worse were my love letters. There were two twins nobody liked—corpulent, loud, and blond. One of them began losing her hair and started wearing hats. As a practical joke in eighth grade, I wrote a fake love letter to the girl—it's lost, but I distinctly remember one of the lines: "I get horny at the sight of your hair."

The principal called two of my friends and me into the office, where the mock object of my affection sat, howling through tears. I was suspended from school for two days for sexual harassment and ordered to scrub toilets alongside the janitors after school for two weeks. The worst part about it was calling Mom from the office and explaining what I had done. When I came home, my mom locked herself in her room and cried. Mami expected that kind of behavior from Elsa, whom she placed in Catholic school because Elsa was hanging out with the gangster girls who populated our neighborhood, but not from her golden son.

No junior high moment was worse—that is, besides the time during silent reading period in English class when I rested my legs on the small desk of my school chair and farted loudly—than when I made it to the finals of our honors English class's speech contest. The winner would earn a trip to Disneyland, location of a countywide tournament. During the preliminaries, I focused my oratorical skills on the glory of Notre Dame football in a speech that ended with a rousing rendition of the school's "Victory March." Everyone loved it the first time around. It helped that I wore a FIGHTING IRISH jacket that hung down to my knees.

My competitor's speech, meanwhile, was lame and included her shouting, "Choo-choo!" (I can't remember why.) I was ready to slaughter. I memorized my speech, added new flourishes— included Grantland Rice's description of the Four Horsemen, memorized the succession of Notre Dame coaches from Rockne to Holtz. My classmates ate it up. As I began the conclusion . . . my voice cracked. Loudly.

The class—which included a couple of kids from Jerez— roared. Even the teacher had to suppress her chuckles. I was furious—at everyone for ridiculing me, but mostly at my vocal cords for not being able to put off puberty at least one more day. I recited the rest of my speech as fast as possible and unfolded the handwritten version from my back pocket. In front of everyone, I crumpled the paper up into a compact ball, tossed it in the air, and punted my speech into the back of the room as I stormed out. My rival won and ended up winning the countywide title as well.

School sucked, but I was having better luck on the home front. After years of fighting, Mami and Papi had calmed down to an uneasy détente brought on by my baby brother, Gabriel, born a couple of months after my Papa Je passed away. Through scrupulous saving, my parents had become financially secure enough to hire a live-in nanny from Jomulquillo—she was probably an illegal immigrant, but who cares? She cooked great enchiladas. My father, after years of neglect save for A.A. meetings and Stetson prodding, tried to take a more active role with me, much to my embarrassment.

I had always wanted to play Little League baseball when I was younger, but he never signed me up. My cousins on both sides of the family tree were preternaturally gifted, earning all-league honors in high school baseball and wrestling. I, on the other hand, was a runt. To compensate for my lack of athletic experience or skill, I walked to the Anaheim Public Library every weekend and read hundreds of sports books—biographies, histories, Wade Boggs's hitting tutorial. In PE, I wowed my classmates with trivia when they weren't pantsing me, stumping even our coaches. I was enjoying sports in my own way. But in seventh grade, my dad suddenly decided I should become Fernando Valenzuela, the Los Angeles Dodgers pitcher whom every Mexican family worshipped during the 1980s and 1990s like the Virgin of Guadalupe.

My baseball career lasted from seventh to ninth grade. Forget the Pittsburgh Pirates: I was the worst manifestation of baseball *ever.* One season, I didn't eke out a single hit in at least fifty at bats; another year, two. I never played anything but right field, safely distanced from the action, but I still made errors that cost my team games. I fell for the hidden-ball trick. Twice. I think I might be the only Little Leaguer ever *paid* to fake an injury— Little League requires that teams play everyone not injured during a game, so a coach offered me five bucks to tell the umpire I was sick when we faced off for the league championship.

Redemption among my fellow players was achieved through my loud mouth and inventive heckles, which mostly involved yelling gibberish in French that I picked up from a dictionary. More helpful was when I was suspended for seven games. During a blowout, I was riding the umpire too much. Coach asked I tone it down. "Fuck you," I snapped back. I was already angry at him for thinking of me as deadweight.

"What did you say?" he replied, furious.

"Fuck you," I reiterated, as the other players laughed.

"You're not playing today," he huffed. "Because you cussed at me, you're automatically suspended two games."

I wasn't going to stick around—I had an El Cargadero dance to prepare for, cousins to chase. I hopped the dugout fence and walked home despite his protestations. Leaving a game without a coach's permission—two-game suspension, on top of the two games for cussing at him. Each suspension automatically earned a one-game suspension, and I received another game for wearing a Mercedes-Benz hood ornament around my neck earlier in the year.

I returned home to find my beaming dad. He had recently undergone his citizenship ceremony: he was now officially an American. He was proud that day in a way I've never seen him since: years of citizenship courses, paperwork, and fees earned him a little American flag Mom placed next to our mailbox. None of us children went to see him take the citizenship oath or even cared. We knew who Papi was: despite his limited English, despite his predilection for dances, despite the gossip of the old country swirling around his *pocho* son, he was the most American man we knew. Mami and Papi celebrated by going off to a dance—a wedding, I think. I stayed home and played Genesis until midnight.

FREEWAYS

Interstate 5 spans the county from Buena Park through San Clemente and is usually crowded only going north toward Los Angeles County. Interstate 405 touches in from Seal Beach up to where it meets the 5 in Irvine at what's called the El Toro Y. Pacific Coast Highway runs from San Clemente to Seal Beach; the 91 cuts through North County from La Palma to Anaheim. Orange County–only freeways include the 22 (Orange to Garden Grove), 55 (Anaheim to Costa Mesa), and the 133, one of the most beautiful freeways on earth as it cuts through canyons and empties just before the Pacific. Toll roads dominate in the eastern and southern sections of Orange County, but only because people who live there are Satan's spawn.

The Beaner-Bashing
Capital of America

The Garden Grove Women's Club in—where else?—Garden Grove is a dilapidated structure, a relic of days when men and women joined civic organizations to spread goodwill. Nowadays, it hosts as close to public Nuremberg rallies as you'll find outside a Tom Tancredo Fan Club meeting. If you're interested, drop in the last Wednesday of every month. In the building's main room, individuals hawk CDs or pamphlets, friends laugh and hug, newcomers grab a pen and sticker to write their name and paste it on their shirts. Lots of Old Glories on clothing. A $5 admission fee for nonmembers. The crowd is mostly middle-aged to elderly, which means anyone under thirty-five gets doted on like a grandkid. Almost everyone is white. Nonwhites can enter, but expect stares, if not confrontations. Say hi to the big, bearded dude carrying a bowie knife!

A couple of minutes after the scheduled 7 p.m. start, people sit in rows that span the room's length. The Pledge of Allegiance is recited. A few in the audience might shout UNDER GOD! in memory of the aborted effort by the Ninth Circuit Court of Appeals a couple of years ago to render that phrase unconstitutional. And then the beaner bashing begins.

This is the monthly meeting of the California Coalition for Immigration Reform (CCIR), a Huntington Beach–based group that's done more to fan the anti-immigrant flames in this country than any crew since the Know-Nothing party. Listed on the Southern Poverty Law Center's list of domestic hate groups, CCIR birthed the Minuteman Project and wrote Proposition 187, the 1994 California ordinance that has inspired dozens, if not hundreds, of similar anti-immigrant resolutions nationwide. But its most important contribution to the country's roiling immigration debate is their monthly meeting, which always advertises a keynote speaker. It's where Minuteman Project's Jim Gilchrist got his start, where border vigilante Chris Simcox and conservative blogger Michelle Malkin found sympathetic ears before exploding onto the national scene. Speakers have claimed that Cuba, China, and Mexico are engaged in a triple axis to rule over the United States à la *Red Dawn;* insisted illegal-immigrant children are vessels for tuberculosis; and pound the drum of Reconquista, the theory that Mexicans are crossing the U.S.-Mexico border to reclaim the southwest United States for their *patria.* A high school senior revealed he wanted to kill Muslims for a living—not terrorists, not Al Qaeda, not even Osama, but Muslims. CCIR members cheered, no doubt unaware that across the street from the Women's Club is a hookah lounge where Muslims peacefully smoke the night away.

In Santa Ana, about fifteen minutes away from the Garden Grove Women's Club, stands another decrepit structure: the Yost Theater. For decades, the Yost was one of Southern California's most prestigious Latino performance venues, an art deco movie palace where megastars from across Latin America staged shows to crowds into the thousands. When musicians weren't performing, the Yost imported films from Mexico or screened first-run American movies with Spanish subtitles. The lines never diminished from the day the Olivos family opened the theater in 1952—*el Yost,* Latinos called it, always pronouncing the *Y* as a *J.* But, city officials shut down the Yost in 1986, looking to redevelop the Mexican business

district around it out of existence. They told the Olivos clan to seis-
mically retrofit the theater or face foreclosure; when the family told
Santa Ana's redevelopment agency they couldn't afford the fixes,
the city bought the building for $650,000 with the promise they'd
pay for the retrofit, then sell the Yost back to the family. Instead,
Santa Ana sold the Yost to a developer for $50,000, breaking the
hearts not just of the Olivos, but Latino OC.

Santa Ana officials promised residents that the Yost would
soon reopen, but the theater sat mostly quiet for more than
twenty years, opened only for Pentecostal churches that didn't
allow nonevangelicals inside unless they pledged fealty to the
Rock of Ages at the door. Only the marquee didn't change during
those years: YOST spelled in a curving, peeling, sans serif font, a
symbol of dashed dreams.

A week after the CCIR held their October 31, 2007, meeting
(insert ghoul joke here), the Yost bustled as it did in its glory days,
if only for a night. Hundreds of people—young, old, white, black,
punks, children, but mostly Mexicans—streamed into the aged
theater. Older people walked around in tears; others swiveled
their heads at the engraved ceiling and bemoaned the whitewashed walls that once featured murals and movie posters. The
fogies told stories of their youth, and the young patrons actually
listened. Everyone bounced on the still-springy seats. At the concession stand, two teens did a brisk business selling pan dulce,
Snickers, soda, and popcorn drizzled with Tabasco. The air filled
with a nervous, awestruck energy.

A young woman dressed in a baptismal white dress climbed up
the stage around 8 p.m. The volunteer from the nonprofit Centro
Cultural de Mexico thanked everyone for spending their Friday
night at the Yost, then launched into an impassioned manifesto in
English and Spanish about "reclaiming the space, the community,
what was once before and will be again." The crowd applauded,
even if her speech left them a bit perplexed.

Sam Romero, on the other hand, smiled while standing in the lobby. He owns a Catholic gift store next door to the Yost. Romero has spent all of his seventy-odd years in Santa Ana, most of them fighting city bureaucrats who want to turn his tiny shop into a hipster boutique and gentrify his Logan Street barrio out of existence.

"We used to come here all the time," Romero told me. "There used to be great movies here, and all types of movie stars from Mexico. But I remember before this became a Mexican theater, when the city was mostly white.

"You know what's my fondest memory of those days? After we'd buy our ticket, the ushers would greet us and say, 'Upstairs, spic.'" Romero repeated the admonition, then cracked up and went to find his seat.

CCIR and the Yost: a microcosm of Orange County, a parable for the United States, the ultimate Orange County epic. More than religion, more than politics, the art of war against immigrants—sometimes Asians and blacks, but always, always Mexicans—has defined the county. We are the Mexican-hating capital of America—not Phoenix, not Oklahoma, not even wherever Lou Dobbs's considerable shadow may swallow the sun with his black heart. It's Orange County where politicians harvest anti-immigrant sentiment into an electoral platform, one so potent that even Vietnamese candidates—many having arrived in this country subsidized by taxpayer dollars—tell appreciative audiences they came to America "the right way" and photograph themselves next to the U.S.-Mexico border fence to plaster the pictures on campaign literature.

Anti-immigrant activists from across America see our county's immigration wars as a how-to manual, a veritable training camp where outlandish ideas and statements get trotted out, accepted, and finally become law. Give cops immigration powers? Our idea. Deny public education to illegal immigrants? That's us. Fight a court order demanding the integration of schools? Yep. All-Latino city councils that try to gentrify Latinos out of barrios? Why not? Our racist sneezes become national hurricanes.

The rhetoric you hear in Washington, the viciousness with which the various amnesty proposals were shot down in 2007, the way talk show hosts blubber about a supposed Mexican takeover of the United States through welfare fraud, pregnancy, and/or spicy salsa—you're listening to Orange County's siren song. You've learned well, America—blaming immigrants (especially Mexicans) for our national ills is again a pastime, and states, cities, and counties are tripping over themselves trying to out-anti-Mexican each other. But beware our tale, because not only did the chickens return to roost, but they're laying eggs without end: Orange County now has more minorities than whites—and Mexicans are the biggest ethnic group. Imagine that: good, white, conservative Orange County now has more coloreds than whiteys. And remember that as Orange goes . . .

Wake up and smell the tacos, *cabrones*.

> **Seal Beach:** Such a nice town—boring, but near the sea; charming, but no Anaheim. There's nothing to say about it except that whoever lives there probably thanks God every day for the blessing of no worries—at least until the Seal Beach Naval Weapons Station gears up for the coming China War. **Best restaurant:** I'll be the first to admit that **A Slice of New York Pizza** isn't going to make a New York wiseguy forsake his mama's cooking, but how can you not patronize a restaurant that has a John Riggins with the New York Jets football card hanging on the wall? *142 Main Street, Ste. B, Seal Beach, (562) 493-4430.*

Orange County didn't wait for the United States to arrive before making xenophobia the county's creed. In the 1820s, a Franciscan friar at Mission San Juan Capistrano named Gerónimo Boscana wrote *Relación histórica de la creencia, usos, costumbres, y extravagancias de los indios de esta Misión de San Juan Capistrano llamada la nación Acagchemem* (A Historical Account of the Origin, Customs, and Traditions of the Indians at the Missionary Establishment of St. Juan Capistrano, Called the Acagchemem Nation). It was the first book devoted to the Juaneños' religious beliefs and customs before the Spaniards forced them into Christianity. As valuable as Boscana's anthropological documentation was to generations of historians, his opinions of the Mission's wards were even more precious:

> *The Indians of California may be compared to a species of monkey; for in naught do they express interest, except in imitating the actions of others, and, particularly in copying the ways of the* razón *[men of reason] or white men, whom they respect as beings much superior to themselves; but in so doing, they are careful to select vice, in preference to virtue. This is the result, undoubtedly, of their corrupt, and natural disposition.*

Another Boscana gem:

> *The Indian, in his grave, humble, and retired manner, conceals a hypocritical and treacherous disposition. He will deceive the most minute observer, as has been the case with many, or with all, who have endeavored to learn his character, until time has revealed to them his true qualities. He never looks at anyone, while in conversation, but has a wandering and malicious gaze. For benefits received, he is never grateful; and instead of looking upon that which is given, he beholds only that which is withheld. His eyes are never uplifted, but like those of the swine, are cast to the earth. Truth is not in him, unless to the injury of another, and he is exceedingly false.*

Boscana's study wasn't made public until after his 1831 death, when the Mission's archivists presented the manuscript to Alfred Robinson. Robinson was one of the first Americans to live in California, having married into a Californio family from Santa Barbara. In 1846, he published *Life in California during a Residence of Several Years in That Territory* (why can't we authors come up with such baroque titles anymore?) and included Boscana's manuscript as an appendix, slapping on the title *Chinigchinich* after the Juaneños' creation god.

In his account, Robinson showed up at Mission San Juan Capistrano long after its glory days had passed. "This establishment was founded in the year 1776, and, though in early years the largest in the country, yet is now in a dilapidated state, and the Indians are much neglected," he wrote in *Life in California*. As he and a friend rode into Capistrano, a curious incident occurred:

> *Several straggling Indian boys were seen about the gates, and two or three approached as we alighted; they said nothing, but stood gazing at the great staring eyes of friend G, which were considerably magnified through the spectacles he wore, till at last a sudden light seemed to break upon their dull comprehensions, and, with a cry of* "Cuatro ojos, cuatro ojos," [*four eyes, four eyes*] *they darted away. This soubriquet* [sic] *we instantly adopted, and G was ever known throughout the whole coast by the nickname of* "cuatro ojos."

Even then, the native brownies were creative with their antiracist comebacks.

Though Robinson's journals were sympathetic to the Indians and Mexicans, most American chroniclers weren't so magnanimous. Richard Henry Dana might've declared Capistrano "the only romantic spot on the coast" in his *Two Years before the Mast*, but he wasn't so kind toward the Mexicans who inhabited the region:

In the hands of an enterprising people, what a country this might be! we are ready to say. Yet how long would a people remain so, in such a country? The Americans (as those from the United States are called) . . . are indeed more industrious and effective than the Mexicans; yet their children are brought up Mexicans in most respects, and if the "California fever" (laziness) spares the first generation, it is likely to attack the second.

The stereotype of Mexicans as lazy and ineffectual—i.e., like the Indian—seeped into the Orange County mind as whites moved in to displace the Californios. It's a part of Anaheim lore that when Juan Pacifico Ontiveros—owner of a rancho that spanned what's now Fullerton, Anaheim, and Placentia—sold the 1,165 acres that became Anaheim for $2,300, he supposedly told buyer George Hansen that the desiccated lot couldn't support a single goat. Hansen and his German investors proved him wrong within a decade, turning the plot into a profitable vineyard. It's mentioned in most Anaheim and Orange County history books, yet there's no primary document or interview tying Ontiveros to those foolish words. And no one bothers to look for it because there's no need—if it deals with Mexicans and underachievement, it's true.

Orange County's acceptance of its Anaheim German colony established an interesting double standard: while European immigrants were welcomed and even prized (Basques settled in northern Orange County and immediately set up sheep farms, while a small Polish colony was established around the home of famed actress Helena Modjeska in the canyon that now bears her name—Susan Sontag retold her story in her 2000 National Book Award–winning novella, *In America*), the native Mexican population was distrusted, maligned—even lynched. "Though Anglos and Mexicans shared the same soil," wrote one historian, "they were separated by language, custom and inherited conflicts, and their two worlds flowed along together like oil and water."

Orange County's first convicted felon was Modesta Avila, a native of San Juan Capistrano born in 1869. She helped her mother maintain a small house, which sat on land that the mighty Southern Pacific Railroad coveted. It laid track just feet away from their home. Avila complained to authorities that the rumbling trains didn't let her chickens sleep or lay eggs. Nothing came of it.

Avila devised a wonderful protest: she strung a laundry line across the railroad tracks. When that didn't get the company's attention, Avila stuck a post in the middle of the tracks. On it was a note to the Southern Pacific: "This land belongs to me. And if the railroad wants to run here, they will have to pay me ten thousand dollars."

Punishment was quick. Prosecutors trotted Avila before the recently opened Orange County Superior Court and charged her with a felony to obstruct a moving train. After her first trial ended in a hung jury, a second trial found the young woman guilty and sentenced her to three years in state prison. Avila served only a year before dying of fever in San Quentin at age twenty-two in 1891.

Avila is a folk heroine to Orange County Latinos, but the official histories haven't treated her kindly. One book described her as a "charming dark-eyed beauty . . . who relied more on her beauty than her intelligence to keep food on the table and a roof over her head." Charles D. Swanner, in his 1965 memoir *50 Years a Barrister in Orange County,* was less forgiving: noting Avila's prison sentence, he commented, "No doubt she found the peace and quiet she desired in her new surroundings!"

The same year after Avila's death came another case that ended badly for local Mexicans. Francisco Torres worked at Helena Modjeska's ranch. He was a native of the state of Colima, twenty-five years old, and quiet. During the summer of 1891, Torres argued with the ranch foreman because $2.50 was withheld from his usual $9 salary. A struggle ensued, and Torres murdered the foreman with a pickax. He fled for San Diego, trying to cross the Mexican border toward freedom.

The murder made headlines across California. Newspapers added crimes to Torres's name with little proof. A posse captured him a week after the murder and returned him to Santa Ana. His captors advised the Orange County Sheriff Department to transport Torres to Los Angeles instead of Orange County because angry Orange Countians were calling for frontier justice. Hundreds awaited Torres at Santa Ana's train depot as he arrived from San Diego. Orange County sheriff Theo Lacy nevertheless placed Torres in the Orange County jail, where he pleaded self-defense.

Not only did the county want Torres dead, it didn't think much of Mexicans at large. The *Los Angeles Times* claimed he was "in no way better than an Indian" and remarked, "There seems no doubt that the accused man has many friends among the Mexicans in this locality, and it is likely that they will assist him in the trial. The main witness for the prosecution is a Mexican woman, and it is probable that every effort will be made to weaken and break her testimony."

Early on the morning of August 13, a mob broke into the Orange County jail, dragged Torres to a telephone pole on the corner of Sycamore and Fourth streets, and hanged the young man. Pinned on Torres's chest was a sign reading CHANGE OF VENUE. No one was ever convicted of Torres's lynching, but years later Lacy's son told a historian that "the most prominent men of the town" perpetrated the crime. A local newspaper, for its part, declared it "the neatest and best executed job of lynching ever performed in California."

Mexicans weren't the only minorities who suffered in Orange County's early days. In 1906, health officials found a Chinese man who they claimed suffered from leprosy and ordered Santa

Ana's Chinatown burned to the ground. "No event in Santa Ana caused more excitement during the period around the turn of the century than the burning of Chinatown," wrote Swanner. A couple of years later, the city council approved the construction of City Hall on the ruins. Twenty years later, the Ku Klux Klan won four of the five city council seats in Anaheim, and nine of the ten members of the police department were in the KKK. No records exist if the Klan ever lynched anyone, although they burned a cross in front of St. Boniface Church and held a rally that attracted twenty thousand people at what's now La Palma Park. The city fathers tired of them and recalled everyone. Nevertheless, rumors exist to this day about the Klan continuing to run Anaheim from the bowels of Disneyland.

That the Ku Klux Klan found such a welcoming environment in Orange County isn't surprising, and not just for the obvious reasons. The man who wrote the first bill proposing to secede Orange County from Los Angeles was Victor Montgomery, a Confederate veteran who served as a scout for General Nathan Bedford Forrest, the Klan's first public leader. Dr. William Henry Head, the Assembly member who took Montgomery's bill to Sacramento, was a proud Klansman who kept his robe and the KKK's founding documents decades after Forrest ordered the Imperial Empire to burn such mementos in the early 1870s. In 1916, Head posed for a picture in his Klan regalia for Annie Cooper Burton's pamphlet *The Ku Klux Klan,* an unabashed celebration that described the group's purpose as "to scare into submission the unruly free negroes and the troublemaking carpetbaggers."

"It was strange how the old feeling came back to him," Burton wrote about photographing Head. "He felt, he said, as if he were breaking his secret oath in thus displaying his uniform. Certainly, he did look guilty and a little self-conscious as he emerged from the funny-looking garment." Will you find this anecdote in respectable Orange County histories? Is the pope Jewish?

Orange County's reputation as Klan heaven scared most African-Americans away, and those who dared move in unsurprisingly faced problems. In 1926, the city of Brea crafted a restrictive covenant that stated, "No part of said premises shall ever be sold, conveyed, transferred, leased or rented to any person of African, Chinese or Japanese descent." That same year, a mysterious fire engulfed the Pacific Beach Club, a resort built exclusively for African-Americans in Huntington Beach. County residents fought hard to ensure that investors couldn't build the club, going as far as lobbying railroad companies not to extend their tracks to the club; city planners refused to provide the club with water or electricity. The county Board of Supervisors even mulled condemning the property. No one was ever arrested for the fire, which occurred three weeks before its grand opening.

Even worse was the treatment that sixteen hundred Jamaican immigrants received in the mid-1940s. Farmers brought them to Fullerton and La Habra to alleviate a labor shortage during the Good War. As long as they quietly picked, residents tolerated the presence of these Caribbeans. But once the *hombres* went out on the town, people became furious. "Their numbers, appearances and [customs] were strange and frightening," wrote Leo Friis in his 1965 book, *Orange County through Four Centuries*. Farmers had to teach them how to use restrooms; after payday, the men swarmed into stores, scaring customers and merchants. Hundreds of county residents protested the Jamaicans' presence, but the growers didn't ship them back home until they went on strike.

Still, no group suffered as much in Orange County as the Mexicans. They occupied a singular place in those days—on the outskirts, acceptable only as cheap labor, relegated to citrus camps or the barrios next to them. Successive waves starting with the Mexican Revolution doubled the county's Mexican population almost every decade. Growers at first accepted the immigrants, paying for their Americanization programs and even spon-soring baseball teams between different citrus workers' camps.

Avila and Torres notwithstanding, brown and white got along in a Jim Crow sort of way until the Great Depression. An anti-immigrant wave spread across the United States, and thousands of Mexicans in Orange County were deported—legalized residents, children born in this country, and illegals alike. This exacerbated the Citrus War of 1936. Two years later came the Great Flood of 1938, the largest natural disaster in Orange County history. The deluge covered approximately a third of the county and left about forty-five people dead, three-quarters of them Latinos, almost all of them children under twelve. Most of those Latinos built makeshift homes near Placentia and Anaheim, near the Santa Ana River, which had flooded with catastrophic regularity since the days of Father Junípero Serra. For years, the Board of Supervisors tried to pass bonds to build a dam northeast of Orange County that would tame the river, but Orange County voters—knowing that a flood would most likely not affect them—consistently rejected the proposals. They finally approved the Prado Dam bond measure a couple of months before the flood. On the day of the flood, the *Anaheim Bulletin* wrote that the Prado Dam "will be a splendid achievement, but it never will bring back one of the lives lost, nor will it restore any of the property destroyed. The realization that it need not have been necessary must increase the feeling of respon-sibility borne by those who [opposed it]. The tragedy of it all is that we know it need not have been."

Shortly after the flood, a group called the United Spanish War Veterans went before the Board of Supervisors to complain that all the aid to "indigent Mexicans" came at the expense of helping "solvent citizens." The board, according to a newspaper account, "expressed sympathy with the viewpoint."

❊   ❊   ❊

> **Santa Ana:** First off, pronounce it like the natives—
> contract and combine the *A*'s so the city sounds like SanTana.
> So significant I devoted a couple hundred words to it—flip to page
> 59. **Best restaurant:** For a city that's proportionately one of the
> most Mexican in the United States, the lack of good Mexican food
> is shocking. Instead, head over to **Bangkok Taste,** which features
> dishes from across Thailand. *2737 N. Grand Avenue, Santa Ana,*
> *(714) 532-2216.*

Thankfully, World War II shook county minorities out of their complacency.

County Japanese tried valiantly to oppose internment but ultimately failed. As a result, Seima Munemitsu arranged for Gonzalo Mendez, a native of Mexico who grew up in OC, to oversee his Westminster farm until the Munemitsus returned. Gonzalo relocated his family to Westminster and enlisted them to tend the farm. In 1944, Mendez's sister Soledad Vidaurri tried to enroll her children and Gonzalo's son and daughter into a nearby school for the city's white schoolchildren. School officials allowed Vidaurri's children because they were light-skinned but barred the darker Mendez children. They suggested Gonzalo's children go to the "Mexican" school about a mile away.

During the 1920s, school districts across Orange County opened Mexican-only schools at the behest of administrators and teachers who insisted Mexican children had no aspiration toward higher education and were better suited to pick crops. These facilities were shoddier than those of their white counterparts, most of the times located far from the students' homes. It was technically illegal to discriminate against Mexicans in California because the government considered them "white." That didn't stop "real" whites, though. When Mexican parents complained about the discrimination, Anglo parents complained louder—in 1918, a Santa

Ana PTA asked district officials to keep Mexican kids away from theirs since segregation was "eminently desirable from a moral, physical and educational standpoint."

Gonzalo talked with other Latino families who also wanted their children to attend better schools. In 1945, the Mendezes and other families sued the Westminster, Santa Ana, Garden Grove, and El Modena school districts to challenge Orange County's segregated education system. Administrators tried to argue before a judge that Mexican children weren't worthy of much scholastic attention since they didn't understand Mother Goose rhymes and argued their policies were constitutional thanks to *Plessy v. Ferguson*. U.S. District Court judge Paul J. McCormick wasn't pleased: he ruled in favor of the Mendez family, writing in his 1946 decision, "We think such practices clearly and unmistakably disregard rights secured by the supreme law of the land." Filing an amicus curiae for the National Association for the Advancement of Colored People was Thurgood Marshall. The governor of California at the time was Earl Warren, who signed a law outlawing segregation in all California schools in 1948. The two played an instrumental role in *Brown v. Board of Education,* the case traditionally cited by historians as desegregating American schools.

Times were changing in Orange County for minorities, slowly, barely, but surely. Olympic gold medal winner Sammy Lee—the first Asian-American to win a gold medal, in the ten-meter platform dive—tried to buy a house in Garden Grove in 1955 but was rejected; a national outcry led by Vice President Richard Nixon and Ed Sullivan allowed Lee to purchase a home. A similar fate awaited Jesse Flores, a former pitcher for the Philadelphia A's who grew up in La Habra's citrus camps. After retiring for good in the early 1950s, Flores tried to buy a house in the nicer part of his hometown. But when he met with the Realtor, Flores discovered the sale was off—no Mexicans allowed outside the barrio in La Habra. After he complained, city leaders offered Flores a deal: deliver us the Latino vote in the upcoming elections, and the house is yours. Flores refused and bought a house in a nicer part of the barrio.

Lincoln and Dorothy Mulkey, a young African-American couple, tried to rent an apartment in Santa Ana in 1965 and were denied on account of their race. Housing discrimination in California was legalized the previous year through Proposition 14, passed by voters to overturn the state's antidiscrimination laws in housing. The Mulkeys sued, but lost their case in Orange County Superior Court and in California's appellate level. They persevered, fighting their case to the Supreme Court. In 1967, the Warren-led Court ruled in favor of the Mulkeys and overturned Proposition 14 in *Reitman v. Mulkey,* ruling it violated the Fourteenth Amendment.

Despite the civil rights advances, the county's population stayed almost exclusively white through the 1970s, with most migrants being Americans from other states. But the demographic deluge was coming—and fast.

Westminster: Only last year did Westminster finally wake up and decide to be a great city by proclaiming it needed to save Little Saigon from extinction. Nevertheless, its place as one of Orange County's most racist cities (and that's saying something) is secure—it says it right there in *Mendez v. Westminster.* Don't be surprised that the South Vietnamese flag flies next to the Stars and Stripes through much of Westminster—and if you don't like it, don't say a word unless you want to invite thousands of elderly Vietnamese to stage weeklong protests outside your home or business. **Best restaurant:** Little Saigon has one of America's great ethnic dining experiences and also hosts the best meal deal in history at **Banh Mi Cho Cu:** a footlong Vietnamese sandwich—pickled carrot, daikon, jalapeño, and your choice of meat inside a soft-yet-crunchy baguette—for about two friggin' bucks. *14520 Magnolia Street, Unit B, Westminster, (714) 891-3718.*

* * *

Barbara Coe is a tiny virago with a butch haircut, shar-pei face, and large glasses—the mean aunt you always ignored. In 1991, her friend died in a nursing home, and Barb blamed his death on the nurses, who supposedly didn't know enough English. Coe was already furious with immigrants—in her role as a data specialist for the Anaheim Police Department, she told her superiors that Latinos were prone to commit crime. "I learned that the majority of these nursing facilities employ illegal aliens and most of the patients are illegal aliens," Coe told a biographer. "I also learned that illegal aliens were receiving Medi-Cal and Social Security benefits by the billions, but my friend was denied benefits. This terrible injustice toward a loyal American citizen, combined with the Anaheim Police Department's refusal to deal with the illegal-alien crime explosion, was my incentive to do something about our immigration problems."

The following year, Coe sent out an invitation to different groups asking them to form a coalition to fight the "immigration invasion." And American history changed.

The demographics of Orange County had dramatically changed in the nearly twenty-five years since *Reitman v. Mulkey*. In the 1970s, hundreds of thousands of Vietnamese refugees landed in Camp Pendleton and the El Toro Marine Air Corps Base, the first stops in America before the government tried to disperse them across the country so they could assimilate more easily. Instead, most drove up the 405 Freeway to Westminster, the same town that had segregated Mexican children thirty years before. The city was mostly farmland and bogs, and its housing prices were among the most affordable in Orange County. Around Westminster were churches and nonprofits that helped the Vietnamese put their new lives in order—St. Barbara's Catholic Church in Santa Ana, Garden Grove's St. Anselm of Canterbury Episcopal Church, among others. Instead of settling across the United States, these refugees stayed close to each other and their patrons. They spread across Westminster and the neighboring cities of Garden Grove, Fountain Valley, and Santa Ana, and thus the hub got a name: Little Saigon, the largest community of Vietnamese outside Vietnam.

Today, conservatives praise the Vietnamese as immigrants who did everything the "right" way—assimilate, succeed—mostly because they consistently vote Republican. In reality, the reception the county gave them was similar to that of Mexicans. Harassment of Vietnamese students in schools was frequent; gangs sprang up in defense, leading to sensationalistic news stories even though membership was just a fraction of Orange County's total gang population. In 1989, vandals tarnished a freeway sign directing commuters on the 22 Freeway to Little Saigon, first by draping an American flag over it, then by chopping it down altogether.

Many Orange Countians applauded the move. "[The vandal is] expressing a lot of our opinions," one lady told an *Orange County Register* reporter at the time. "I'm living among these people who can't drive and can't speak the language and own all the businesses. I don't think we should be advertising it." Others bought bumper stickers that stated "Will the last American to leave Garden Grove bring the Flag?"

The Vietnamese became somewhat accepted by the mid-1990s, although outsiders still view the community with curiosity, especially when refugee politics comes into play. In 1999, a Vietnamese merchant hung a picture of Ho Chi Minh in his video store, incurring the wrath of his fellow refugees, who protested outside Hi-Tek Video in Westminster for weeks; at one point, a rally attracted more than fifteen thousand Vietnamese. In response, police monitoring the protesters described them as "gooks." And when refugees spent more than a year rallying outside the offices of *Viet Weekly*, a Vietnamese-language weekly that dared print viewpoints praising Ho Chi Minh and criticizing the

Vietnam War, surrounding businesses responded by blasting loud American music in an effort to scare them away.

While Little Saigon experienced its growing pains, other immigrants continued to migrate into the county. Significant chunks of Chinese, Persians, Koreans, Middle Easterners, Eastern Europeans, and Filipinos filled the cities of Anaheim, Santa Ana, Westminster, Fountain Valley, Stanton, and Garden Grove, burbs once reserved for lower-class whites but now home mostly to older white homeowners who had a direct connection to the turbulent 1950s and 1960s.

Coe and her cohorts—including Harold Ezell, a former INS official and Newport Beach resident who told the *Los Angeles Times* in 1985 illegal immigrants "should be skinned and fried" and described a Latino opponent as a "fat burrito eater"—tapped into the growing unease of OC's white population. In January 1994, they formed the California Coalition for Immigration Reform and began collecting signatures for what they called the Save Our State Initiative, which became better known as Proposition 187. Their timing was perfect. Orange County was in the midst of a recession, the county had just declared bankruptcy, and many of the factories that had allowed the Greatest Generation to live comfortably were shutting down. Incumbent California governor Pete Wilson used illegal immigration to reinvigorate a floundering campaign, providing a much needed media boost. Proposition 187 passed by a comfortable margin in 1994 but never became law because opponents tied up the resolution in courts for years. Nevertheless, CCIR set an example that has been followed across the country.

Over the years, Coe's group has kept up the fight. She and her members have traveled across the country telling their story, advising and inspiring other activists. In early 2005, after attending CCIR meetings, retired Aliso Viejo CPA Jim Gilchrist started the Minuteman Project, which organizes private-citizen patrols of the U.S.-Mexico border. Later that year, Costa Mesa mayor Allan Mansoor announced he wanted the city's police officers to check anyone's immigration status—the first such program for a police department in the United States. Mansoor even allowed the Minuteman Project to hold a barbecue fund-raiser in a park for him and spoke before the CCIR to an appreciative audience. Shortly after, Mansoor's boss, now indicted Orange County sheriff Mike Carona, proposed doing the same for his department. They were just following in the footsteps of Coe's Anaheim Police Department, which pushed for a similar program in the city's jails after Proposition 187 but instead got an immigration agent to check the background of immigrants—the first instance in the country.

Mansoor (now a Costa Mesa council member) also eradicated Costa Mesa's day-laborer center. In 1989, Costa Mesa officials built the first such city-funded day-laborer center in the country after complaints from residents that Mexicans were loitering in Lions Park. Now, the Mexicans stand on street corners across the city. Other cities in Orange County are following Mansoor's footsteps, passing laws to make it tougher on immigrants—expect your local city council to plagiarize Costa Mesa in the coming years, if they haven't already.

Ultimately, though, these anti-Mexican efforts are for naught. The war is lost—the Mexicans won. Census reports released last year project Latinos will become the majority in Orange County within thirty years. When that day arrives, expect a big party at the Yost. After that November 2007 concert, the building's owner decided to open the theater again after hearing how packed the seats were. The long-shuttered venue is now hosting weekly shows ranging from movies to plays to concert performances in English and Spanish. Coe and Gilchrist, meanwhile, spent 2008 fighting each other in court, accusing each other of graft. The Reconquista is not only happening, it's bilingual. And did we mention Gilchrist owns a Chihuahua?

FAMOUS PEOPLE RAISED IN
ORANGE COUNTY WHO NOWADAYS
WANT LITTLE TO DO WITH US

Steve Martin, Michelle Pfeiffer, Diane Keaton,
Will Ferrell, Gwen Stefani, Jackson Browne

My Mexican Awakening

I trembled before the Anaheim Union High School District's five trustees. Speech time. My striped rayon tie was loosened; long-sleeved blue shirt, itchy. Scuffed Doc Martens. Hair shiny with brilliantine. Shielding me from the AC chill of the meeting room was my mother's cheap windbreaker.

More than a hundred people filled the AUHSD school board chambers that summer night in 1999, and hundreds more protested outside. We wanted the board to know that their planned lawsuit against Mexico seeking $50 million for educating the children of illegal immigrants was insane and *muy* racist.

"My name is Gustavo Arellano, Anaheim High School class of 1997 and son of a former illegal immigrant," I nervously began.

Many of Southern California's prominent Latino activists and organizations were there. Each waited patiently to scream at the AUHSD board. But, by divine providence, I was first.

"We are not Mexican or American, legal or illegal—we are humans first and foremost," I sputtered, clutching a wrinkled white paper upon which I had scribbled out my thoughts an hour earlier. "We should not castigate others simply because of the status of their legality; we should help them and welcome them.

"The problem is not in the influx of illegal immigrants," I continued, getting progressively angrier with each sentence, syllable, thought. "There is no amount of money in the world that can make people care for us. You can give us all the technology you want, but if you don't care about us, you don't give us anything. . . . Who cares if my taxpayer money goes to the education of an illegal immigrant? I am helping a fellow human being."

Having recently reread *The Catcher in the Rye*, I was overusing Holden Caulfield's constant dismissal of people as "phonies" that year. So I decided to emulate the enfant terrible and concluded by complaining to the AUHSD board they were "phonies . . . and if you continue these actions, we will get all of you out of here."

The crowd roared. I walked away from the podium happy and sweaty. At the age of twenty, I had finally become a Mexican.

That's right: until I screamed at the AUHSD board, I never truly considered myself Mexican. It was my culture, sure, in the genes I inherited, the social milieus I was forced to participate in, evident the way I mispronounced English words years after it became my primary language (you should *still* hear me try to pronounce *gamut, persimmon,* and *harpsichord*). But there was never a reason to ponder identity issues when everyone around me was mostly from El Cargadero and Jerez, and the only *gabachos* I thought of were politicians, media stars, and the many spurning my crushes.

If anything, being Mexican bothered me. America had assimilated this humble wab so thoroughly that family, friends, and others constantly ridiculed me as a *pocho*. In addition to the aforementioned bout of Stetson-phobia, my diminishing Spanish skills drew chortles from everyone. Between elementary school and my freshman year of high school, I lost the ability to roll my *R*'s or remember common words. Once, I wanted to tell my mother that Elsa was embarrassed. Grasping for the proper English-to-*español* translation, I mentioned to Mami that her daughter was *embarazada*. Mom was driving me back from school, and she became livid.

"*¿Con quien?*" she demanded.

"What do you mean 'with who'?" I replied, befuddled. "She's *embarazada.*"

"*¿Por cuanto tiempo?*" Mom said, her face reddening.

"I don't know for how long!" I squeaked. I realized we were lost in translation. "Don't you say *embarazada* if someone's 'embarrassed'?"

A look of relief and disgust crossed Mom's face. "No, Gustavo," she sighed. "'She's embarrassed' *es* '*tiene vergüenza.*' '*Emarazada*' *es* 'pregnant.'"

I didn't get why everyone was upset I wasn't Mexican enough. You can only expect so much Mexican fervor from a child of Mexican immigrants who didn't dance, wear a Stetson, or make his pilgrimage to Mexico every spring and Christmas. Besides, I tried to argue with any naysayers, we were in the United States. There was more to living than trying to retain the culture of a country our parents fled when they were young. The *gabachos* didn't care about how Mexican I was—why should anyone else?

A few racists made me reconsider my ethnic apathy. One October afternoon during my sophomore year in the fall of 1994, I was walking home from Anaheim High School when a group of white guys in a truck and wraparound shades pulled up next to me. "187!" they yelled, speeding away while flipping me off. I kept walking, having no clue what excited them so much.

No one was home when I arrived, but the television was tuned to the local news. The newscasters were reporting on the increasing furor surrounding Proposition 187, a ballot measure drafted in Orange County for the fall midterm elections that year seeking to deny illegal immigrants government benefits and force government employees to report anyone they thought didn't possess legal papers to *la migra*. A reporter interviewed a couple of Proposition 187 supporters who promptly began railing about "aliens" invading the United States.

Who could possibly have anything against illegal immigrants?

I thought. My father was once one, as were so many of his friends from Jerez. They were all good people—a bit too wabby for my tastes, but good. I didn't consider them threats, yet those white people were screaming as if illegal immigrants were a tad less savage than Saddam Hussein. As those protesters continued to talk, I remembered what those truck-driving *gabachos* had yelled about an hour earlier. I wasn't an illegal immigrant, yet those white guys who yelled at me didn't care!

Proposition 187 became a bellwether in California, even national, politics—read the previous chapter for more info. But the measure effectively killed the Republican Party in California. Ever since, Latinos in the Golden State have largely registered as Democrats to spite the GOP for the measure.

Politics were the least of my concerns about Proposition 187 back then, though. I worried about friends and family who were illegals—what would happen to them? Many of my peers felt the same way. High school walkouts erupted across California, and rumor had it that Anaheim High was next.

It finally happened during lunch, a week before the elections. Students took to their usual benches. Suddenly, some knocked down a chain-link fence that separated us from the outside world, and hundreds of my fellow Anaheim High Colonists poured out. They ditched school to join a huge march in Fullerton. Not me. I was one of the few students in most of my classrooms that day— not because I didn't support the marchers but because I was afraid. I was still burned by my sexual-harassment suspension; I didn't want to tempt fate.

That afternoon, I went home and turned on the news. Reporters were interviewing a shaken African-American man. He had tried to march alongside the students but they booed him off. His sin: he carried an American flag and asked protesters to put away their Mexican tricolors.

"I wasn't for Proposition 187 at first, but if Mexicans are going to act like this, I'm going to change my vote," the man said bitterly. He was now against Mexicans because they couldn't put away their pride for an afternoon. "Idiots," I muttered, vowing never to show off my *mexicanidad*.

Huntington Beach: In the Orange County imagination, home to two distinct species of white males. Exhibit A is the bro: tattooed, goateed, sunglasses-wearing, pit-bull-owning, big-truck-driving white men who can snap at the sound of a snicker. More sympathetic is the surfer—unless you bogart his waves. Then he gets all bro on your ass. Something's in the city's polluted water, because two of its recent mayors have been convicted of felonies for abuse of power. Its Fourth of July parade is the largest west of the Mississippi—and tried to bar one of the original plaintiffs from *Mendez v. Westminster* from participating in 2007 for not providing enough entertainment value. **Best restaurant: Tacos El Chavito,** where you can feast on two tacos and free, unlimited pineapple juice for a buck. *On Morgan Street between Slater and Speer avenues, Huntington Beach. No phone number.*

The Proposition 187 protests effectively put the kibosh on my interest in high school activities, both extracurricular and academic. Not that there was much to do: Anaheim High, once the crown jewel of the city and Orange County's third-oldest high school, was in free fall. The once overwhelmingly white student body was now mostly immigrant. About 90 percent of the students were of Mexican heritage, with a sizable chunk of the kids from El Cargadero, Jerez, or other Mexican diasporas. Many of the few black, Asian, or white students at Anaheim High were from Africa, Southeast Asia, and the former Soviet Bloc, respectively. Almost all of us spoke English, but the crush of students meant the school lacked resources, and trailer classrooms kept sprouting every fall to accommodate new batches. Students simply didn't go to college—I think the best university anyone from the class of 1997 went to straight out of high school was the University of California, Los Angeles—a fine university, but hardly the Ivy League.

I nearly became a statistic as well, but only because of my nerdiness. Classes were boring, and I didn't bother with much homework. I was placed in many of the honors classes but frequently found myself underwhelmed. Underachiever? That was me. Classmates and teachers usually thought of me as the kid who knew all the answers but didn't bother to come up with them during tests.

My high school years are best defined by how I grew as a Socratic citizen instead of my grades. Living in such a tight-knit Mexican colony meant individual dissension wasn't tolerated. If someone cut their hair differently from the accepted fashion—a DA for men, modest bangs for women—people talked and ragged. Strange hair? Turning into a *gabacho*. Not a Catholic? Going to hell. Alcoholic? Not a word.

But the worst words were reserved for male homosexuals (lesbianism didn't exist in our Mexican sexual universe). One day, Elsa hosted a pool party, and one of the friends invited was gay. When my dad found out, he ordered us not to swim in the pool following the friend.

I learned well, unfortunately.

A couple of boys were on the school's dance team, and I referred to them as faggots. In their face. My friends always winced; I wasn't deterred, citing the Bible, claiming that homosexuality was a sin, and all gays and lesbians deserve a trip to the gas ovens.

The homophobia changed, however, my junior year, when I took biology with Mr. Elder. He was a Kentucky native, a funny guy—and he once danced. His wife was the pretty head dance instructor at Anaheim. In other words, Mr. Elder's manhood was unassailable. He showed us the film *And the Band Played On*, adapted from the book of the same title—which detailed the early years of the AIDS crisis. Seeing the film was a Saul-on-the-way-to-Damascus moment. For all my immature, ignorant ramblings about Auschwitz, I never wanted any homosexuals to actually *die*—and the government was letting many suffer by not dealing with the disease! It angered me so much I stole the book from my friend, read it, and was angered even more. Within a week from seeing the film and finishing the book, my feelings for gays and lesbians changed for the better. I apologized to the teens I had called fags for years and asked God for forgiveness during confession. Hey, homophobes: learn from me.

Villa Park: Another Spanglish joke: should be pronounced like the Mexican revolutionary, but instead is pronounced like a villa. Gotta be wealthy to live here, as city law mandates that all houses must be on at least one acre. The county's smallest city, so tiny there is only one shopping plaza and two streets that provide access to the rest of the county. **Best restaurant:** Only by default does **Rockwell's Café** win—unless you like chain Chinese food. *17853 Santiago Boulevard, Villa Park, (714) 921-0622; www.rockwellsbakery.com.*

Halfway through my junior year, I decided not to try in trigonometry anymore. The reason: invisible numbers. As long as I could remember, math teachers taught us that the square root of a number never produced a negative, yet my trigonometry teacher now said it was possible. My trust in institutions was shaken forever, so I decided to read the *Los Angeles Times* sports section during class the rest of the year.

Some might try to attribute my disinterest in high school to my parents, to Mexican society's disinterest in education, to institutional racism, but none of them were the culprit. It's all the fault of invisible numbers, and *nada* else. I had a good philosophical point: Why had teachers lied to students all these years? If they lied to us about math, what kept them from lying to us about everything? My catechism teacher had taught us that lying is a sin—but if teachers lied and didn't suffer, what did that mean? And why bother anymore? Told you I was a nerd.

I received an F in trig at the end of my junior year, earning just 25 percent of all possible points. I expected that. I'd have to repeat the class. Fine. I was now in danger of failing high school. Okay. The report card also revealed an unsatisfactory in effort. Accurate. But an unsatisfactory in citizenship? *That* went too far.

The first day of class my senior year, I approached my trigonometry teacher, Mrs. Spykerman, a tiny woman. Skinny like plywood, with big grandma glasses and a haircut out of a Betty Crocker cookbook, she ran her classroom with a general's attention to discipline. I asked her to justify my U in citizenship. I never disrupted her class, I argued. I stayed quiet during lectures. All I did was read newspapers.

She didn't care—or rather, she cared too much: "I gave you the U because you didn't set a good example for your classmates."

A tired look came across her face. "Look, Gustavo, I know you think high school is dumb and boring. But you *need* to get good grades. Otherwise you won't get into college. And trust me— you'll *love* college. You'll be able to study whatever you want. I promise."

Until then, my only thoughts about college involved bowl games. My father had prepared me for the labor force as early as sixth grade, when I'd spend summer vacations rising with him at three in the morning, fastening ropes around the cargo of flatbed trucks. He secured me apprenticeships with other truck drivers and mechanics during the summers through junior high and high school, hoping I might do more than read books. And I was required to work during the school year starting my sophomore year, bouncing around telemarketer gigs until securing a spot as a ride attendant at an Anaheim amusement park.

I didn't want a working-class life. Early in my freshman year, I asked a counselor about scholarship opportunities. She extolled the virtues of vocational training—did studying carpentry excite me? Not particularly. The counselor sent me away.

But Mrs. Spykerman's advice was intriguing. Study what I wanted to study. A couple of days later, I mentioned college to my dad.

He laughed. "Why do you want to go to school for four more years?" He talked about us running a trucking operation together. "You're already working. You should be a truck driver like me—don't waste your time with school."

His ignorant advice didn't hurt. Dad had accomplished a lot in this country without an education—him and my mom—just by their indefatigable work ethic. And I might've followed his advice if not for NAFTA.

Just before I spoke with Mrs. Spykerman, my mother told us that Hunt's was laying off almost everyone. After years of seasonal employment, my mom became a full-time canner at Hunt's shortly after Gabriel's birth. It was tough but worth it for my mom—the Teamsters provided us with health insurance, and her bosses occasionally gave Mami surplus boxes of the tomatoes and vanilla pudding she canned and sorted to bring home.

But Hunt's had decided to cut costs and move their tomato-canning operations north, to California's Central Valley and its acres of tomato fields. For decades, Hunt's stood around acres of farmland, but years of suburban growth and cheap imports meant they had to ship in crops to can. My mom and her friends, many of them women from El Cargadero, were just making too much money to justify the operations.

Mami's last day was in the spring of 1997, her token severance package a cheap blue windbreaker screen-printed with a laurel, the year she started working at Hunt's, and 1997. When she came home that afternoon, I asked Mami if she cried. "A little bit," she said, her voice trailing off, her face begging me never to speak about the subject again. She was now unemployed, with no job prospects, a forty-five-year-old Mexican woman with limited English skills and an eighth-grade education.

"I don't want to be like you and my mom, Papi," I replied to my dad in Spanish. "I see *ustedes* work so hard and get so tired. I think college can help me get a better-paying and easier job."

"You won't find anything good in college," Dad growled. "Just watch."

Screw invisible numbers—I had catching up to do. My GPA was abysmal, and I didn't belong to any student clubs. My only extracurricular was the Kiwanis Bowl, a sort of high school *Jeopardy!* where my nerdiness proved so dominant that my team—me and a couple of warm bodies—won two years straight (my senior year, all of Anaheim's nerds united to try to dethrone me; I nuked them). I joined the newspaper and yearbook staffs; we published just two editions of the former because the school administration wouldn't allow us to print anything bad about school, and we antagonized our adviser so much with the latter that he went on medical leave. I graduated with a 2.89 GPA—hardly scholarly, but enough to get me through.

To my shock, Anaheim High's class of 1997 elected me Most Likely to Succeed. They saw potential that I didn't. And I was picked to give the commencement speech even though I wasn't the valedictorian. I have a copy of it underneath a box of books, but it was basically a jeremiad against the administration for not improving Anaheim High during my four years. Anaheim High's administration sat stone-faced; the students and their parents laughed and cheered. High school was over—onward to college.

Oh, did I mention that my date to senior prom was Thoreau's

Walden? Read it at a Borders Books in Brea. Don't laugh—that book put out more than any girl I could've possibly invited.

Brea: Keeper of North County's last open spaces—for at least one more year, as bulldozers are already grading its pristine hills. Better known during the 1990s for record-setting girls' basketball teams of Brea Olinda High School. Was once an oil town, and derricks still stand in the city, but that's an industry as dead as the orange groves. **Best restaurant:** Yes, you can eat hamburgers anywhere in North America, but when you're in a city as mundane as Brea, **Brea's Best Burgers** is quite the blessing. *707 S. Brea Boulevard, Brea, (714) 990-2615.*

Orange: Its historic downtown has been seen by anyone who has rented *That Thing You Do!, The Man Who Wasn't There,* and the final shot from *Crimson Tide* after Denzel Washington faces a court-martial. City officials passed a resolution trying to drive day laborers out of town; it's not working. **Best restaurant:** Included more for its locale than grub, **Felix's Continental Cafe** serves good Cuban and Spanish food on the city's historic Old Towne Plaza, one of the county's few roundabouts. *36 Plaza Square, Orange, (714) 633-5842; www.felixcontinentalcafe.com.*

Bad grades exiled me to Orange Coast College, a community college in Costa Mesa carved out of the former Santa Ana Army Air Base, where so many Americans initially experienced Orange County. Campus was a twenty-minute drive from my house, far enough that it wouldn't feel like high school, close enough that I didn't have to move out of my parents' house. I snookered my best friend, Art—another smart-but-underachieving Mexican—to join me.

We'd become fascinated by film our senior year at Anaheim High, after stealing a bootleg copy of *Pulp Fiction*. Orange Coast has one of the country's premier juco film programs, and our goal was to become the next Tarantinos, the brown Scorseses. We created films—terrible but amusing shorts involving water hoses, roses, and slam dunks. I prospered in other classes, earning a 3.91 GPA. Mrs. Spykerman was right—college was exhilarating. And OCC also has the hottest coeds on the planet according to *Playboy*—or so says a school urban legend.

I didn't give a thought to my ethnicity during the two years I was at OCC except for one cruel moment. Shortly after graduating Anaheim High, I began dating an Irish girl. My parents liked her, but both hinted that a Mexican girl was more desirable—as long as she wasn't a cousin, of course.

"I don't want to marry a Mexican woman," I proclaimed to my mother one day. "I don't want to marry a woman like you." I complained that I couldn't stand her submission to my father, how she blithely weathered his screams and shouts while my siblings and I retreated to our rooms.

At the time, I hurt her deeply. But my mom loves this story because that Irish girl dumped me for being *too* Mexican.

My cousin Marcelo—the same cousin who taught me how to wipe my *tochis* with a rock when I visited El Cargadero as a young boy—married at a ritzy chapel. He was the last of my cousins to migrate from Mexico, coming to the United States when he was about fourteen. Despite not speaking a lick of English at first, Marcelo not only graduated from high school but ended up earning a bachelor's degree. *And* he married a white girl. All of us Miranda cousins were impressed—this was the most complete assimilation we'd seen.

I told this story to my Irish lass—about how El Cargadero parties were slowly but surely changing from thousand-person soirees in labor halls to genteel affairs. Gone were the live *bandas*—in their place were able DJs and emcees who crafted nights to remember. It was nice, I remarked, but part of me also missed the mega-*bailes* of my youth.

"Well, if we ever get married," she responded, "I don't want any of that Mexican stuff."

"What's so wrong with it?" I replied.

"Too loud! Too many people. Besides, this is America, not Mexico."

I agreed with everything she said, but her tone was mocking, vicious. I told her that.

"Why do you care?" she shot back. "You're American, not Mexican."

She was right. But I didn't find anything wrong with my peers who identified more with Mexican culture, I told her. We fought for a good ten minutes before hanging up. With the exception of two or three e-mails over the years, I've never heard from her since. Hey, Annie, if you're reading this, can I have my CDs back?

COLLEGES

Orange County has no real major university. The University of California, Irvine, has top-notch science and humanities departments, but its only good sports team is its baseball squad. California State University, Fullerton, consistently fields Division I baseball contenders, but the school has little else to offer—even the girls are just so-so, lookswise. Chapman University has one of the largest endowments, but that's only because the school sold its soul to the local Republican Party, many of whose top donors sit on the school's Board of Directors. Vanguard University and Concordia are the local Christian colleges; Soka University in Aliso Viejo is a private university run by a secretive Buddhist sect. But the best education for your pesos can be found at our many community colleges—Orange Coast, Fullerton, Saddleback, Irvine Valley, Cypress, Santiago Canyon, Coastline, and Santa Ana.

LOCAL MEDIA

Despite having more than 3 million residents, Orange County is a bush league for local media. Almost all of its radio and television needs are supplied by Los Angeles, and the only two non-TBN home-based stations—KDOC-TV Channel 56 and KOCE-TV Channel 50—mostly broadcast *Baretta* and PBS reruns, respectively. The news culture, then, is dominated by the *Orange County Register*, which no one respects since it's a major metropolitan daily that still thinks covering the birth of puppies is headline news. The *Los Angeles Times* also gets distributed, but stopped devoting many resources to Orange County about a decade ago—its massive Orange County offices in Costa Mesa are about 80 percent empty. Niche publications geared toward the wealthy (*Orange Coast*), superwealthy (*Coast*), and shit-gold-they're-so-wealthy (*Riviera*) are popular but barely readable. The weekly *Orange County Business Journal* occasionally breaks stories but is a trade magazine people read only to find investment opportunities. Of course, all pale next to the *OC Weekly*. As for blogs, only three must-reads: the conservative OC Blog (redcounty.com), liberal Liberal OC (theliberaloc.com), and schizophrenic, libelous Orange Juice! (theorangejuice.com).

❖   ❖   ❖

After completing two years at OCC, I transferred to Chapman University, a private university in the city of Orange with an annual tuition of about $25,000. My grades earned me grants and scholarships that paid almost all the hefty price. To help out my family with the bills, I worked for a collections agency, checking the credit scores of people who missed their payments to Toyota. This was a good but boring job—about the most I learned from it was that a lot of Armenians live in Glendale, California, and in the suburbs of Boston. My kind bosses allowed me to do whatever I wanted during downtime, though. To waste time, I began to read newspapers for more than just their sports sections.

That's when I discovered Harald Martin. Martin was an Anaheim police officer who doubled as the president of the Anaheim Union High School District and was climbing the city's political ladder. My boss told me about Martin's plan to sue Mexico for $50 million for the cost of educating the children of illegal immigrants. The cop claimed it was for the good of the students in Anaheim junior high and high schools, but his actions spoke louder than words. Martin dismissed opponents as communist, and compared Mexican kids to Tribbles, those legendary furry pests from *Star Trek*, on National Public Radio.

"They came on the ship and everyone loved them," Martin told an NPR reporter in 1999. "They were so cute and fluffy, nice little things when there were four or five of them. Then it got to the point down the road when it wasn't so nice. They were getting in the way because there now were thousands of them on the ship."

I didn't come across this interview until last year—the only radio stations I knew about at the time were Spanish-speaking, or Howard Stern (Baba Booey!). But Martin's proposal—*Star Trek* similes aside—infuriated me in a way Proposition 187 only barely had five years earlier. Proposition 187, while potentially devastating to friends and family, wasn't as immediate. I almost even accepted the case for it. Martin, on the other hand, was directly targeting *me*.

I was one of those students he claimed were destroying Anaheim schools. So many of my peers at Anaheim were the children of illegal immigrants, kids who filled the hallowed positions of an American high school. Our star wide receiver—parents from Jomulquillo. Homecoming queen—parents from El Cargadero. Student body president. Band geeks. Stoners. Geeks—all the progeny of illegals. All good Americans, yet our trustees and administrators treated us the way students treated my mom and her siblings during the 1960s. My freshman year, the lockers for gym were in trailers; by the end of year, the stench of pubescent wafted as far as the parking lot. My chemistry class was also in a trailer. Our principals were uncaring outsiders who cracked down on cherished school traditions such as the Orange Fight (where the football players would gather a bunch of oranges and harmlessly throw them at each other) and painting our school year on the benches of the track stadium, claiming it inspired gang violence.

Anaheim High School definitely had problems, but it wasn't the illegal immigrants or their children who caused them. We all tried our damnedest in spite of a crumbling school—and now a fellow Colonist was going to tell us that we were the cause of our alma mater's ruin?

The *Los Angeles Times* announced that the AUHSD trustees planned a vote on the matter during a board meeting. I wanted to go—I didn't know what to do, but I wanted to be there, as if my presence might trigger a change. I tried to convince my parents and friends to go voice their complaints, but no one cared. I didn't mind. When I arrived, I was amazed by how many people showed up. Old. Young. Latino. White. Black. Martin had his supporters, but most attendees were there to protest him.

I ran into a young reporter. Nowadays, Yvette Cabrera is one of the nation's top Latino columnists, but back then she had just started at the *Orange County Register.* Yvette asked why was I there. I told her my story. She wondered if I was going to address the board. I didn't even know that was possible, I responded. She passed along a green comment slip to me, which I promptly filled in and returned to the clerk.

The rest, as they say, is *historia.*

The presence of hundreds of activists opposed to Martin's resolution didn't dissuade the board from passing it that night, so organizations huddled and decided what to do next. I volunteered my services in whatever way I could help, but quickly became disillusioned because these adult activists started fighting each other. It was dispiriting as a young person to see group meetings devolve into shouting matches. I remember one in particular: a strategy session that dissolved into finger-pointing and screams because they couldn't agree on whose name should go first on a press release. The group vowed to recall Martin, but nothing ever came of it. (Just last year, though, Martin was reappointed to office, and a new generation of activists united to pressure the asshole into resigning.)

I started at Chapman University shortly after my AUHSD howl. Before Harald Martin, I had told myself I wanted no dealings with student organizations—get my grades, make money on the side, and prepare for a doctorate, that was the plan. But Martin unleashed an activist streak in me I never knew existed. During a student organization fair, I searched for MEChA—Movimiento Estudiantil Chicano de Aztlán (Chicano Student Movement of Aztlán). This high school and college group ostensibly taught members about Mexican-American history, but was in reality an outlet to protest discrimination against Mexicans, real and perceived. Many MEChA chapters made their name during the 1994 Proposition 187 protests, mostly by acting like *pendejos*. Anaheim High had a MEChA chapter, but I didn't join—they always used yelling in place of conversation and called themselves Chicano, a term my parents told me long ago was shorthand for "gang member."

Now was not the time to second-guess. I approached the Chapman MEChA booth and talked to two women about what was happening with Martin. Would they care to help us? The two invited me to a MEChA meeting—and that's how I joined the Reconquista.

If you listen to conservatives, MEChA is the Mexican-American equivalent of Hitler Youth, soul brothers to Hamas. It's easy to understand why: the organization's founding documents, the Plan de Santa Barbara and the Plan Espiritual de Aztlán, call for a Chicano homeland called Aztlán and rail about the "brutal gringo" invasion of the American Southwest. I had heard whispers about

MEChA's fixation on protests, the vitriolic speeches bashing everyone who wasn't brown, the inflammatory MEChA clap, where a
student claps and others join rhythmically, louder, faster, until a
Mechista shrieks *"¡Qué viva la raza!"* (Long live the Mexican race!),
and everyone responds *"¡Qué viva!"* (May it live!).

I encountered some extremist rhetoric at my first MEChA
meeting at Chapman—wild ideas such as increasing Latino enroll-
ment on our minority-deficient campus and mentoring at-risk high
school students. All the hype about MEChA as the storm troop-
ers for the coming Reconquista was gibberish. There were other
MEChA chapters that engaged in the idiotic "The Southwest
United States was our land," but Chapman *Mechistas* dismissed it
as the type of rhetoric common among undergrads, from the same
philosophical vein that makes a young adult think that socialism is
ideal, Western civilization is evil, and Dane Cook is hilarious. And
it wasn't just Latinos involved in our radical clique. Members
included African-Americans, Asians, *gabachos* . . . even a Kazakh
student named Amir who proudly wore his MEChA shirt complete with the organizational logo: an eagle gripping a stick of
dynamite and looming over a banner that reads LA UNIÓN HACE
LA FUERZA (Strength through Unity). We were young and idealis-
tic. We wanted to change the world for the better, and MEChA
allowed us to do it.

We protested Supreme Court justice Clarence Thomas when
he christened Chapman's new law school; we supported striking
janitors and held events for all the major Mexican holidays. But
mostly we spent our free time recruiting high school students to
Chapman and holding educational carnivals for elementary
school *niños y niñas*.

Chapman administrators loved our dedication, holding us up
as models of what other students could aspire to. My fellow
Mechistas went on to join nonprofit organizations, to intern at the
libertarian Cato Institute, to consult for the Democratic Party, to

become bankers and psychologists, to make it in Hollywood. Not a single *Mechista* in our group dropped out of college. Revolutionaries in every way.

Outside of MEChA, I didn't involve myself much at Chapman. I switched my major to film studies, deciding not to pursue filmmaking as a career since it cost too much money. (This was just before the advent of digital cameras, pre-millennials, and a full five years before YouTube.) Art dropped out, content to spend his life in front of a Nintendo. Dates dwindled after the Irish Mexican-hater, partially because my social skills were inept, and partially because I still shared a bunk bed with my brother and any attempts at *amor* had to happen in the backseat of my brand-new 1999 Toyota Camry. Still, Mrs. Spykerman was right about college. Chapman forced me to interact with people of all races, no longer solely Mexicans from one particular region. I graduated in 2001 with a 3.89 GPA—a full point higher than what I had underachieved at Anaheim High.

Despite my healthy ego, I've never been one to celebrate myself. But my parents were so proud that I was one of the first cousins in either the Arellanos or Mirandas to graduate from college, they insisted on holding a party in a small labor hall. It was fun—a *conjunto norteño*, tons of *bolillos*, and I dressed in a three-piece pin-striped suit with fedora, which made me look like a G-man, but was done as an homage to my Papa Je—but I didn't enjoy the party as much as I should have. I was already thinking ahead to the fall, when I'd begin my master's program in UCLA's Latin American Studies department. For my thesis, I wanted to make a documentary about El Cargadero.

I wasn't the only person from El Cargadero who was graduating from college, or on the way—there were dozens of others, all with similar backgrounds. We were proof that Mexicans could and would succeed in this country. Our parents, meanwhile, sent billions of dollars back to Mexico each year—why? Why was there such a strong connection between Anaheim and El Cargadero? How did such a small town create such a great batch of folks? The day after my Chapman graduation party, I hopped on a plane with my father to El Cargadero to find out.

Tustin: Sometimes lumped in with South County, other times not, and the city readily shows its dual nature, with run-down barrios and stately Victorian houses within walking distance of each other. Tustin was banking on placing hundreds of homes on an old marine base to bolster its image, but the comatose housing market has left many of the properties vacant, and all others on hold. **Best restaurant:** Tustin is surprisingly one of the best dining towns in Orange County, with many ethnic options, the best being **Dosa Place,** specializing in Indian crepes the size of baseball bats. *13812 Red Hill Avenue, Tustin, (714) 505-7777; www.dosaplace.com.*

It had been fourteen years since my last trip to Zacatecas. Dad warned me that nothing was like it was: "Things have changed a lot. Everyone left—only the old and very young remain."

We landed in Zacatecas's namesake colonial capital, where my father's cousin—a teacher in Jerez, one of the few men from my father's generation in Jomulquillo who didn't go north—picked us up. For two hours, we drove through the Zacatecan countryside until reaching Jomulquillo in the evening. I was dumbfounded. When I was a kid, the same drive had snaked its way through tiny ranchos and dirt paths. Today, a brand-new highway gave us a smooth ride. Jomulquillo was little more than dirt, mud, and empty lots the last time I visited. But thanks to the remittances and fund-raising dances by the *clubes sociales* over the years, Jomulquillo was downright respectable. The streets were paved, although cattle still trotted across town in the mornings and evenings. Potable water was finally available, only during certain hours; natural gas for heating now came from refillable tanks. A bridge now connected the two barrios of the rancho that the rainy season divided every year. Most of the houses were now two stories or featured beautiful wrought-iron fences—but they were all empty. "Everyone's up in the United States," my dad explained. "But you should come during the winter, when all the houses are full and everyone shows off their new trucks!"

A couple of days later, we drove to El Cargadero, and the progress was similar. The houses there were nicer—one even featured a lawn—and an electrician was wiring each residence for phone service. Everything was tranquil, picturesque. The land of my parents was improved, but now dead. I walked the streets— only old men and teenage girls. One of the most depressing times I've yet to suffer.

While in El Cargadero, I befriended a guy who was roughly my age. Amazingly, we weren't related. I asked him if he ever thought of moving to Anaheim.

"I have cousins there, but I want to live here," he replied. "I want to work in a factory. I don't want to go to the United States. I don't want to be an illegal immigrant."

"But doesn't the money that we send back to *ustedes* help the townspeople?" I asked.

"Help?" he snorted. "What help? All that money goes to help yourself—the people who left. If you cared about El Cargadero, you'd use all the money to build factories in the village so that young people like me wouldn't have to leave.

"Look around you! All this richness, so much beauty—and there's no one here to enjoy it! Is money that people send to us helping? No! There's nothing here—El Cargadero is all gone!"

I became good friends with the guy during my visit. He's now in the United States, building houses as an illegal immigrant.

BEACHES

All have their charms. Surfers head to San Clemente State Beach and Huntington Beach. Dana Point was once known as Killer Dana for its great waves, but the city built a harbor in the 1960s that destroyed the surf forever. Our surfing subculture has spawned and housed surfing's vital organs—magazines such as *Surfing*, the Quiksilver and Roxy clothing brands, and the Surfrider Foundation. But those guys and gals are assholes if you try to move in on their waves—don't bogart them, dude! Surfing culture is no longer the domain of working joes, though—hyperdevelopment along the coast has priced the beach bum out of existence. And the prettiest beaches, those on the cliffs from Newport Coast through Laguna Beach? Most of them are in private residences, but California state law prohibits owners from denying access to the coast. If homeowners threaten to call the cops on you while you sneak into their homes on the way to the beach, remind them of the Coastal Act—and then run!

The "Real" Real Orange County Reel, or: About Those Stupid Television Shows, Why Orange County Is "Hip," and What's Really Real and What's Somewhat Real—for Real!

They're trying to kill John Wayne again.

By the time you read this book, the world will already have suffered a multimillion-dollar branding campaign praising Orange County as America's barometer for It, created and waged by our civic fathers, who continue to propagate the fantasy first envisioned by Serra. Did you enjoy the slogan, undoubtedly cute and probably referring to Orange County as "the OC" (don't call it that)? What did you think of the logo, which I'm sure included a motif of waves, palm trees, and definitely, most definitely oranges? Were you motivated to book a flight? Spend money on us? Want to discover the bounty not addressed so far in this book, those mother lodes of pleasure that need no publicizing from me because the capital behind them can fund sub-Saharan economies?

Before I trash this PR spin, let me defend the Duke, 'cause his legacy needs a cavalry. When planners announced their scheme to market Orange County to *ustedes* in late 2007, one of the ideas bandied about was to add "Orange County" in the name of John Wayne Airport. It was a compromise of sorts—in 2004, after the success of the Fox television teen soap *The O.C.*, a supervisor proposed renaming the county's sole airport "The O.C. Airport."

"I think we need to capitalize on the newfound fame," Supervisor Chris Norby told the *Orange County Register* at the time. "O.C. is hot throughout the country. It's something they borrowed from us to make it popular."

Norby received a slew of e-mails, phone calls, and letters demanding the county keep John Wayne. He dropped the issue. Flash forward four years, and the only people left who want to keep calling it John Wayne Airport are his family and this whippersnapper scribe.

Silly Orange County! The damn-tiny airport just off the 405 Freeway in Irvine was already called Orange County Airport . . . until the death of the Duke in 1979. The country laughed—still does—when we renamed it after an actor who wasn't a native but passed his last, booze-soaked years here, never did much to promote his digs, and who best represented a myth. In other words, Wayne's name was perfect for us. In 1979, when the Associated Press asked county supervisor Thomas Riley, now dead, why he pushed for renaming the county airport after Wayne, Riley didn't cite his friend's charitable efforts, a love for Orange County, or even any of the films in which Wayne played a flyboy, such as *The Wings of Eagles* and *Central Airport*. Instead, Riley claimed that Wayne deserved recognition because he "exemplified in his character the qualities of the West—a love of freedom, fundamental optimism, a search for new frontiers, and superstrong patriotism." And when a campaign to remove Wayne's name arose in the late 1980s, Riley reiterated, "In the minds of young Americans, John

Wayne is one of the greatest American patriots in the West." Riley was in his sixties then, so maybe "young Americans" referred to people in their forties.

Sanity on the Left Coast. Crazy California's last bastion of liberty. Orange County has always wished you associate those ideals with us—but now we want more. We want you to envy us. Drive around Orange County for five minutes, and if you don't see a six-figure car, fake tan, or a garish townhome, you're in Santa Ana. This new Orange County perverted Robert Schuller's assurance to congregants that they had "a God-ordained right to be wealthy." Forget the "right"; it's now every Orange Countian's *duty* to mimic Mammon—and yours to desire. Just across the 405 Freeway from the Trinity Broadcasting Network stands South Coast Plaza, the highest-grossing "planned retail center" (read *mall*) in the United States, where Japanese tourists visit to spend tens of thousands of dollars within hours and promptly return to the Land of the Rising Sun. Minutes away from the mall, within eyesight of Newport Beach's gorgeous Back Bay estuaries, stands Fletcher Jones Motorcars, headquarters of the world's largest Mercedes-Benz dealer. Just half a mile away is Newport Lexus, the most expensive auto dealership ever built when it opened in 2006, with a cost of $70 million. America's second-largest BMW dealer is Crevier BMW, which got sweetheart deals from Santa Ana officials to expand and erect a giant marquee that blinds commuters on the 55 Freeway. Dealers sell more Lamborghinis in Orange County than anywhere else in the United States; Aston Martin finds its second-best market here. In 2006, luxury brands accounted for about a quarter of all cars sold in Orange County; the total represented 10 percent of all sales in the United States. My friends swear Orange County is the breast implant capital of America, but I haven't felt enough to make sure. Mega-developer Hadi Makarechian boasts on his Web site that his creation of garish palaces on the Pacific Coast inspired the term *McMansion*. To quote Alfred E. Neuman: *Blecch*.

Why shouldn't we continually burnish our image? We're the place *USA Today* called America's "capital of cool" in 2002, that stodgy *U.S. News & World Report* deemed "Hip's New Headquarters" the same year VH1 gushed "The American Hip Factory." The surf-industry giants—Quiksilver, Billabong, all those clothing manufacturers that turn middle-aged men back into teens—operate from our coastal towns. The makers of Botox, the saviors of so many middle-aged women, concoct their Injections of Youth in Allergan's Irvine headquarters. And, of course, the television shows! *The O.C.*! *Laguna Beach: The Real Orange County*! *The Real Housewives of Orange County*! *Newport Harbor*! Probably another show has been green-lighted since I finished writing this book! Great bands! Disneyland! Aren't you glad I haven't examined that blight yet and only will in a Mickey Mouse way?

Laguna Beach: As famous former resident Louie Pérez of the group Los Lobos once told me, where the billionaires are crowding out the millionaires. That this city is quickly becoming part of Orange County's Money Belt is surprising, since rents and housing were affordable just a decade ago, when Laguna Beach was one of the most gay-friendly cities in the United States and hippies still populated Main Street. Nowadays, a nicer Newport Beach. **Best restaurant:** A lot of high-end eateries here, but all pale to the essential joy of eating a hamburger topped with pastrami from **Husky Boy Burger** while you watch the sun set on the Pacific Ocean. *802 N. Coast Highway, Laguna Beach, (949) 497-9605.*

The Orange County I've written about isn't the Orange County of renown but it's the background to understand the modern region that garnered so much attention this decade. *That* Orange County is the star of about a half dozen television shows and numerous specials, magazine spreads, or news profiles in the past five years. You know these shows or have at least seen their commercials. They depict a region of wealth, of malls that don't measure themselves by size but by the number of obscure Italian designers they can attract, of multiple homes and never-ending plastic surgery, day spas, and housemaids. A yearlong Hamptons, the new Beverly Hills, Park Slope with tract housing.

Many county residents criticize these shows for highlighting just a fraction of the county—mostly the reptilian Rockefellers between Huntington Beach and Laguna Beach—while excluding everything else—the minorities, the diversity, the history. All valid points. But these whiners—myself included—sell the shows short. Like those beautifully fraudulent orange-crate labels whose perfection masked the county's reality, but also revealed our projected self-image, during the first half of the twentieth century, the Orange County–based boob-tube programs of this millennium serve as an advertisement for an ideal but also—often unwittingly— as biting commentary on the county.

Before these shows, Orange County's Neanderthal reputation prohibited it from achieving much pop-culture fame. The success of Disneyland in Anaheim, while phenomenal, seemed an apt fit for Orange County—manufactured to perfection, with no tolerance for dissension. The first real rumbles of Orange County coolness came via its beach bums. In 1966, Huntington Beach native Robert August grabbed his surfboard and, along with fellow surfer Mike Hynson, surfed around the world, an adventure immortalized in the documentary *The Endless Summer.* August gave many Americans their first surfing visuals; the sound of surfing had already been pushed by homegrown artists such as Dick Dale and the Chantays, while the Beach Boys and their rivals sang the praises of the county's treasured surfing spots: Laguna Beach, Huntington Beach, Trestles, Dana Point. But the song that best celebrates this easygoing ethos is the A-side for the maniacal "Wipe Out" (you heard right: "Wipe Out" was a B-side) by the Surfaris: "Surfer Joe."

"Down in Doheny where the surfers all go / There's a big bleached blondie named Surfer Joe," the track starts, as the Surfaris sketch out the pristine beauty that was the early 1960s Orange County coast. Joe, the Surfaris lead singer warbles, haunts "the playground of the surfers, Doheny Beach," and sweeps contests up and down Pacific Coast Highway. Until Uncle Sam ruins his idyll: the marines draft Joe, who goes AWOL and flees to the sanctuary of Trestles, then gets captured and relegated to kitchen duty. The message of "Surfer Joe" was poignant: Orange County was beautiful, but disappearing—and if you tried to counter the civic fathers, watch out. By the way, one of the Surfaris' original members leads music services at a Calvary Chapel outlet in South County. God rules here, dude.

Surfing remains an obsession in Orange County. In 2006, Huntington Beach officials trademarked "Surf City U.S.A." so they could sell products with the slogan, going so far as to fight the city of Santa Cruz for the rights. Plans are under way to erect a mammoth surfboard on Pacific Coast Highway with that slogan, yet another hubristic homage in a county that plows them over every couple of years with no sense of irony.

After the 1960s surf craze fizzled, Orange County returned to its dull reputation, with only its wacky conservatives garnering consistent headlines. Not until the 1990s did the county's cred experience a resurgence in American pop culture. Bands such as the Offspring, Social Distortion, Lit, Sugar Ray, Korn, and No Doubt spun suburban anger into national bestselling albums. They sang of a different Orange County, one of boredom and drugs, defiance and sarcastic pride. No Doubt, in particular, understood what their fame meant to the county's old myths: their smash 1997 album was titled *Tragic Kingdom*, and the cover was a mock-up of an orange-crate label—except the orange tree was barren and the fruits had holes in them.

But no Orange County native better attacked Orange County than Zack de la Rocha, the front man of Rage Against the Machine. De la Rocha grew up in Irvine—his mom was a graduate student at UC Irvine, and de la Rocha took classes at University High, the same high school from which Will Ferrell graduated. In many interviews, de la Rocha has recounted the story that a biology teacher mentioned in a class passing through Orange County while returning from San Diego and having to slow down for "the wetback station"—the immigration stop right before San Clemente. The class laughed—except for de la Rocha, who's been getting his revenge ever since, by using the anecdote as fuel for his . . . well, rage.

Thanks to the music, Orange County had "buzz" (sorry to use that horrible cliché, but it's absolutely necessary in this context) just before the television shows broke out. The first earnest volley to pass off Orange County as a hipness nexus was the 2002 film *Orange County,* starring Jack Black and Tom Hanks's son Colin. Its plot was borrowed from every other high-school-themed film ever shot: a young, smart man itched to get away from his hometown and start anew. "It's just not a place—it's a state of mind" read the film's slogan, but the flick didn't do much to show what exactly constituted the place or the state of mind. It didn't prove particularly popular at the box office despite Black's turn as a hilarious stoner older brother.

The year *Orange County* was released, another nationally screened fantasy introduced America to the county anew. For decades, the Anaheim Angels were synonymous with devastating ineptitude. They weren't Cleveland-Indians-at-Municipal-Stadium bad: the Halos consistently made the playoffs and signed future Hall-of-Famers like Rod Carew, Reggie Jackson, and Nolan Ryan. Because of this, their failure to win a pennant was especially excruciating. The notorious example was when the team came within one strike of beating the Boston Red Sox in Game 5 of the 1986

American League Championship Series; instead, reliever Donnie Moore gave up a home run and Boston eventually rallied from a 3–1 deficit to win the series (Moore would commit suicide over this failure).

But in 2002, a ragtag collection of misfits, near midgets, a rally monkey, and one precocious reliever propelled the Angels into the World Series against the San Francisco Giants and the mighty Barry Bonds. National media did their requisite parachute dispatches about Orange County—"Where the heck is Anaheim?" *All Things Considered* asked, throwing in the requisite jibes at Disneyland, conservativism, and master-planned suburbs. The thrilling seven-game series showed those *pendejos*.

Orange County was important, though, because it reintroduced America to the county's beachfront, which boosters were now calling California's Riviera. Just twenty years earlier, the coastal communities—from north to south, Seal Beach, Huntington Beach, Newport Beach, Laguna Beach, Dana Point, and San Clemente—were an eclectic mix of industrial use, cute bungalows, hippies, yachts, and miles of pristine hills and cliffs extending inward. It didn't stand a chance: in the 1980s, the Irvine Company and other developers began erecting resorts, and multimillion-dollar homes, gentrifying every city along the way into overpriced sameness.

This is the Orange County of *The O.C.* and *Laguna Beach: The Real Orange County*, the two shows that followed Jack Black's worst film (I'm going to give *King Kong* a pass because it had a giant ape). Each show simultaneously depicted the old and new Orange County—what was lost, what remained, and what was changed to reflect the county's preferred image.

Of the two shows, *The O.C.* is the more influential, and not just because it premiered first (in August of 2003). Its setting is Newport Beach, the county's historical center for old money. All you need to know about this charming town is one of my personal anecdotes. A couple of years ago, I attended a fund-raiser on behalf of the *Weekly* at the Balboa Bay Club—the Russian Tea Room of OC and John Wayne's favorite drinking well—and while I was standing in line for a horrid Mexican buffet, a skinny, prissy thing approached. She asked if I could serve her refried beans. I laughed. While I waited for the valet later that night, the same woman asked if I could grab her car. "Not unless you want it on cinder blocks," I replied. My Camry arrived. I paid the $5 charge and slipped the Mexican valet an extra $20.

Newport Beach *is* that moneyed and aggressively ignorant about the rest of Orange County, and *The O.C.*'s success solidified that groupthink. Though much derided by pompous folks such as yours truly, *The O.C.* wasn't that bad of a show as far as teenage tripe went. Bad boy Ryan Atwood is taken in by his lawyer, Sandy Cohen, leaving the civic hell named Chino (a city just over the Orange County–San Bernardino County border) to try to reconstitute himself in Newport Beach. Ryan strikes up an immediate friendship with Cohen's son, Seth. Through these two, we see a typical teen's life: love, mansions, dysfunctional adults, and enough indie-rock music to make you long for the days of Benny Goodman.

The O.C. stereotyped its setting to an absurd degree but portrayed a truthful comedy of errors. The rich were suicidal or merely miserable. Caleb Nichol invoked for many Irvine Company head Don Bren, not in the plots or dirty details, but in his aura of power. Latino roles were limited to hot gardeners, subservient maids, and a pregnant girlfriend. The real problems Orange County was facing—immigration, changing demographics, escalating home prices—and the way the show's creators dismissed them were hinted at through vague references that most likely drew little more than head scratches nationwide, but drove actual Orange Countians loco. In one episode, Seth's aunt recounts banging heads at a heavy-metal concert in Anaheim with a Newport Beach friend. Seth can't believe it—but the aunt is even more incredulous: "I can't believe [the friend] went to *Anaheim.*"

Unlike its TV brethren, *The O.C.*'s character development and plotlines cast a skeptical eye on the riches of its protagonists. The wealthier you were in the show, the more miserable everything was. It didn't matter: instead of viewing the drama as a cautionary tale, many county residents adored the bling and the national attention it brought them. Newport Beach's mayor even presented the cast with honorary keys to the city within a year of the show's debut. The show was a launching pad for up-and-coming indie bands such as Phantom Planet and Matt Costa and even popularized a new religious term, *Chrismukkah,* a holiday Seth claimed to have invented to properly celebrate his Jewish and Christian roots. Worst of all, Orange Countians and other Americans began referring to the county as "the OC"; series creator McG (the fool behind the *Charlie's Angels* boobfests, who graduated from Newport Harbor High) claimed Newport teens called their hood "the OC," ironically to convey how unthreatening their lives were. If Denver is the Sally Field of American municipalities, as a friend of mine once opined, then *The O.C.* revealed that Orange County is Mariah Carey—talented at times, flashy, but delusional.

On the heels of *The O.C.* came *Laguna Beach: The Real Orange County,* a show green-lighted specifically to ride the wave of "the OC phenomenon." This show was more remarkable than *The O.C.* because it rewrote history with every shot of the squabbling, spoiled, stupid high schoolers it showcased. Laguna Beach is probably the county's prettiest town: the only two access points to the city are Pacific Coast Highway and Highway 133, a gorgeous road that takes you from the traffic of Interstate 5, through hills, past canyons, and finally spills you out on the Pacific Ocean and Main Beach. For decades, Laguna Beach was one of the few liberal respites in Orange County, a place that maintained a vibrant gay community and a bohemian atmosphere up until the late 1990s. It first achieved fame as an artists' colony, and Laguna's main civic event is still two concurrent art festivals (the Pageant of the Masters and the Sawdust Art Festival), which draw thousands of tourists every summer.

Starting in the mid-1990s, housing prices outpaced even those in the rest of the South County market, pricing out the hippies and the middle class as the superrich moved in. Those new immigrants, we'll call them, have slowly drained the city of its lefty charm—the Democrats still dominate, but the hippie havens of yore and legendary gay bars such as the Boom Boom Room are giving way to boutique hotels, hipster hangouts, and luxury resorts. In a sign of the times, the boys' high school football team changed its name from the limp-wristed, historically relevant Artists to the Breakers—more aggressive, manlier, and definitely no longer fruity.

Laguna Beach: The Real Orange County highlighted this new Laguna at the expense of the old. Its format was a classic Orange County ruse—despite passing itself off as a documentary, many of the scenarios were staged. Fittingly, one of the students presented in the first season was the daughter of Robert A. Schuller, son of the Crystal Cathedral's founder and its current pastor. The show proved popular enough to not only expand and feature a new city—Newport Beach, surprise, surprise!—but also rewarded the world with a spin-off series: *The Hills*, the reprehensible MTV show that in turn cursed the world with Heidi Montag and Lauren Conrad.

The O.C. and *Laguna Beach*, as entertaining as they could be, were primarily about the spoiled kids of Orange County. It took *The Real Housewives of Orange County* to focus the camera on the people who really make the OC the OC—the bitches.

The epicenter of this "real" OC is a place I can't get into: the gated community of Coto de Caza, tucked next to Rancho Santa

Margarita and Trabuco Canyon in deepest, prettiest South County: think grassy hills, rolling streets, grumpy security guards, and one of the county's last extant orange groves. This unincorporated neighborhood is the principal setting for *The Real Housewives of Orange County*, the Bravo cable-channel reality show that ran from 2006 through 2008 and purported to capture the life of an average megamillionaire working girl. I wish I could tell you the unvarnished truth about Coto de Caza, give you the scoop behind the show, describe the multiacre estates, but an individual can only enter the community's gates if his or her name is on a list—and mine isn't. I'm sure I could sneak in—pose as a gardener, perhaps—but even that's difficult. That's Coto de Caza: exclusivity. We're in, you're not—consider the translation of its name from Spanish: "private reserve."

Coto de Caza first gained publicity during the 1984 Summer Olympics, when it hosted the pentathlon competition. At the time, only a club, equestrian facilities, other athletic areas, and modest homes dotted the area's hills. After the world saw its placid gorgeousness, Coto de Caza's developer, Arvida Corporation (then a subsidiary of Walt Disney Productions), announced plans to cram six thousand homes onto its holdings; about half that number eventually went up. This wasn't the county's first gated community, but Coto de Caza did represent a new wrinkle to local status seekers—an attempt by the superwealthy to segregate themselves from the merely wealthy. A microcosm of a microcosm.

You only have to watch about ten minutes of *The Real Housewives of Orange County* to understand this. The show was created by Coto resident Scott Dunlop, who pitched a Coto series to executives at Bravo in 2006. He wasn't a Hollywood player; he ran the Dunlop Group, a consulting firm that in typical Orange County can-do spirit sells itself as "pursuing authentic and contrarian thinking for our clients & ourselves." Calling the show *Behind the Gates*, Dunlop proposed a satirical take on his master-planned neighborhood, hoping to enlist Cotoans to improvise their day-to-day lives for public consumption—*Curb Your Enthusiasm* among the silicone set. Instead, Dunlop's proposal morphed into a reality show documenting four Coto women and one staying in nearby (but no less affluent) Ladera Ranch. The new show's title was an amalgam of what it professed to show: a documentary about Orange County coupled with the cattiness of *Desperate Housewives,* the hit television show not based in Orange County but concocted by OC native (and gay Republican—go figure!) Marc Cherry.

The Real Housewives of Orange County has filmed three seasons and is gearing up for a fourth, further testament to the cruelty of the cosmos. As a show, its only selling point is schadenfreude, except the miseries depicted are mitigated by moola. Each of the principal characters goes through the familial pains and personal emotional hardships of any human being—Tammy Knickerbocker dealt with her ex-husband's death from a heart attack, Jeana Keough separated from her husband, former big-league pitcher Matt Keough, Lauri Waring's son entered rehab, and Vicki Gunvalson is a workaholic—but the show concentrates on capturing the "Orange County lifestyle," a nebulous phrase that makes sense only to them. All of the ladies own palatial homes and openly admire their own accumulation of wealth. "We show our love by buying each other things," Keough once said, and ain't that the truth. The show rarely ventures from South County, specifically from Ladera Ranch, Coto de Caza, and Mission Viejo—and the few times it does, it's usually on business trips or leisure outside of Orange County. Sons are apathetic and living off their mothers' salaries; the daughters usually head off to the beach, whether to sunbathe or hawk energy drinks in ultratight bikinis. In one episode, Jeana's children fought because one was getting a hand-me-down Mercedes-Benz convertible as a present.

In spite of the hardships, none of the women remain sympathetic for long. I once felt sorry for Keough, a former *Playboy* Playmate who is the show's requisite fattie, because of her marital problems and demon spawn—but in a Season Three episode, she cracked jokes about a Latino waiter after he politely served her. Then again, who am I to judge? I can't say I've seen every episode—I'm more of a *SportsCenter* guy. But America is watching—*The Real Housewives* has earned stellar ratings throughout its run and even spun off a New York City sister show, offering evidence that even the worst Park Avenue princess has nothing on an Orange County diva. Still, one can dream: I want to load up a truck of day laborers, crash through the gates, and let the Mexicans run amok—no pillaging, no raping. Just wander those immaculate streets and terrorize the bejesus out of everyone with our swarthy presence.

Laguna Hills: No different from Laguna Niguel, which is lame blandness.

Laguna Niguel: No different from Laguna Hills, which is lamer blandness.

I've only ever seen two television shows nail Orange County perfectly. In 2005, *South Park* screened an episode involving a group of kids from "the OC" who challenged Cartman and the gang to a hip-hop dance-off. While eminently enjoyable (I won't say what happened but it involves Butters tap-dancing), the depiction was heresy: the OC group was multicultural! Black got along with white got along with Asian got along with Mexican! No wonder the OC kids died.

The best effort to document Orange County's foibles, its hilarious hypocrisies, and its irresistible pull was *Arrested Development*. For three Emmy-winning, cult-followed, low-rated seasons, this Fox television show was the real-life equivalent of *The Simpsons*. The commoner could enjoy the show sans context and the social critic could appreciate it, while cynical Orange Countians worshipped it for the brilliant exposition of the county's power structure and ways.

The program focused on the Bluth family, who terrorized Newport Beach as residents and developers. In the first episode, the Securities and Exchange Commission arrested family patriarch George Bluth for defrauding investors by using their money to build tract homes in Iraq for Saddam Hussein. Obedient, good-hearted son Michael assumed Dad would give him control of the Bluth Company, but George instead handed the presidency over to his wife, the maniacal, forever-sloshed Lucille. She promptly appointed the youngest son, Buster, as president to run the company from the background—except she couldn't help without slurring her martini-fueled words. This arrangement couldn't last, so the family—which, save for Michael, had never worked a day in their collective lives—turned to Michael for salvation.

The series took off from there, weaving in everything from British spy shows, magic, the pompous caterwauling that is Europe's "The Final Countdown"—and an Orange County hardly seen on any national, or even local, level. Several *Arrested Development* plot devices were parodies of actual Orange County landmarks. The frozen-banana stand where the Bluths made their fortune? A simulacrum of Sugar 'n' Spice, a small ice cream shop on ritzy Balboa Island that sells frozen bananas and whose mascot is an anthropomorphic banana. (By the way: the owner is a cranky old woman who told me *Arrested Development* had "ripped off" her place yet has an autographed poster of *The O.C.* cast members displayed on the wall because one episode featured

Sugar 'n' Spice. And while we're bitching, *The O.C.* also once mentioned the *OC Weekly,* but only for about a second. Damn straight we're bitter.) The art show involving live dioramas of famous paintings where George assumes the role of Michelangelo's God creating Adam only to escape from the Feds? The Pageant of the Masters, a Laguna Beach institution that has impressed out-of-town rubes since the 1930s.

But these were details. *Arrested Development* captured Orange County perfectly with its synthesized characters. George Oscar "Gob" Bluth, the egomaniacal eldest son with no tact who ridiculed ethnics, was a stand-in for our arrogance; George, most any of our GOP officials. Lucille Bluth was realer than any Real Housewife, played with dripping sarcasm and alcohol. Michael's only son, George-Michael, represented the spoiled, sheltered child of any white family in Orange County. George-Michael's girlfriend, Ann, was a fundamentalist Christian who spent her free time protesting *Desperate Housewives.* Even George's hippie brother, Oscar, was a classic county type—a relic of 1960s Laguna Beach.

The most important skewering in the series, however, involved the interaction between the Bluths and Mexicans. In the first season, Michael and Gob fought over the affections of Marta, a Mexican telenovela star. When Michael and Lucille hobnobbed during an awards show, Lucille openly wondered why there were so many Mexicans in tuxedos yet none of them were refilling her drink. Later in the series, Michael and Gob each lost a chance to move in on Marta because they didn't understand a basic Spanish word—*hermano.* It means "brother," and I assume even folks in Iowa know the term, but in the *gabacho* mouths of the two it comes off as a slur. Fistfights and hilarity ensued.

None of the Bluth children, however, were more foolish about Mexicans than Buster. In Season Two, Buster tried to go AWOL from basic training in the army but didn't know how to properly execute his plan. When he overheard that Michael was offering to give the family maid, Lupe, a ride home, Buster assumed "home" was Mexico. Excited, he snuck into the trunk of Michael's car and went to sleep, expecting a long drive south.

Of course, Lupe's house was in Santa Ana.

When Buster felt the car stop, he popped out of the trunk and wandered around Santa Ana, assuming he was in Mexico. He marveled at how similar Mexico and Orange County were, but— true to his slack-jawed ways—decided to sleep under a trampoline in Lupe's front yard. "This will keep me safe from the hot Mexican sun," Buster said to himself in a stereotypical Mexican accent. When Lupe asked Buster in English what he was doing, he replied with this accent, "I'm trying to find a place to live."

"*Ahora tengo que cuidar para retardo,*" Lupe says to herself. On the television screen, the subtitles flashed, "So now I must take care of Buster," but . . . well, if I have to translate it for you, then you are the *retardo*.

Lupe led Buster into her well-kept house, and Buster marveled at how everything was so similar to the United States. He told her children that their clothes looked like his childhood clothes, and that the seat shaped liked a massive hand was just like the one he used to own. Previous episodes had shown Lucille giving Lupe hand-me-downs and also checking her purse every day to ensure she wasn't stealing forks.

Later on, Buster partied with Lupe's family and loved it. "Oh, I love this way of life!" he proclaimed to Lupe. "This is where I belong. I love being Mexican."

A Mexican man approached him and said in unaccented English they were leaving the party for a night shift. A serious look crossed Buster's face. "Oh, no, no, no, I'm going with you," he replied. And then, the Mexican accent again: "I am one of you now. ¿*Sí?*" He jumped into an overcrowded van, giggling and remarking, "We're like slave buddies!" before running into a kitchen to begin his new job as a dishwasher.

A show this brilliant was doomed. The satire and parodies were simply too bright, too hot, too much of an affront to the now enshrined OC, and too lost on too many American television viewers.

A couple of other shows—*Ocean Force: Huntington Beach, O.C.* and one about people throwing big parties—haven't captured the national imagination. Our time in the national spotlight is over, but we don't particularly care. "Orange County" in the American mind now represents greed, vacuity, but at least everyone talks about us, right?

And so we return to the bronzed Duke, standing alone at the airport that bears his name—for now. He's not looking too good. That half-smile is a grimace. His Orange County is galloping toward the sunset, and his ingrate grandchildren now run the asylum. Leave it to Orange County to make the days of Birchers and segregated communities seem quaint.

Rancho Santa Margarita: Ranchland until the 1980s, when it suddenly exploded into developments for people who wanted to escape South County. Only real feature is Santa Margarita Catholic High School, which produced Heisman Trophy–winner and long-suffering Cincinnati Bengal starting quarterback Carson Palmer. **Best restaurant: Celinda's Mexican Deli,** but focus on the chile relleno burrito. *29941 Aventura, Rancho Santa Margarita, (949) 589-0354; www.celindas.com.*

Becoming "The Mexican"

In May of 2007, I sat on the second floor of a Barnes & Noble in Orange and waited. Earlier that day, my sister had called to excitedly report that the book version of my *¡Ask a Mexican!* column was finally on sale. She'd bought two copies and promised to buy more. "Stop it," I told her. "Strangers need to buy the book. They need to buy it *now*."

After a day of interviews and blown deadlines, I'd stopped by the Barnes & Noble to look for *¡Ask a Mexican!* It was near the entrance, on one of many tables advertising new releases, on a small shelf between *E = Einstein* and a random novel. This wasn't good enough, I thought. I grabbed a copy, propped it on top of the other new releases, and fled toward the Sudoku section. From there, I watched.

It was a slow night, and most of the customers sped past my table on their way to whatever had brought them here. A couple of them stopped. Hope? Nope. They flipped through Lee Iacocca's latest and that damn Einstein book. All of the books but mine.

I took the escalator upstairs and found a seat next to the humanities section that afforded me an eagle's-nest view. Only fifteen more minutes of spying, I promised myself. Another half hour passed. I flipped through books to kill time. Judy Chicago is overrated save for *Red Flag*. Which Persian emperor was the best friend of the Jews—Cyrus, Darius, or Xerxes? There must be a better reason why the Brits have such bad teeth besides drinking tea. *Under the Banner of Heaven:* need to buy that book. I did.

After even another half hour, a customer finally reacted to my masterpiece. A little girl yelled, "Daddy, look!" She pointed at ¡*Ask a Mexican!* The father shook his head and muttered words I couldn't quite hear. Their dismissive laughs, however, still ring in my ears. I left Barnes & Noble shortly thereafter, fearing that my writing career was nearing the end.

THE YOUNGSTERS

Orange County has produced vital bands in the past, such as Rage Against the Machine, No Doubt, Social Distortion (catch them on Guitar Hero IIII), even Jackson Browne. But the county sound has sorely lacked any breakout acts for the past decade. The biggest names, the Cold War Kids and Matt Costa, create shimmering melodies at hipster breeding grounds such as Detroit Bar and Avalon's in Costa Mesa and Anaheim's Chain Reaction. Main problem: scenes get shortchanged due to city regulations that insist last call is at 2 a.m. and businesses close around 11 p.m. Anaheim used to have the world's premier Latin nightclub in J.C. Fandango, a strip-mall room where the biggest names in tropical, Mexican regional, and rock *en español* performed weekly, but the club gave up on impressing the world because of familial squabbling by one genius brother and two idiots.

The reason you're reading this book—the reason a publishing company ever offered me a contract, the reason I'm not an orange picker—has a lot to do with two jokes with spectacularly unexpected ramifications.

Around the spring of 2000, I was volunteering for a city coun-

cil race in Santa Ana. My involvement with MEChA had motivated me to improve the lot of Orange County's Latino community, and I was trying to meet hot activist ladies. One night, while
stuffing envelopes in a cold garage with two volunteers who were
expecting hot chicks and not a sausage party, I noticed a newspaper in the trash can called *OC Weekly*. I had never heard of the
paper, but the sex ads in the back were appealing.

It's like any alternative newspaper in the country—scandals,
snarky columns, sex ads, and music reviews. The issue I picked up
was a special April Fools' edition that saw the newspaper transformed into an Orange County version of the *Onion*. Stories
included coverage of a congressman's anus from which the sun
shone, politicians declaring everything was okay, and other such
silliness. One article caught my attention, in particular: "Five Latinos We Really Like." One was Taco Bell's CEO. Another was Tom
Fuentes, the head of the Orange County Republican Party and
persona non grata among county Latinos for his role in the 1989
poll-guard incident. Yet another was my man Harald Martin.

The article was ignorant, offensive, and brilliant. It was the
funniest satire I'd read since *Weekly World News*. I also knew that
uptight Chicanos like the ones who ruined the Harald Martin
recall wouldn't get the joke. And I figured the *Weekly*—which I
noticed didn't feature any Latino writers on its masthead—would
probably apologize for the furor out of PC piety.

I wanted to have fun. So I wrote the following letter:

> *Dear* OC Weekly: *I am writing to express my outrage*
> *concerning "Five Latinos We Really Like." Forgotten among*
> *these pillars of the Latino community is the matriarch of*
> OC *Latinos, the incomparable Barbara Coe. How could the*
> OC Weekly *forget this leader of Latino rights? Her myriad*
> *achievements in helping the Latino community include being the*
> *president of the California Coalition for Immigration Reform;*

playing a major role in Propositions 187, 209, 227 and "Son of 187"; and supporting Voice of Citizens Together, the noted Latino advocacy group. Let us also not forget the beautiful billboards her group has put up across our state giving Latinos free advertising. Babs also full-heartedly supported the proposal of noted Latino activist Harald Martin (who, thankfully, made this list) to save Latino students from themselves. A woman with such a proven record of activism in the Latino community should not have been excluded from this list, and I will boycott this newspaper and encourage others to do so until an apology is written to all Latinos concerning this issue.

To their credit, the *Weekly* ran my letter and—surprise!—next to another similarly toned thought, except the writer was a Chicano Studies professor and he was *serious*. Point made—but no apology on their part to either of us. This rag was better than I thought.

After the *Weekly* printed the letter, I e-mailed a thank-you note to the paper's editor, Will Swaim. By chance, I had seen him the previous week on a local political talk show. Tall, dashing, with a chin like Jay Leno and hair like James Dean, Will had torn apart a conservative yakmouth with humor, logic, and brutality. My kind of intellectual. I commended Will on his performance and asked how I could convince the *Weekly* to cover a particular story. Martin was still on the AUHSD board, and a couple of activists were trying to boot him from office again. I also wanted the *Weekly* to cover the Santa Ana council race for which I was volunteering. Will didn't have much interest in the race, but run-ins with Harald Martin got his attention. He set up a meeting between me and one of his investigative reporters, Nick Schou.

I mispronounced Nick's name the first time we met (it's "Skow," *not* "Shoe"), and the Martin angle fizzled. Nick asked if I had any other story ideas. I told him the saga of El Cargadero, figuring there was nothing to lose. Rather than reject my proposal, Nick was enthusiastic. He promised to pitch Will the idea. Will loved it.

For the next couple of months, Nick followed me around to speak with different *cargaderenses*. I served as a guide for him at *la cafetería*, at my Mama Chela's house, even at a dance for the El Cargadero *club social*. My aunts and mom told him the Miranda tale, from Mama Pacha to my battles against Martin. Meanwhile, I kept feeding Will story ideas, not out of any expectation to write them, but in the hopes of getting issues covered in the *Weekly*. Finally—out of genuine interest or in an attempt to shut me up, I'll never know—Will asked me to write about how the Democrats were using the ghost of former California governor Pete Wilson during the 2000 presidential elections to scare Latinos into voting for Democrats.

I wasn't up for it. The only articles of any kind I had ever written before were opinion pieces: two essays for the *Orange County Register* regarding Harald Martin, and letters to the paper's editor regarding its racist Letters to the Editor section. But Will persisted and promised to help edit me. I wrote my Pete Wilson piece—even interviewed a Chicano Studies professor. The article ran in the same issue that splashed Nick's El Cargadero article on the cover. Will radically rewrote the intro and cut my conclusion, but, otherwise, most of the words were mine. And I earned $100.

I called Will to express my gratitude. Despite our steady correspondence over six months, this was our first phone conversation.

"Thank you so much, amigo," he replied in a patrician tone that revealed his South County upbringing. He raved that my Wilson story was great and asked if I wanted to become a regular *Weekly* contributor. I expressed reluctance—I wasn't a journalist. Then he asked, "How old are you?"

"I'm twenty-one years old," I replied, not really knowing what he was getting at.

"No way!" he exclaimed. "You write like a forty-five-year-old man! You have amazing talent for your age!"

On and on he praised my nonexistent talents before offering me another idea. An Anaheim swap meet held *lucha libre* matches every Sunday. Since none of his reporters were Latino, he asked if I had any interest in writing about it.

Will assumed I was familiar with *lucha libre,* and I let him think that. In reality, I was a WWF fan and felt *lucha libre* was just another Mexican oddity. But the thought of contributing more to the *Weekly* excited me. I accepted the challenge and submitted a draft about two weeks later. Will liked it so much he told me to write more. He also mentioned that the *Weekly* was looking for food reviews. I pitched him a review of an Anaheim Thai restaurant, claiming it was delicious. I had never tasted Thai food.

The two articles were published in one February 2001 issue, just a couple of days after my twenty-second birthday. I celebrated the occasion by playing Genesis.

Over the next two years, Will molded me into the journalist I am today. I started by mostly covering music, slowly inching myself toward hard news and food writing. Soon, I outproduced even the weekly's prolific staff writers. Writing was amazing, liberating, and it paid.

What was better was learning from a brilliant man who wasn't afraid to trash me. Not since Mrs. Spykerman in high school did an adult challenge me every day—but whereas Mrs. Spykerman did it with tough love, Will used insults. He rejected half of the ideas I pitched him, three-quarters of the articles I submitted, and actively rewrote everything that made it into the paper. *Terrible* and *crap* were the nicer invectives he used. He also once told me that licking a dog's asshole would be preferable to reading the article I'd filed.

Rather than take offense, I asked Will to explain what was so reprehensible about my writing, and to help me improve. I also asked for a tour of the *Weekly* offices. We agreed to meet for lunch, and he showed me around the cramped offices, just down the street from John Wayne Airport. I shook people's hands, met editors, interns, and freelancers. Everyone was pleasant, until one person remarked, "When I saw your name, I thought to myself, 'I didn't know our paper delivery drivers were also reporters!'"

"No, Mexicans know how to write, too," I snapped back. Will and I left.

I continued to freelance for the *Weekly* throughout my senior year at Chapman and my first year in UCLA's Latin American Studies master's program. After my second semester at UCLA, I knew journalism was for me—not only did I love seeing my name in print every week, but grad school had proven to be the ivory-tower existence I dreaded it might. I wrote an anthropological paper comparing the El Cargadero Social Club to primitive societies through analyzing their dances and the gift-giving ceremonies of Pacific Northwest tribes—less of a stretch than you might think. A fellow grad student suggested I submit it for publication in a journal, but the thought that it would take at least a year to appear in some obscure magazine read by a couple hundred professors while hundreds of thousands of people could read a three-hundred-word music review I cranked out in a half hour was bothersome. More important, I saw how favoritism and the buddy system protected those who were lame.

In one of my first-year seminars, on the first day of class, the professor strolled in late, accompanied by a shapely female companion and a small dog that he allowed to scuttle across the table where we sat. The "scholar" operated without fear: he had earned tenure decades ago and hadn't needed to do anything since then. The students looked on, annoyed but intimidated. During the break, I walked out and e-mailed Will. I wanted to become a journalist.

To my surprise, Will suggested I finish graduate school. I was still raw as a reporter, he explained, and since I was halfway through a two-year program, it was foolish for me to leave. I asked if I could join the staff of the OC *Weekly,* and he said there weren't any positions open—however, he suggested I apply for a diversity grant through the Association of Alternative Newsweeklies, a trade organization for alt weeklies in the United States and Canada. I did, and I won.

I also sought advice from other journalists. I sent e-mails to any reporter I found with a Hispanic surname and went to readings of Latino authors. Only two writers ever responded: Rubén Martínez, essayist and author of multiple books on the Latino experience, and Sam Quinones, currently a writer with the *Los Angeles Times* but in those days a freelance reporter in Mexico who had published *True Tales from Another Mexico,* a collection that anyone who loves great writing must own. Not only did Rubén and Sam offer me advice, but the two also connected me with editors they knew—that's how at age twenty-two, even as Will was ripping my articles, I was writing op-ed pieces for Pacific News Service and the *San Francisco Chronicle.* Advice to anyone who gets approached by a young person seeking advice: give it in droves.

❊   ❊   ❊

Aliso Viejo: The worst city in Orange County by far. Its beautiful hills are populated mostly with gated communities, meaning its long sidewalks are as empty as Hiroshima after the A-bomb. So newly incorporated that the city council still meets at an industrial-park facility. **Best restaurant:** For years, I couldn't find an eatery worthy of recommendation in Aliso Viejo until stumbling upon **Siamese Express,** a Thai restaurant that sells purple tamales. *26952-C La Paz Road, Aliso Viejo, (949) 831-0882.*

After I graduated from UCLA, Will stayed true to his word and hired me as a full-time staffer. By that point, I had expanded my reporting—not only was I assigned to Latino culture pieces and hard news, but Will also made me the food critic. Me, the guy who had never tasted ethnic food other than instant ramen and pizza until reviewing that Thai restaurant I lied about. I didn't care what the assignment was—I wanted to write. And I did—so much that I felt resentment build among the *Weekly*'s reporters. Where others wrote two pieces a week, I frequently published five, even seven. Only Nick had the decency to pull me aside.

"Gustavo, did I ever tell you about my father when he spent a summer at a factory?" he told me during lunch one day.

No.

"One summer when he was a teenager, my dad worked at a factory," Nick began. "He outperformed everyone because he was a hard worker. He worked so hard that an older man pulled him aside and said, 'Look, kid, you gotta slow down, you're making us all look bad. If you don't, some of us guys are probably going to break your legs.'"

I didn't care for parables—I just kept writing. I reviewed restaurants, did film reviews, everything. I started doing commentaries for NPR's *Day to Day* program in the fall of 2003—and the grumbles grew louder at the office.

Still, I was just a cog in the *Weekly* machine until November 2004, when Will called me into his office. By that point, we had moved offices to Santa Ana. Will had just driven up the city's Main Street, where a massive billboard for KSCA-FM 101.9 loomed over downtown featuring a smirking Mexican DJ wearing a Viking helmet. This was El Piolín, a former Santa Ana resident who would use his syndicated radio show to promote pro-amnesty marches in 2006 that attracted millions and is the most-listened-to DJ in the United States, with a daily morning audience of at least 19 million. But El Piolín was still unknown to *gabachos* in 2004, so, when Will saw the goofy billboard, he asked me about it.

I explained El Piolín to Will—his rise from illegal immigrant to student at Saddleback High School in Santa Ana to popular Arizona DJ who returned to Southern California. Will was interested, but his mind was elsewhere. "That guy looks as if you could ask him any question about Mexicans, and he'll know the answer," Will said, looking outside his fifth-story window toward Main Street. "Why don't you do it? Why don't you ask readers to send in questions about Mexicans, and you answer them?"

I laughed. Will had often come up with ludicrous ideas that evolved into amazing stories (e.g., the April Fools' issue), but the idea of entertaining readers' questions about Mexicans didn't appeal to me. Not because I thought it would be incendiary— rather, I thought no one cared much about Mexicans. Will persisted. We were desperate to fill our news section that week—the *Weekly*'s long-running column *Burning Bush* (where we published conservatives criticizing the president) was shutting down because Dubya had just swiftboated John Kerry's ass. Besides, Will promised, we would scrap it if no one paid any attention.

That afternoon, I slapped together the following question and answer:

Dear Mexican: Why do Mexicans call white people gringos?

Dear Gabacho: Mexicans do not call gringos gringos. Only gringos call gringos gringos. Mexicans call gringos gabachos.

We called the column *¡Ask a Mexican!* and paired it with an illustration by mad genius Mark Dancey of the most stereotypical Mexican man imaginable—fat, wearing a sombrero and bandoliers, with a mustache, stubbly neck, and a shiny gold tooth. This was a logo we'd used in our recent Cinco de Mayo issue, which was devoted to Mexican-hating in Orange County. No one had appreciated the logo, and we patiently fielded complaints from numerous readers. We decided to use Dancey's illustration again for the new column, convinced it was even more appropriate for the outrageousness of the new column.

The response was instantaneous. Liberal-minded people criticized the logo, the column's name, its very existence. Conservatives didn't like how I called white people *gabachos*, a derogatory term a tad softer than *nigger*. Latino activists called the paper demanding my resignation and threatening to boycott the *Weekly* (those yaktivists and their boycott!). But, more important, people of all races thought *¡Ask a Mexican!* was brilliant. And, more surprising, the questions poured in.

We've run *¡Ask a Mexican!* every week since (save for special issues), expanding the column to two questions per week in May 2005. Soon after, I answered questions live on KABC-AM 790's *The Al Rantel Show*. More questions came in. Still, I thought the column was just a silly little thing until the *Los Angeles Times* called toward the end of 2005 and asked if they could profile me. It turned into a Column One, the *Times's* famed section for literary journalism. And that's when everything changed.

❋   ❋   ❋

Laguna Woods: Formerly Leisure World. The only city in California where only senior citizens can live. One of the few cities in Orange County where Democrats outnumber Republicans, mostly because liberal geezers are rich enough to live in a retirement community, while conservative coffin dodgers hire Filipinos to oversee them during the infirm years in one of their many houses. **Best restaurant:** Whatever they're giving the comatose patients through an IV tube tomorrow.

I'd like to think ¡Ask a Mexican! spread across the country on its own merits. But I'm realistic: the Los Angeles Times made me acceptable to America. The profile (written by Daniel Hernandez, who is writing a book about Mexico City coming out next year via Scribner—buy it!) became an Internet sensation. It was the most viewed and most e-mailed story on the Times Web site for days. I started receiving e-mails from across the country—almost all of it positive. Agents called like the sharks they are—dozens of them, film and literary. One kept calling, convinced I was the next Cantinflas. The Times invited me to submit editorials, a gig that morphed into a contributing-editor role. And then came the talk shows: Nightline, Today, Good Morning America, Tucker Carlson's old MSNBC program, local radio programs from Minnesota to South Carolina, Glenn Beck to Michael Reagan's fill-in. Shortly thereafter, newspapers began picking up the column—it now runs in thirty-five weeklies, with a combined circulation of over 2 million.

I was able to land a two-book deal (you're reading the second one) with Scribner. When my book deal was announced to the staff, one of my colleagues cried out of admitted jealousy. Colleges and organizations began inviting me to speak about the column; in one case, the Association of Hispanic Advertising Agencies asked if I could serve as a mestizo Bob Barker for their Ask a Latino! game show. I agreed, spent a week in beautiful, sultry Miami, and made the crowd laugh.

Needless to say, the column is controversial. I've heard reports of Chicano Studies professors slamming my columns in class, of high-minded Hispanics calling bookstores to demand they pull ¡Ask a Mexican! from the shelves. A man in Newport, Oregon, was suspended from his duties as a hospital handyman for five days without pay for passing one of my columns around. The charge? Racism and sexual harassment. (The offending column said Mexicans and Irish were "drunk, degenerate, fornicating

Catholics" and also that Mexican men treat women the same as chickens: "as purveyors of breasts, eggs, and little else.") In the various markets across the country, right after a paper introduces my column, self-proclaimed Latino defenders insist on meetings with editors and demand they drop me. None have, so far, *inshallah*, except a fish wrap in the Daytona area. The reaction in each market has been just like that in Orange County—outrage, followed by condemnation, followed by acceptance, and concluding with popularity.

So much more. A reporter jokingly blamed me for her losing out on a prestigious fellowship because she expressed affinity for the *¡Ask a Mexican!* column to the panel of judges. A *Los Angeles Times* reporter called me the Paris Hilton of Latino journalism. Too many of my friends have had to defend me against random outraged *pendejos*. New Year's Eve 2008, a friend introduced me to her friend at a party. "He writes *¡Ask a Mexican!*" my amiga excitedly proclaimed.

"Yeah, I know who he is," she proclaimed, her lips pursing. "I'm not too particularly fond of his work."

Chula, I wasn't too fond of the spare tire around your midsection, but I had the good taste not to mention it. Well, until now.

It can get tiring defending the column, especially when *Weekly* readers know I also write about plenty of non-Mexican issues. Yet *¡Ask a Mexican!* now marks me like a big cactus on my high forehead. My mug has been broadcast enough times such that I get recognized by fans about once a week. This isn't an inflated head on my part; it's the truth.

¡Ask a Mexican! made me into an N-list celebrity and allows me to target the Harald Martins of America. On a selfish level, I will always hold the column dear to my heart because it was the last push I needed to fully integrate into America.

Through college, through grad school, through writing for the *Weekly*, I roomed with my brother, Gabriel—shared a bunk bed with him. Non-Mexican-Americans my age ridiculed me, even though that's how everyone in El Cargadero did it—no one moved out until after marriage, unless you were going to school out of state, and what was the point of doing that? The subject of leaving home just wasn't discussed—if you were in a Mexican family, you stayed. While attending UCLA, I suggested to my parents that perhaps I should get a dorm room, since I had to endure a tortuous commute—about two hours in traffic each way, three times a week. The two immediately shamed me into silence. "Why are you trying to break up the family?" my mom pleaded. "Rents are too much, Gustavo!" my dad implored. I shut up.

Day to day, living at home wasn't a big deal. I left for work early and returned home late. Weekends were devoted to finishing stories at home and surfing the Internet. I loved my family—liked to bug my siblings and watch movies with them. There was only one problem: sex.

When I was younger, and the two girlfriends I had also lived at home with their parents, staying the night with them wasn't an option since the girls had curfews. Nooky, then, was limited to car rendezvous and the occasional motel rental—not that I was getting any, mind you. I didn't even lose my virginity until I was nineteen, and the lovely experience lasted all of ten seconds.

As I grew older and started pursuing women who had their own pads, my approach just wasn't going to cut it with these liberated *muchachas*. More than once, the mere *mention* of my sharing a bunk bed immediately turned a woman off. I saw it in their faces—a glimmer of attraction turned to a snicker within seconds, then apathy, then no returned phone calls.

It didn't help that rancho mores had turned me into a gentleman so damn respectful he couldn't get his fingers onto a bra strap without asking the girl for permission. The summer after I graduated from UCLA, I ran into a former classmate at a rock *en español* show in Los Angeles. I remembered her immediately—I thought she was heavenly. A Ph.D. candidate in history, she expertly analyzed arcane papers in our seminar class. Argentine, tall, with long, wavy hair and hips that moved like hydraulics. At the show, she did nothing but flirt, smile, and virtually jump on me. I thought nothing of her gestures until driving home, when I had a wit-of-the-staircase moment—you *baboso,* she was hitting on you!

I e-mailed her that night, and we went out on three dates before I made my "move"—a chaste kiss on the lips. We'd laughed over dinner. We'd seen *Lost in Translation.* We went dancing—and then she invited me home at one in the morning. The excuse? She wanted to burn me a copy of OutKast's *Speakerboxxx/The Love Below.* In those days, burning a CD lasted a solid hour—and keep in mind, that album was a double disc.

What did we do until three in the morn? Sat at a table and talked—I might've touched her shoulder.

As I said, I did peck her at the end of the night, but I sensed a coldness the next time I saw her that hadn't existed before. We went to a concert, then I drove her home. I made it into her kitchen again and told her she was "wonderful."

"I knew you liked me," she responded calmly, coolly. "But sorry—you're too physically timid."

To this day, it's the worst insult I've ever heard—and I've heard people call my mom a "monkey whore."

I moved on and fashioned the semblance of a dating routine, but no relationship lasted longer than three months. Even the girls who seemed most interested didn't understand why I always went home at four in the morning. Eventually, a helpful ad girl at the *Weekly* informed me that if I slept with a woman, I should spend the entire night with her; otherwise, no one would take me seriously.

To remedy this, I started making up stories for my parents. I had to go to Tijuana to see a rock concert. We had to pull an all-nighter at the office. I needed to travel for the job. See, I couldn't admit that I was going to spend the night with a woman—are you kidding me? I'm sure they still think I'm a virgin.

But lying to Mami y Papi didn't solve my problems. I still couldn't find a good relationship. Women told me I was immature. It wouldn't be a problem if I were dating a girl from El Cargadero, but that just wasn't going to happen. Since I hadn't regularly patronized rancho dances for years, I'd lost access to all the eligible, but conservative, women who were predisposed to going out with someone from El Cargadero or Jerez because of shared values and heritage.

There was one *cargaderensa*—she was older than me. I was friends with her younger sister, and our friend (one of the second cousins I courted during high school) set us up. We went on a couple of dates, and all was well. Then one day we started talking about the Catholic Church sex-abuse scandal, and she asked why I didn't write any "positive" stories about the Church. The last time I saw her, she ignored my offer of a tortilla chip.

After the *Los Angeles Times* profile ran and the column increased my visibility, I knew it was time for a change. I realized that I had to leave the sanctity and security of the family if I wanted to mature. I had to move out.

Surprisingly, my mom accepted the decision without rancor. But my father wouldn't have it. He told me that paying rent when I could live at home was foolish. He said I was needed in the house to make sure my brother turned out all right, even though the kid is as placid as a Quaker. When all else failed, my father nearly had a bawling fit and forbade me to move out. But I had an escape plan—he was going to Jomulquillo on vacation.

While he was gone, I packed up my room—about a thousand books, my computer, and clothes—and moved into an apartment in Santa Ana. Joining me was my best friend, Art, who had bugged me for years to get an apartment. It was a tiny dump—the former attic of an old home—but it was ours. When my father returned, he was furious. To this day, he keeps saying I never needed to move out, that the family would be much stronger. But part of me believes he's secretly proud. Like father, like son.

THE ARTS

It says a lot about the county that our most famous artists are Thomas Kinkade, who paints simplistic pastoral designs, and the singularly named Wyland, famous for massive murals of freakin' *whales*. The clash between nouveaux riches, starving artists, and old money creates bewildering situations. The Pacific Symphony, which plays at the new Segerstrom Hall, is good, but who cares about classical music nowadays? Its next-door neighbor, South Coast Plaza, is most famous for staging *A Christmas Carol* and the Latino-themed *La Posada Mágica,* but also fosters young play-wrights drawn from a vibrant, poverty-stricken theater scene.

The Mexican. I still find it hilarious that I of all people became "The Mexican." My first language might have been Spanish, my parents unassimilated Mexican immigrants, but I grew up with no particular appreciation for my mother culture. It was a given, but so was my Americanness. I was neither and both at the same time, and I didn't care either way.

Not until Proposition 187 did I realize that I and the millions of my Mexican-American peers were regarded as dangerous by a large section of America. I didn't understand where all the hatred came from. I still don't. Oh, I know the historical and sociological aspects of xenophobia, especially when it comes to Mexicans in the United States. But I'm part of that invading horde anti-immigrant activists rail about along with everyone from El Cargadero and Jerez, and we just don't see the doomed America they do. And as soon as I joined the *Weekly* as a freelancer, I realized few in Orange County agreed with me. The column's success validated that disturbing point on a national level. The furor I get from both sides tells me we'll be fighting about Mexicans for years to come.

And so, I write.

The culmination of my odd rise to quasi-fame was marked by a July 2006 appearance on *The Colbert Report*. I've graced other, lesser shows—*Hannity & Colmes, Good Morning America, Your World with Neil Cavuto,* and various Fox News and CNN programs to opine on Mexican stuff. The *New York Times, Houston Chronicle,* the Reuters newswire, and others have written glowing profiles. But to appear on *Colbert* meant a joke understood a joke. Satire across America translates into a better nation.

Colbert's handlers flew me out to New York and put me in a boutique hotel. Once I got to the studio, talent bookers promptly handed me a swag bag—three bottles of vodka, every flavor of Altoids imaginable, a gift certificate for custom-made shoes. A six-pack of mini-bottles of Shiraz. Hangover pills. Other randomness. A *Colbert Report* tote bag. And granola bars. All the *Today* show gave me was ranch dressing.

Before the taping, Colbert stuck his well-coiffed head in the greenroom and thanked me for agreeing to be his latest punching bag. "*Gabacho, gringo, gaijin, geek*—why do so many names for outsiders begin with the letter *G*?" he rhetorically asked. "Gustavo, too," I lamely cracked. He laughed—a sincere, warm laugh. I still bombed.

After a commercial break, I was led into the studio. It was cold; the audience, unimpressed. Not only did Colbert mispronounce my last name twice on-air, he also had to rerecord the opening because he stuttered through *Arellano*. It's okay: I called him a French-Canadian.

While on the show, Colbert asked me what was the Spanish word for patience. "*Pacencia,*" I asserted. Wrong—the word is *paciencia.* Within minutes of my returning to the hotel after the taping, angry Latinos from across the world had e-mailed in to bash me.

These e-mails provided the only existential moment I've ever had about the column. I received hundreds of them—gently chiding, laudatory, but most calling me a Hispanic Lou Dobbs. A *vendido*—sellout. On the JetBlue flight back home, I started doubting the validity of the column. How much of an authority was I, I wondered, if I stumbled over freshman Spanish words such as *paciencia*?

I skipped through the channels offered by JetBlue during the flight and noticed that Comedy Central was reairing *The Colbert Report* episode. I cringed and switched the channel to ESPN2. I nearly flipped when I noticed the lady next to me had settled on the program. My segment was up in about ten minutes.

After a final commercial break, I appeared. I stole glances at the lady's screen, shooting between her erupting laughter and my on-air fidgeting. About two minutes into it, her laughter stopped. She looked at me, looked at the screen, and looked at me again. "Is that you?" she asked with a twinge of doubt in her voice. Yes, I nodded. "Good job—you're funny!"

And then I thought about my error. I had always translated *patience* as *pacencia*. I never recalled my parents correcting me, unlike so many other Spanish mistakes. What was wrong with me? Was I woefully lacking in Mexican credentials and therefore exploiting my mother culture?

Upon landing at Long Beach Airport, I immediately drove home to my parents' house. Everyone I knew saw the show and called me or texted me in the days following the appearance to congratulate me. None of them mentioned my flub. I worried.

"Congratulations, macho man!" Papi proclaimed upon my return. I was hungry and heated up the stove to make a quesadilla. But first, I needed to know the truth.

"¿Papi, como se dice patience *en español?"* I asked nervously, fearing the answer.

"Pacencia," he responded with little hesitation. *"Pacencia."*

I turned to my mom. *"¿Mami, sí se dice* patience *así?"* I asked. "Is that how you say *patience?"*

"Pues no—se dice paciencia," she replied. *"Pero así se dice en el rancho."* But that's how they say it in the rancho.

Almost forty years after my parents had left El Cargadero and Jomulquillo for the States, the old country still was in their American son. I smiled, turned on the rerun to see myself on *The Colbert Report,* and e-mailed the haters to go fuck themselves.

San Clemente: Southernmost point in Orange County. The much heralded Spanish Village by the Sea. Frequented a lot by the marines just down the 5 at Camp Pendleton, which means this picturesque town gets bloodied more than any city other than SanTana. **Best restaurant: The Surfin' Chicken,** home to the best charbroiled chicken on earth and killer shark tacos. *71 Via Pico Plaza, San Clemente, (949) 498-6603.*

Insert Concluding
Orange Cliché Here

The family of my second girlfriend was everything Uncle Sam wanted in His WWII generation. Her parents weren't natives of Orange County but moved to Anaheim in the 1960s, buying a large house in a middle-class neighborhood. Their four daughters all served as cashiers next door at the La Palma Chicken Pie Shop, an Orange County institution where the 1950s have never ended: pot pies and grilled-cheese sandwiches are on the menu, served by fifty-year-old waitresses who bark orders at the Latino cooks. The parents retired, bought a Ford Taurus, and became grandparents. The future was bright. Everyone accepted me as one of their own, although I vaguely recall the mom cracking about her daughter's new boyfriend's ability to read in English rather well.

(Yes, romance and my *mexicanidad* have never meshed well. As I've illustrated, the girls from El Cargadero never liked me because I wasn't Mexican enough. The one Mexican girlfriend I had was from Mexico City and thought I was too rural in my Mexican ways. My current girlfriend frequently says, "We're not in the rancho," when I ask her to stop an annoying habit. But the worst reaction a girlfriend's parents ever had toward me was with a Vietnamese *chica*. Her parents never warmed up to me solely because

I was a Mexican—never mind that I was earning my master's degree at UCLA at the time or that I was respectful toward their daughter. These refugees, whose English was worse than my parents', didn't want their daughter dating a Mexican—period. The girl, on the other hand, dumped me because I wasn't a radical Chicano. Only in America. Now, back to the story.)

Everything changed for my sweetheart's family in late 1997, when her father fell off a ladder after a Mexican accidentally tipped it with a forklift. Her father went into a coma and died within a couple of weeks, and the family soon frayed after that. The girl broke up with me about three years after his death, and we never spoke again.

I've lost track of the family over the years—I know my ex-girlfriend moved out shortly after our breakup, and one of the sisters married a marine, but that's about it. I do think about them frequently, in large part because I have to pass by their former home almost every week. It's about a minute away from my parents' home, in a neighborhood near Interstate 5 that offers commuters a quick shortcut through Anaheim. When the girl and I were dating, she openly complained about how their neighborhood was turning more and more Mexican every year. They were soon the last white family on the block.

Earlier this year, I saw a FOR SALE sign on the front lawn. But, as I passed by, I wasn't prepared to digest what I saw: a big, fat Mexican guy in the doorway, gazing toward God knew what. Not only had my second girlfriend's family moved away, but now *these* Mexicans were leaving the house as well.

Signs of dilapidation were everywhere in the neighborhood. Graffiti. A computer monitor in the street. Too many cars. Corn in the front yards. Badly kept lawns. Flaking paint jobs. Loud music. Men sitting in garages, clutching beers. The supermarket that had operated next to the Chicken Pie Shop for decades was being turned into a Latino-themed furniture store. The Orange

County of the girl I once loved no longer existed—and it wasn't even appealing for some Mexicans, either.

This kind of change would anger just about any American—hell, it pissed me off. But then I drove up to my parents' house. It, too, had changed in the nearly two decades since Mami and Papi had scrounged up enough money to get us out of the shack on Philadelphia Street. When we moved in, the apartment complexes on our street housed gangs, prostitutes, and drug dealers. Carl Karcher, the hamburger baron, leveled those slums six months after we moved in, building a spiky fence between our house and the new residences. White people still lived in the neighborhood, but they were readying to leave.

The neighborhood has never been pristine—graffiti goes up every once in a while, and I'm sure the house on the corner is one of vice, either sex, drugs, or illegal immigrants. Sketchy characters still rent the "new" apartments, and my mom grows rosebushes and bougainvillea to discourage teens from passing through our front yard. Really, the neighborhood is like any other in the United States—only you better know Spanish if you want to speak to the adults. Us kids, on the other hand, prefer English.

The same happy ending doesn't apply to our Philadelphia Street dump. Gangs now live throughout the barrio. Developers somehow squeezed more apartments into what was already a crowded neighborhood. But change is afoot. Where once a factory paid livable wages, new faux brownstones are being built, just like the ones down the street near the Sunkist Packing House. The free market is reinvigorating (read *de-Mexicanizing*) my old hood. I drive by there every once in a while and squeeze my Camry through the narrow alleys to gaze at the worn-down granny flat where we lived. There's the same gravel pit my dad poured so long ago because the dirt below kept ruining the paint on his old Thunderbird. But gone is the big home that a *cargaderense* family owned, replaced by spanking-new apartments. None of the peo-

ple I grew up with there live in the neighborhood anymore—
everyone abandoned their degrading barrio, damn the memories.
Change is good. Change is bad. Change happens—deal with
it. I do, for better or worse.

> **Dana Point:** Named after Richard Henry Dana, the first
> American commentator on Orange County (and if you don't
> know whom I'm talking about, it's time you read the rest of this
> book). Home to two of the most beautiful resorts in the world—the
> Ritz-Carlton, Laguna Niguel, and the St. Regis Resort, places where
> you can get butlers to walk you to the beach and surf. *Lame.* Also,
> a city that banned day laborers after residents claimed they shit
> on public streets. **Best restaurant:** I usually don't advise folks to
> spend more than $30 per couple on a meal, but I'll make an
> exception for **Stonehill Tavern,** which insists on a sophisticated
> approach to American cuisine. In layman's terms, hope you enjoy
> your $28 truffle cheeseburger! *One Monarch Beach Resort, Dana
> Point, (949) 234-3318.*

In the first chapter of *Fast Food Nation,* Eric Schlosser asked
Karcher if he ever missed the old days, when he ran just a couple
of restaurants and Orange County was rural and bucolic. "No,"
Karcher replied. "I believe in Progress."

Schlosser was trying to portray Karcher as the prime example for
the food industry gone awry—an entrepreneur whose dreams were
fulfilled but got the best of him. To a child growing up in Anaheim
during the 1980s, Karcher was one step below God. His signature
was on the gift certificate for a free Carl's Jr. kids' meal that elementary teachers gave to students with good grades. My family ate at
his restaurants almost weekly. A Carl's Jr. stands right across Broad-
way from Anaheim's Central Library, where I spent so many hours.
The gentle giant prayed at morning Mass daily at St. Boniface,

always sitting in the front pew. Instead of living isolated from the burger-eating public, Karcher resided in a modest two-story house within walking distance of Latino-heavy Pearson Park. I never mustered the courage to ask the tycoon for one of the free-hamburger coupons he kept in his wallet the way most of us keep credit-card receipts, but my friends who did said he handed them out with a smile as large as his restaurant's trademark Happy Star logo.

By the time Karcher passed away earlier this year, Carl's Jr. was a joke of a brand—it's best known for lame double-entendre-packed ads featuring Paris Hilton, Dennis Rodman, Hugh Hefner, and other sex fiends hawking messy, massive burgers. Karcher had lost control of the company after expanding too fast and nearing personal bankruptcy. The profits remained, but the vision didn't— *Portfolio* magazine revealed that toward the end, Karcher was saddened by the direction of his company but was powerless to do anything. To eat at Carl's Jr. in Orange County was once a journey in goofy provincialism. Now? No different from McDonald's.

Nevertheless, Karcher went to his Creator happy. In sixty years, he had witnessed the county transform from its pre-WWII days into a modern madhouse. In this way, he was Mr. Orange County—an entrepreneur who believed change was not only Progress (capital *P* in the original, just as he insisted Schlosser quote him in *Fast Food Nation*), but inevitable. It's the Orange County Story—and don't just believe me. Many Orange County historians subscribe to this Cult of the Orange Crate, talking with nostalgia about the changing of ownership from Serra to the Spaniards to Californios and finally to the United States, whose citizens reinvent this fertile land again and again, and conveniently forget the nasty bits.

That's what we're taught from an early age—to always move forward, never look back except to mythologize. But this train of thought betrays fear and insecurity that exposes an outlandish flaw.

Consider the worst reception I've ever received; not in front of a group of Republicans or one of the many times I've popped up on the Fox News Channel (Sean Hannity wasn't as bullying as I've seen him with other guests, but that might be because he had spent the previous ten minutes screaming at a Muslim activist). No, the spittle came from a South County chapter of the Orange County Democratic Party. I was a keynote speaker at their June 2006 meeting, held at El Adobe de Capistrano, a San Juan Capistrano institution that served as a barracks for Spanish soldiers centuries ago but became famous after Richard Nixon told the press corps it was his favorite Mexican restaurant. Problem was, El Adobe wasn't a Mexican restaurant—it served continental cuisine to everyone but Nixon, who ate Mexican dishes specially prepared by the executive chef. El Adobe went exclusively Mexican shortly after its spotlight moment lest reality contradict Nixon's declaration of the Orange County ideal.

My speech topic seemed innocuous for this crowd—politics in Orange County and how the *Weekly* covers it. But it wouldn't have mattered what I said—the audience had their own agenda. The moment I asked the audience for questions, the scene turned rancid. "Why can't Mexican kids learn English?" one person asked to a round of applause. They did, I tried to explain, and I'm proof of it. Few bought my response. "Why don't any Mexicans want to become Americans anymore?" another lady asked to a round of applause. I began to reply, but another person interrupted, which led to other people arguing—a shrill septuagenarian insisted second-graders in Orange County no longer spoke English, which drew a rebuke from me, which drew heckles. Fun for Rush Limbaugh listeners—but weren't these the Democrats? Finally, the nice woman who had invited me to speak had to yell above the crowd to restore order. It didn't help that two whiskeys (always served neat) were filtering through my bloodstream. Finally, I had enough.

"You know what?" I sneered to the room. "I feel sorry for you. I feel sorry that you don't believe Mexicans can become Americans. I'm one of them. I know we can do it because we do. I have faith in America. You don't." And with that, the audience jeered.

I've been attacked with uglier rhetoric before, at lectures and on the radio, but that's the only time I've ever blown up in public (even when a lady called my mother a "monkey" during an interview on Chicago's WGN-AM, I managed to laugh and tell the woman that I loved her). Every time I hear this lie, that Mexicans resist assimilation, I cringe. The immigration wars, once the domain of Orange County crazies and their philosophically inbred cousins nationwide, are now widespread. When Colorado congressman Tom Tancredo held a fund-raiser for his failed presidential campaign at the Richard Nixon Library in mid-2007, an adoring audience presented him with devil's horns and a blowtorch in honor of his scorched-earth approach to the New Americans. The Republic has learned well from Orange County. Progress is good—unless it involves Mexicans. But change is inevitable—and it's going to involve Mexicans. Why can't anyone accept it?

COMMON NICKNAMES FOR CITIES, SOME NICE, MOST NOT

Anaheim: Anacrime, Anagrime, Anaslime, Wabaheim. **Costa Mesa:** Costa Mexico, Costa Misery. **Garden Grove:** Garbage Grove. **Huntington Beach:** HB. **Irvine:** Illvine, Scurvine. **La Habra:** Guadalahabra. **Leisure World:** Seizure World. **Santa Ana:** Saint Anne, SanTana. **Stanton:** Stanton. **Surf City:** Surf Shitty. **Yorba Linda:** The Land of Nixon.

My dad continues to visit Jerez twice a year—for a week in April and two weeks at Christmas. My mom occasionally accompanies him on trips, but she's tired of it. Not only are El Cargadero and

Jomulquillo empty, but the fabric that once connected so many *cargaderenses* from Anaheim to Zacatecas is now stretched so thin that no one much bothers to maintain it.

The El Cargadero migration grew too big. My dad still goes to *la cafeteria* every Sunday, and my parents attend parties as they always have, but too many *cargaderenses* are in Anaheim to keep up appearances. Look at my *tía* Maria's family, for instance. She lives a couple of blocks from my parents, the widowed mother of eleven adult children and too many grandchildren for me to document. Seven of her children live on the same street, all owning their own homes. Another daughter lives down the street from us. Two more live in Anaheim. Between them, they have a get-together almost every weekend. And since our family's house has a pool, my family usually hosts the celebration.

But I rarely go to those parties, or any other *cargaderense* fiesta. I don't feel superior, don't feel alienated. I love going to those parties—eating carne asada, talking sports, and generally killing time. I'm just too busy—my need for community has waned. I'd rather work. I'm just too American.

And that's not a bad thing. Almost all of the people I grew up with—the girls I courted with no luck and the guys who ridiculed me for not wanting to dance—are the same. All the anchor babies who entered school speaking only Spanish, who didn't move out until marriage, and who still speak to their parents only in *español* even though those parents have lived in the United States for almost thirty years—we're psychologists, schoolteachers, grad students, professionals, contractors, all white-collar and well-paying blue-collar trades that Mexican kids supposedly avoid like *la migra*. Few of us own homes yet, but that's only because the housing market is so horrific for a young person in Southern California. That's okay—our parents scrimped and saved and are in no danger of losing their houses to the subprime-mortgage scandal. We live rent-free!

And those are just the *cargaderenses* I know about. Last year, I gave a reading from *¡Ask a Mexican!* at the Anaheim Public Library's Central branch, the same place my mother let me read for hours as a child. My audience gathered in the basement, in the room where every Saturday librarians screened science movies and cartoons for all us kiddies. There wasn't much publicity for the reading—just a plug in my column and flyers. The room was packed mostly with high schoolers from my alma mater who showed up only because teachers promised extra credit if their students attended. More unexpected, however, were the dozen or so *cargaderenses* in the audience. Only one of them was familiar to me, but I'd actually never met her before—she was the young niece of one of my pretty second cousins.

I discover these never-before-known *cargaderenses* all the time. Chicana author Helena Maria Viramontes's father is from El Cargadero—she grew up in East Los Angeles. Andrés Bermudez, the Mexican-illegal-immigrant-turned-millionaire-tomato-farmer who made international headlines in 2001 when he ran for mayor of Jerez? From El Cargadero—he was supposedly one of my aunt's boyfriends when they were teens. In Northern California lives the Gamboa family. My mom picked tomatoes with the patriarch during the 1970s. In the 1980s, their sons Billy and Danny were my close friends in Anaheim. I don't remember much about them because they moved away when I was in first grade. But after a concert in Santa Ana one evening, I began speaking with a fan of mine, a stranger. He asked about this book, and I mentioned my El Cargadero roots.

"I have a friend from El Cargadero," he said. It was the Gamboas.

We were both stupefied. Of all the ranchos in all the world! Turned out that the Gamboas were now millionaires—after moving north, they transitioned from tomato pickers to tomato farmers. One of the brothers is a pilot for the air force; the other is an insurance agent. Almost everywhere I go, I find these stories of successful *cargaderenses*.

And we're finally moving out of Anaheim. There are *cargaderenses* across the United States. I've never met the *cargaderenses* who live in Chicago, in Fremont and Porterville in California, even those brave souls who grew up in Santa Ana. They are foreigners to me. But the connection to El Cargadero is still there. It's a kinship, a sense of identity that forever ties us to a small rancho up in the mountains, a cemetery of Mexico's failures but a Valhalla for our vision. We're all assimilated, and our children will be even more so and adopt what sociologist Herbert Gans identified as symbolic ethnicity—in other words, a Cinco de Mayo–style Mexican, a Yom Kippur Jew, a St. Patty's Day mick. To use one of my favorite clichés—we're as American as nachos. Why the fear?

I'm ever grateful for the ¡*Ask a Mexican!* column. It enabled me to travel for the first time, rewards me with a nice chunk of syndication lucre, and allows me to promote my writings. But it also cost me my idyllic *Weekly,* while at the same time saving my plans. Change.

In late 2005, the *Weekly*'s parent corporation, Village Voice Media, was bought out by the New Times, a chain of papers based in Phoenix that our original corporate overlords had long preached to us was the devil. New Times was supposed to be everything the *Weekly* wasn't—establishment, neoconservative, uncaring of the plight of the downtrodden and generally a mess. Cookie-cutter journalism. The barbarians from Phoenix, we called them. But I read New Times' papers every week and was impressed by their stories, by the way they nabbed bad guys—in other words, how they were identical to us. As panic spread through the *Weekly* office when news of the merger hit, I wasn't bothered. I knew the *real* New Times, I thought, and as long as I was allowed to do the stories I wanted to do, I would stay.

Corporate took an immediate shining to me. After my first *Los Angeles Times* profile hit, a suit came to me with ideas for marketing the column and getting it into more papers. I never had any ambitions to do so, but I agreed to let him try. He promised the moon but delivered only one paper outside of the Village Voice Media family. "I guess there isn't as much interest in the column as we thought there was going to be," he said, pawning the syndication efforts off to me. By myself, I nabbed twenty papers within a year, and with only a half-assed effort.

Toward the end of 2006, there were whispers that Will Swaim, the man who'd rescued me from grad school hell, wanted to leave the *Weekly* and start a paper in Long Beach, just across the Orange County line. I knew he was chafing under VVM leadership, who asked him to stay as editor or publisher of the *Weekly*—but not both. This wasn't a rumor. He announced his resignation in February 2007, and within a month three-quarters of our small staff had left to join him.

Everyone expected me to leave. I was Will's protégé—without him I would've still been a data monkey. He had allowed me to sit in on meetings with potential advertisers and learn the art of that newspaper lifeblood, allowed me to sit in on interviews, and groomed me like an heir. So when he asked me to join his new paper, I'm sure he expected me to defect as well. We were walking near his home in Irvine on a blustery, sunny day. "It'll be the *OC Weekly* in exile," he told me.

I had no choice. "No." And for that, I was viewed as a corporate stooge by many of my coworkers. I said no for a couple of reasons. *¡Ask a Mexican!* the book hadn't been published yet, and to antagonize Village Voice Media by quitting meant losing a valuable platform for promoting the book. I also didn't want to be in the same office with the staff that had left or were planning to leave—those who didn't openly despise me did it behind my back. Matt Coker—our former managing editor, and one of the funniest fucks in the world—wrote a story for the *Sacramento News & Review* about his time with me.

"Other staffers routinely would complain to me privately about Gustavo this and Gustavo that, their language peppered with insinuations that our boy suffered from the ol' inflating-head syndrome," Matt wrote. I wasn't surprised.

But the main reason I didn't leave is because the new paper was going to cover Long Beach. It's a great town, with its own unique history and problems, and right next to Orange County, but I have no interest in Long Beach. I told this to Will, and he wasn't pleased. "Long Beach is no different from Orange County," he said. "All the stories out there will always be the same—corruption, man on the street, food reviews, everything."

His protest surprised me. It was Will, after all, who drilled into me the idea of making a newspaper tell you about the community it covered. If you read the *Weekly* under Will's regime, it was a grand, Dickensian tale in which you found out a little bit more about the county every week, where music reviews hurled jokes at politicians and you had to read every entertainment listing for the latest obscure reference to a bit of Orange County history. It wasn't enough to merely publish any piece that came along; you had to tell a *story*. A saga.

The relationship between Will and me has been strained ever since. His Long Beach paper, the *District Weekly*, is a great paper—read it at thedistrictweekly.com. And the OC *Weekly* is still a great paper, but I'm one of two staffers born and raised in Orange County. The paper shrinks every week, and everyone worries about the future of print journalism—except me. Corporate still loves me, and I always overwork, not to curry favor with the bigwigs but because that's just how I am. Thankfully, the people around me finally seem to respect that. If I do lose my job and

¡Ask a Mexican! becomes as dated as *The Katzenjammer Kids,* I can always return to El Cargadero and live among ghosts.

Placentia: Historically, one of Orange County's most Latino cities due to the orange groves that covered the city during the first part of the twentieth century. As a result, the small city suffers more than necessary. A couple of years ago, students had to whitewash a mural in one of the city's barrios because a *gabacho* complained it promoted nonassimilation. The sinning images? Latino students typing on computers and wearing graduation robes. Currently the city owes the state of California millions of dollars thanks to a previous city council that spun a redevelopment scheme into felony indictments for the former city manager and the planning director. **Best restaurant:** All the white folks enjoy **El Farolito** because the owners speak English, but much better food is down the street at **Q-Tortas,** a drive-through that sells the Mexican version of hoagies. Wash your *tortas* down with a large pineapple juice. *El Farolito, 201 S. Bradford Avenue, Placentia, (714) 993-7880; Q-Tortas, 220 S. Bradford Avenue, Placentia, (714) 993-3270.*

Change is happening. To Orange County. To America.

In 1934, a pamphlet titled *Thunder in California* tried to discredit the California gubernatorial campaign of author Upton Sinclair. The protagonist was an Orange County native, returning after years abroad so he could "again see the white Orange County farmstead, where he was reared." But times were different—socialism ruled the land, and minorities were more prominent. On the cover of *Thunder in California* was a dark, bearded man, planting his red flag on the Golden State.

Earlier this year, the *Orange County Register* ran a story wondering out loud if Orange County had jumped the shark, pegged to coincide with the season finale of *The Real Housewives of Orange County*. Simultaneously, the paper announced layoffs and the death of its business section—this in a place where Fortune 500 companies frequently relocate their operations to. We always celebrate change, only look back when politically or culturally expedient. We are the Garden. Everyone wants to be us. Until now. With a population of over 3 million, over half of which isn't white, we're falling out of favor. We're like any other community sprawl in this country. Suburbia's dead. Next is whatever follows—postsuburbia? Exurbia? Even worse—urbanization? The prospect scares us shitless.

In this way, Orange County, the self-anointed leader, has become a follower. And now we worry mightily about the future. My question to everyone: why?

I believe in Progress as well. I've lived it—how else can you describe going from strawberry picker to C-list celebrity in one generation? Or seeing an entire displaced community become assimilated, successful, proud of their heritage, yet wholly American within twenty years? The residents of El Cargadero are Progress—that we're Mexican is secondary in our mind, yet most, if they consider this, think us the exception to the beaner rule.

We're not. El Cargadero's story isn't that unique. Across the country, you'll find similar epics: of entire Mexican ranchos uprooted and placed in one locale. In Anaheim alone, you'll also find hundreds of residents from two *municipios* in Jalisco: Arandas and Jalostitlan. I grew up with their progeny as well, and we usually argued about whether their rancho or El Cargadero was superior. The arguments were always in English, and we'd have them over dinners at our respective dances.

We're so American, so Orange County, that even we're prone to romanticize a past that never existed. The adults always do it—can't tell you how many times my dad threatens to move to Jomulquillo for good after another hard day driving his truck, then heads off to a senior citizens' center to challenge elderly *gabachos* at pool. Even the kids get delusional. A couple of years ago at a birthday party, I debated the children of my *tío* Ezequiel. His sons Victor and Plácido were my favorite cousins growing up, even if they teased me beyond belief. They lived in Anaheim until my *tío* became the first of my aunts and uncles to leave Anaheim, buying a two-story house in the wealthier part of Placentia. Even with all this splendor, Victor and Plácido still wistfully recalled their early sojourns to El Cargadero and even expressed a desire to live there one day.

I was astounded. They had well-paying careers, DirecTV in their bedrooms. Plácido collected comic-book figurines; Victor, mostly pornos. I laughed at them. They were spoiled and blind to El Cargadero's morguelike modern existence. Victor and Plácido wouldn't hear it. Life was simpler back there, they said. America was nice, but they'd drop it for El Cargadero instantly.

That was a couple of years ago. Plácido is now the father of a beautiful girl and pays a mortgage in Anaheim. Victor drives a BMW and will probably marry his Vietnamese girl.

As for me? I'll just stay in Orange County, this Eden on the Coast, Gomorrah by the Sea. My Paradise. My Hell. Home.

Acknowledgments

Because the El Cargadero–Jerez diaspora is so freakin' huge, to list all the people I'd have to thank for making this book possible would take up another book. To remedy that, let's wipe out a couple of pages thusly: *gracias* continues to apply to everyone I thanked in *¡Ask a Mexican!*—unless you've talked trash about me behind my back in the past year and a half. In which case, pride goeth before the fall.

Since I had to decide which parts of my and El Cargadero's lives would most appeal to a national audience, I had to leave out *a lot* of great, crazy anecdotes, especially those involving my family. To remedy this, I'm going to list all my cousins and their children. *Primos y primas:* please forgive me if I don't list all of you or your spouse, but we're such a huge family, I sometimes forget who's who! That's what I get for not going to family parties anymore, huh?

From my dad's side:

Tía Nacha: Meño and his daughters; Victor and his kids; Angie and Cassie and her little boy.

Tío Jesús: Chito and his kids; Ramiro; Erica and her kids; Veronica and her kids.

Tía Mela: Jose Alfredo and his kids; Omar and his kids; Maribel and her child; Monica.

Tío Santos: Rudy, Leti, Diego, and Susan.

Tía Paula: Felipe and his kids; Araceli; Arnulfo and his kids—hope I didn't miss anyone else!

Tía Chayo: Sergio and his kids; Griselda and her kids— hope I didn't miss anyone else!

Tío Gabriel: Beatriz and her kids; Ramon and his kids; Nena and her kids; Cristina, Steve—and I'm forgetting someone else!

From my mom's side:

Tía Meme: Hito and his child; Richie; Ferny and his kid; Carlos and Miranda; Bobbo.

Tío Ezequiel: Victor; Plácido and Addy; Julia and her child; Danny; Adriana; Mariana and Samuelito.

Tía Maria: Jesús and Jaime, Chuy, Angel, Alex, and your guys' sister; Chepe and your four wonderful boys; Angela and Angel, Rubencillo, Esteban, and David; Joaquincillo and his kids; Javier and his ever-mischievous boys (like father, like son, eh?); La China and Rosalva, Yoli, Arturo, and Rafa (I think I forgot the youngest); Beto and his four boys; Lalo; someone else and Vivi; your guys' brother, whom I never met because he died when I was young—may he rest in peace alongside your dad; Fernando and I'm not sure if you have kids!

Tía Angela: Luz Elena, your youngest, and Irene; Marcy; Sammy and your kids; Chava and his kids—David and Angie (may you rest in peace; your cousins miss you dearly).

Tía Mariana: I remember meeting you folks only once, when Papa Je passed away. I try not to involve myself in the Byzantine politics that engulf any large family (and especially Mexican *familias*), but, seriously: don't be strangers.

Tío Casimiro: Same applies to *ustedes*.

Tío Jesús: The same applies to his older children. As for everyone that follows Marcelo: I remember you guys when I visited El Cargadero in 1987, how nice *ustedes* were to Elsa and me, and how strange I thought it was that I had cousins living in Mexico. I remember you guys living in the house where *mi tío* Ezequiel's family once lived, that small shack. I remember the older kids not knowing a lick of English—yet all of you are now success stories. Marcelo, Mina, Chuyito, Irene, Alicia, all your younger siblings, and any kiddies *ustedes* may have: you're an inspiration to us all.

Tía Belen: Betty, Adriana, Celina (and your kids), and the little one; Nena and your badass boys; Chava and your children; Ricardo and your kids (we'll get Santa Ana Unified yet); Eva and your kiddies.

Tía Licha: Obo.

I'm sure I missed a couple of you here—know it's because I'm such a nerd and get involved in the minutiae of the world instead of the things that matter. I humbly ask for your apology and trust that I'll receive it. *Los quiero a todos.*

Another subsection could be devoted to all the wonderful people from Jerez—mostly El Cargadero, Jomulquillo, and the city proper (and a shout-out to all the people in our colonies in Fremont and Porterville, California; Los Angeles; and anywhere else we may be), but a couple of folks from the smaller ranchos as well—that influenced my life, the friends of my mom and dad who saw me grow up and always excitedly call them whenever I appear on KMEX-TV Channel 34. To limit space, how's about this: if you or your parents know me and your last name is Saldivar, Barrios, Fernandez, García, Ureño, Gamboa, Miranda, Casas, Guerrero, Acevedo, Perez, Arellano, or Viramontes, thank you. Except for one person—you know who you are. Jerk. And everyone else from Jerez and its ranchos, whom I haven't had the pleasure of meeting; you guys rock!

The above thanks cover hundreds of people, so now I'll focus on those who don't fall under those rubrics. William Lobdell, for offering feedback on "Gimme That OC Religion"; in a way, I'm glad you don't cover religion anymore because that means I have no real competition covering our county's religious crazies, but in a bigger way I think it's a tragedy that good people have lost one of the greatest religion reporters ever—you are a mentor and colleague to me. Scott Moxley, for offering feedback on the Republican chapter. The Kevin and Bean gang, for having me on once a month—love how you rip me off! Nicole (and her cool friends), Dino, and Robin. Sweetpea and Milo's House of Hugs and Kisses, with Nina, Tiki, and Leilani as junior associates. Victims of the Orange diocese sex-abuse scandal, the county's only true secular saints. Assembly member Hector de la Torre, for being foolish enough to nominate me for a Latino Spirit award. All the people who have given me awards—what were you thinking? Justin Manask and my Hollywood crew—we can reach *Entourage* yet. I don't think I thanked you, Ryan Gattis, in my first book, so here you go—and if I did, you rock! To Brant (my Chipper Jones–loving

editor), Susan Moldow, Nan Graham, Kate Bittman, Meredith
Wahl, Anna deVries, and the rest of the Scribner *familia—gracias*
for believing in me. Brian: You owe me a Pueblan dinner!

There are so many more people to thank, but I can't think of
them right now. . . . Wait: to all the great restaurants I've patronized over the years, *gracias* for feeding me. . . . Okay, the thanks
are getting ridiculous at this point, but can you understand why?
I came from next to nothing, and can now boast of having published two books for a major American publishing company
before turning thirty. So my greatest thanks go to this country:
America. God bless you, and please get your act together.

Now, onward to the third book. . . .